Channah ~

Congrats on all your success
CRISTA! You Are like a DAVID.
Marketplace w/ the wisdom of ABIGAILO
Call to CHRIST like Lydia. MAY the FAVOR
the Lord continue to follow you + may the
Charisma of CHRIST surround your career!

Scott Hogle
PSALM 5:12

Praise for
DIVINE INTELLIGENCE

"Succeeding in life requires that you execute winning plays consistently. *Divine Intelligence* will be like a coach at your side each day, one devotion at a time."

—Dave Canales,
Quarterback Coach, Seattle Seahawks

"Many love [going to] church on Sunday because it recharges the batteries in us that work depletes all week. Imagine how much better life would be if work was worship! *Divine Intelligence* is a masterclass in how to use your faith to fuel all that you do every day, in every way."

—Tony Coles,
Division President, iHeartMedia Multiplatform Group
and President, Black Information Network

"The terrain of today's corporate world demands excellence and peak performance. *Divine Intelligence*, written by a seasoned corporate executive and teaching pastor, covers dozens of topics to help you succeed in work and life by bringing your relationship with God into all you do. True to the biblical metal it is forged from, this daily devotional is inspiring and practical, providing reliable armor for the workday ahead."

—Wes Paz,
Creative Production Manager, Nordstrom

"Nestled within the pages of *Divine Intelligence*, you will discover the depths of love God has gone to so you could walk through your day in His Spirit of wisdom and revelation. Your journey with Jesus will never be the same."

—Yvonne Yanagihara,
Market Enablement Manager Hawaii,
SPECTRUM Enterprise

"Scott Hogle's skill as a seasoned executive and teaching pastor comes through loud and clear in *Divine Intelligence*. He unpacks how to apply God's design to reach your destiny, one day at a time. Get this book and put God's wisdom to work in your life."

—**Michael Little,**
Former President and COO,
The Christian Broadcasting Network

"*Divine Intelligence* is one of the most powerful and practical devotionals you will ever read. It brings Scripture and leadership principles to life with easy-to-follow steps you can apply. It is an incredible book that will change how you face your day and live your life with Jesus at the center."

—**Dr. Lori Salierno-Maldonado,**
Author, Speaker, Founder, and CEO of
"Teach One to Lead One"

"*Divine Intelligence* is a breakthrough book to grow your relationship with God and learn how to bring His wisdom into your workday."

—**Harry Hargrave,**
Chief Executive Officer,
Museum of the Bible

"This book is fantastic for Christians working in corporate America. If you're serious about bringing God's presence into your career, *Divine Intelligence* is filled with common workplace situations that call for a faithful response."

—**Denise Lewallen,**
Strategic Account Lead 3,
AT&T ACQ-Retail West

"It is both refreshing and timely to read a devotional that practically aligns one's Christian walk with their business life. As ambassadors for the Kingdom, *Divine Intelligence* will be a welcome read for the person who desires to keep their faith at the center of all they do."

—Monte Montemayor,
Microsoft, Director of SMB Cloud Strategy

"You won't find a better work-life devotional than *Divine Intelligence* for growing in your relationship with Jesus and using your calling in your career to glorify God. Buy this book today and put its principles to work for your best life."

—Jan Higa,
Commercial Broker, Jan Higa & Company LLC

"*Divine Intelligence* ties the Bible and faith directly to daily life more than any other Christian book you will read. The applicability and specificity will inspire you to a deeper, richer walk in your faith."

—Dr. Kent Keith,
President Emeritus, Pacific Rim Christian University
and Author of *The Christian Leader at Work:
Serving by Leading*

"*Divine Intelligence* is a book that goes where many business books dare not to go—that is, showing you how to join your relationship with God with your professional life. This daily devotional reminds readers that great things are possible when you involve God in all your daily agenda."

—Vincent Claudio,
Senior Vice President Operation,
Gerber Collision and Glass

"As a leader, have you ever felt lost, alone, or uncertain about your purpose or direction? Scott Hogle's *Divine Intelligence* serves as a compass to help guide you into deeper spiritual insights to give you the faith to act, solve problems, and overcome limiting beliefs of fear, doubt, and uncertainty."

—Rich Arriaga, Senior Director, Pfizer

"*Divine Intelligence* is a must-read for anyone seeking that extra boost or edge to succeed in business and in life. This daily devotional captures the most relevant Scripture verses to live by then unpacks and presents them in a way that you can readily apply to your life pursuits. This is one book that will, without a doubt, raise amazing leaders with the traits and character of our Biblical heroes."

—Steve Sombrero,
President, Cushman & Wakefield ChaneyBrooks
and Founder, Aloha Beer Company

"Are we career professionals who happen to be followers of Jesus, or are we followers of Jesus who happen to be career professionals? *Divine Intelligence* provides the Biblical perspective and skill set you need to succeed as a disciple in the work world."

—Scott Thayer,
Sales Director, Enabling Technologies

"Scott has written a pioneering daily career connection to God that is long overdue. Using the Scriptures, he speaks deeply and profoundly to working men and women of God in a heartfelt and personally experienced voice. If you want to discover how to make your work your worship with God as your mentor, start here. *Divine Intelligence* is a devotional masterpiece."

—T.J. Malievsky,
Vice President of Media, CRISTA Ministries

"Scott Hogle has given us a very practical and spiritually relevant devotional book for the workplace believer in *Divine Intelligence*. He has covered every major area that a workplace leader experiences. The format allows the reader to engage with Scripture combined with practical application for the workplace. It's a devotional that needs to be read and applied daily."

—Os Hillman,
Author, *TGIF: Today God Is First in All Things*
and President, Marketplace Leaders

"God has given Scott the mind and courage of Daniel. You will see this demonstrated throughout the pages of *Divine Intelligence* as Scott shows people how to combine work and worship in this pioneering devotional."

—Wayne Cordeiro,
Founding Pastor and President,
New Hope International

"The boldness with which Scott holds together his inner walk with God and his outer life in the marketplace is something he is in a unique position to speak on in *Divine Intelligence*. This book will be a great find for those who read it."

—Chad Lewis,
Biblical Scholar and Senior Pastor,
New Temple Evangelical Church

"I see things in Scott's writing I have never seen in other books before; his writing is borderline brilliant. Pick up a copy of *Divine Intelligence* and see what I mean."

—Judy Slack,
Sr. Editor and Writer,
Tom Hopkins International

"*Divine Intelligence* is a bridge between what you hear in church on Sunday and how to create success on Monday in your work world. We meet together on Sunday to worship God and learn more about His great love for us. Starting each Monday, we are challenged on how to bring His love and wisdom from weekend worship into our work routine. This book will help you keep and grow your faith!"

—Stuart Epperson,
Co-Founder and Chairman of Salem Communications

"Whether you identify as a Christian or Catholic, *Divine Intelligence* brings unity to our purpose in discovering God in all we do, especially in our work and not just our worship."

—Bishop Larry Silva of the Roman Catholic Church

"Just a few years past the 500th anniversary of the Protestant Reformation, Scott Hogle has followed in the footsteps of Luther, Calvin, and the other Reformers in reminding us that all *believers are priests* and that the most effective way to live the Christian life is to remove the thinking that divides our lives into a false secular/ sacred dichotomy. *Divine Intelligence* gives us 52 weeks of devotionals that reflect various aspects of that truth to form a beautiful spiritual kaleidoscope that, like a fine diamond, invite the reader to inspect God's character and intelligence. I highly recommend *Divine Intelligence* as a refreshing way to, as Brother Lawrence famously urged us centuries ago, 'practice the presence of God.' Scott shows how God's practical truths can be demonstrated in the marketplace during the week, where most of us spend much of our time, but can also guide us on Sundays."

—Danny Lehmann,
Director of University of the Nations,
Youth With A Mission

"*Divine Intelligence* takes complex biblical topics and communicates them simply and masterfully in a 52-week devotional. Scott Hogle demonstrates a remarkable ability to teach even the learned Bible student how to apply Scripture to everyday life. Scott has walked out many of these areas personally and especially when it comes to divine wisdom, revelation, and intelligence in regard to his supernatural healing. He truly is an inspirational friend, writer, and communicator!"

—Bryan Nutman,
Director of Post Education and Ministry Relations,
Andrew Wommack Ministries

DIVINE INTELLIGENCE

Discover God's Wisdom for Your Work Life

Scott Hogle

MADE FOR
GRACE

Made for Success Publishing
P.O. Box 1775 Issaquah, WA 98027
www.MadeForSuccessPublishing.com

Copyright © 2022

Distributed by Made for Success Publishing

First Printing

Library of Congress Cataloging-in-Publication data

Hogle, Scott
  Divine Intelligence

   p. cm.

LCCN: 2021947774
ISBN: 978-1-64146-742-1 *(PHYSICAL)*
ISBN: 978-1-64146-741-4 *(eBOOK)*
ISBN: 978-1-64146-690-5 *(AUDIO)*

Printed in the United States of America

For further information contact Made for Success Publishing
+14255266480 or email service@madeforsuccess.net

TABLE OF CONTENTS

WEEK

WEEK

WEEK

FOREWORD

Christians sometimes struggle with how to practically bring God into all they do. They tend to separate weekend worship from weekday work. However, by design, God created you to be with Him 24-7. God desires to be brought into *all* you do. Like the French Monk named Brother Lawrence he writes about, Scott has found a way to remain in an attitude of prayer and worship even while he goes about his day-to-day work. This is a brilliant expression of the Apostle Paul's admonition to "pray without ceasing."

Remember how God walked and talked with Adam in the garden? Why did God make it a point to meet with Adam each day, and what did they talk about? As a father, I like to interact with my kids and grandkids to encourage them and tell them how much I love them. When I consider what God and Adam might have talked about each day as they walked the garden, I imagine God talked to Adam about his work there. God likely affirmed Adam and his work, problem solved with him, listened to what Adam had to say, and also asked questions that would cause Adam to think. The Father wants to do the same with you today—not just one day a week, but *every* day.

The book you hold in your hands will unpack the many dimensions of the Father's hope, heart, and wisdom for you. Scott will challenge you to bring God into all you do, and when you do, you will hear the Father's feedback in a new way.

Do you know your assignment? God has assigned something specific to each person. First, to full-time fellowship with Him, and second, to success and significance you can only experience by involving Jesus in every area of your life. Whether your calling is to full-time vocational ministry or the marketplace, *Divine Intelligence* will be helpful to you in your career, your calling, and most importantly, in developing intimacy with God.

It's time we stop compartmentalizing God and limiting him to our weekend worship. You cannot reach your potential in this life without bringing Jesus into all you do. This pioneering work brings both the person and principles of Jesus together in a practical, applicable, and actionable way so you will know how to apply the Scriptures to your life. You will enjoy the breadth and length Scott goes to in outlining the character, competency, and communion Christ desires for you.

To church leaders and laymen alike, I want to say that I share your passion for getting the "church out of the church." It's not enough to build big ministries; we must build big people, then send them out to worship in the world so they can shine their light bright among people. Did you know that almost 90% of Jesus's teachings were in the marketplace and had a workplace context? I can't think of a better time to bring God back into everything we do. Instead of taking God out of schools, culture, and the workplace, this breakthrough devotional proposes to bring God back into everything, especially the work environment where people spend most of their week.

The wisdom of God is simply to know what God would do in any situation. Within this book, there are hundreds of ways to practically do so. I echo the prayer of Paul that the "eyes of your heart may be enlightened" so that you can experience all Jesus has for you in this life. The joy is found in journeying with Jesus. *Divine Intelligence* will inspire you and reignite your passion for Scripture.

Divine Intelligence is a clarion call to our generation that points to the need to involve Christ in every aspect of our lives by showing Christians how to bring the person and principles of Jesus into the workplace. Issues believers face today will require wisdom greater than that of Solomon, and the Scriptures give us access to this "greater wisdom" through the mind of Christ which exists within every Christian. You will see many examples of the mind of Christ applied in *Divine Intelligence*. "The Baby and the Sword" is one example of how everyday people can apply the principles of emotional intelligence or EQ, which God demonstrates through Solomon. (1 Kings 3:24-27)

I have had the privilege of working with Scott for years in ministry work, on the board at New Hope Oahu, and now as a teaching pastor. You will enjoy his practical approach to dividing the Scriptures in a way that can be applied simply. God has given Scott the mind and courage of Daniel, which you will see in his Biblical writing style. Whether you are longing for greater intimacy with God or are in search of His wisdom for a problem you are facing, you will find hundreds of nuggets nestled within the page of this daily devotional.

Divine Intelligence is a "career calling" devotional for your assignment. There is a depth and intimacy that will enter your life the moment you begin to bring Jesus into your "everyday everythings," and I'm confident you will love it.

—Wayne Cordeiro

Dr. Wayne Cordeiro is President of New Hope Christian College, founder of New Hope Oahu and New Hope International, from which over 150 church plants and almost 100,000 salvations have occurred worldwide. Dr. Cordeiro is the Sr. Pastor of New Hope West in Eugene, Oregon and has authored over a dozen books.

Of his writings, Scott credits Wayne's book *The Divine Mentor* for changing the way he approached Scripture and discovered the depths of God's wisdom for every aspect of life.

ACKNOWLEDGMENTS

I t is impossible to list *all* the people in my personal and professional life who have contributed to shaping my character, calling, and commitment to Christ, but here is a short list.

To my family: Generationally, my grandparents Paul and Olga Malijewsky, and my mother, Helen, showed me my first example of what it meant to be a Christian growing up. Then, my uncle T.J. Malievsky, who would become the "Paul to my Timothy," mentored me with thousands of lessons in marketplace and ministry as I grew into adulthood. I am so incredibly thankful for their imprint on my life.

To Dr. Wayne Cordeiro, Founder of New Hope International, and Sr. Pastor John Tilton of New Hope Oahu: I am eternally grateful for the inspiring example you have set of love, leadership, and what it means to be Christlike.

To Chad Lewis, Biblical Scholar and my theological editor: Thank you for editing *Divine Intelligence* and taking my thinking about God to higher ground.

INTRODUCTION

Have you ever felt like you had to pick between a career in the marketplace or serving God in the ministry? Well, you don't! God has designed you for both. In fact, bringing God into your daily routine makes your Monday through Friday work as important to Him as your weekend worship. Why? Because *your work becomes your worship when* you involve Him in your daily doings.

Over the years, I've discovered that many of the principles, skills, and tools needed for success in the marketplace come straight out of the Bible. This book will be a bridge to bring to light many of the principles of God's wisdom found in the Scriptures but not taught in the church, yet essential for Christians to reach their potential in Christ. *Divine Intelligence* will help you bring your worship and work-life together as you discover that God is with you while you work, not only when you worship.

Did you know that of the 132 public appearances of Jesus, 122 (over 90%) were in the marketplace? Jesus told 52 parables, and 45 (86%) had a workplace context. Needless to say, God cares about your work. Which is why I would like to dedicate this book to the majority of Christians who spend their careers working in the marketplace.

I believe that *Divine Intelligence* will empower you to "walk worthy of the vocation wherewith ye are called." (Eph 4:1 KJV)

Chad Lewis, author and biblical scholar, eloquently reminds us that "Martin Luther believed that he could do more good by walking with God in the midst of the real world than by shutting himself up in a monastery. Most Christians would agree in word, but very few are able to carry it out in deed. We still tend to separate the religious and the secular, idolizing pastors and looking askance at business people, politicians, lawyers [and the like]."

In these pages, I will show you how to bring Jesus into your "everyday everythings." Whether you work in an office, at a job site, a retail store, or as an entrepreneur, what you sanctify to God becomes part of your worship, including your work life.

FIRST THINGS FIRST

I went into business when I was 20 years old. My job was to sell advertising to business owners who were often two to three times my age. Too young for my job and in way over my head, I needed more than great earthly mentors—I needed God's mentorship.

Early in my career, I struggled to attain success until I learned God had a better way: a system, a set of principles, and an ever-present help to guide me in my career. My heart hungered for relationship with God, and I knew His ways would create success, so I went on the hunt in the Scriptures. While I was growing up, there wasn't a roadmap for career-oriented Christians. The world embraces the principles of Jesus that create success but ignores the person of Jesus. In the opposite way, many Christians embrace the person of Jesus but reject His principles for their life, so they struggle. However, you cannot succeed in today's world as a Christian without embracing both. Jesus's commands are clear that we are to occupy, multiply, and make disciples of the nations. But first, He will call you into a deeper and abiding relationship with Him.

WHAT ARE YOU ON THE HUNT FOR?

After you've interfaced with these devotionals, you will never look at the Bible the same way again. For every problem you face, there is a biblical solution to help you navigate your situation God's way. When I think about sales, leadership, and communication, I notice how Paul persuades, Moses leads, and how Jesus moved his audiences with questions. If I need wisdom, Solomon is the man I study. Other biblical mentors like Joseph, Ezra, and Esther teach me about diligence and perseverance, service and surrender. Ruth teaches me about loyalty and steadfastness, while Joshua reminds me to be bold and courageous and that God has a strategy for every battle I face.

Nehemiah teaches me how to build in one hand and defend with the other. Being able to multi-task earthly and eternal priorities is essential for your success. Paul shows me how to find common ground when speaking to an audience, and Mordecai demands that I step up in season when timing is critical. I learn about developing a heart of worship from David so "as the deer panteth after the brook," so my soul, too, be trained to long after God.

Whatever you are in need of, God's divine intelligence has an answer. When facing the end of my career, reading Daniel saved my job… but it wasn't the written word on the page that did it. It was God's whisper to me, the spoken (Rhema) word that came alive as I read. As I did, I instantly knew what to do about the crisis I was facing.

THIS COULD BE THE SECOND MOST IMPORTANT BOOK YOU WILL EVER READ!

Will you let God train you? King David once said that "God trains my hands for war." Said another way, God wants to train *you*. You will see hundreds of applications for how God wants to train your heart and hands for your daily work and worship.

There is not a problem on earth that Heaven cannot solve. Some of the topics we'll delve into will feel like sitting in on a masterclass on communication, the art of sales and leadership, emotional intelligence, and relationship building. Why did I include such depth of subjects in this daily devotional? Because God felt it necessary to put them in the Bible so you could exercise them in your career and excel in everything you put your hand to. Since most tried and true success principles can be traced back to the Bible, I've created *Divine Intelligence* as a roadmap to help you discover them.

This one-of-a-kind devotional will show you how to:

- Problem solve like *Joseph.*
- Persuade like the *Apostle Paul.*
- Learn to ask questions like *Jesus.*
- Adapt under pressure like *Abigail.*
- Lead like the great statesman *Daniel.*
- Grow in emotional intelligence like *Solomon.*
- Create a team to build and defend like *Nehemiah.*
- Embrace divine appointments in your life like *Esther.*
- Discover and develop your slingshot skills like *David.*
- Learn to use your business for the kingdom like *Lydia.*
- Unlock God's promises through obedience like *Abraham.*

A SPIRITUAL SWISS ARMY KNIFE FOR YOUR LIFE

Have you figured out how to put the Scriptures to work for your situation? A Swiss Army knife is one of the most versatile tools. It's small, portable, and depending on your situation, it can even save your life if you know how to use it. Many buy this legendary knife but only use a few of the tools. They never take the time to learn and discern how to extract ALL the usefulness the designer put into the tool.

I wrote *Divine Intelligence* as a spiritual Swiss Army knife to help you extract the wisdom and ways of worship in which God desires you to walk so you feel His presence in all you do. This devotional will help you walk out what you are reading about while you remain in an attitude of worship throughout your day, meditating and making sense of the Scriptures for your life. What you seek is within your reach, closer than you may realize. My prayer for you is that you discover joy unspeakable as you bring Jesus into your "everyday everythings."

GETTING STARTED

Congratulations on joining the journey to bring Jesus into your "everyday everythings." The simple act of involving God in all of your daily doings will work wonders for your faith walk. Each devotion in this book can be read or listened to in audiobook form in about five minutes each day. You may choose to read alone, with a group, or add in a journaling practice. Whatever way you decide, I know you'll find great impact through these pages. If you'd like to incorporate journaling, you can find a free downloadable version of a work-life journal on my website, which is linked at the end of this section.

Here are a few helpful tips to get you started:

SOLO DEVOTIONS: If you decide to go through this devotional by yourself, I highly encourage you to pick a time and place to consistently meet with God one-on-one each day. You can do this at home in a favorite chair, at your desk at work while on break, in an empty conference room, or during your lunch break. Wherever and whenever you choose, the key to growing in intimacy in your relationship with God is consistent pursuit of Him and His ways.

SMALL GROUP DEVOTIONS: You can also go through this devotional with a group of like-minded believers. Starting a small group is as simple as grabbing a friend you would like to grow with and taking time to read and pray together. You, them, and Jesus make a majority. Successful small groups often have a facilitator leading the group in discussion (this could be you) and encourages group members to do the exercises in the free downloadable **WORK-LIFE JOURNAL**.

REFLECT TO CONNECT: At the end of each devotional, there is a section with questions to reflect on what you've just learned. If you're doing solo devotions, you can journal through these questions, and if you're doing a small group, the facilitator can lead the group through a discussion.

JOURNALING: God often uses journaling to clarify through the pen what the Spirit wants to speak into your life. As you read in the presence of God, I encourage you to enter with expectation and write down what you hear as well as your impressions from the reading.

The key to growing during daily Bible study is to discover the relevance in the topic of the day and how to incorporate it into your life. As you do this and apply what you learn, you will go from strength to strength in your walk, work, and relationship with God.

Download the free WORK-LIFE JOURNAL at
www.ScottHogle.com

WINNING WITH PEOPLE

Therefore encourage one another and build up one another,
just as you also are doing. 1 Thessalonians 5:11

hroughout Scripture, the theme of "edification" shows up time and again. Putting others first, being selfless, giving honor where honor is due, and not withholding good to whom it is due when it is in your power to do it are all ways of building others up so they feel encouraged. "To edify" means to build another up, and to build others up is the process of strengthening them. When we speak to the "best" in others, it brings the best out of them. Why is this important? One, because it is the right thing to do. But also, because when people feel their best, they perform at their best, and we all know when we are our "best selves." You have the power within yourself to draw the best out of others, regardless of your position.

You must see value in someone before
you can add value to them.

Adding Value to Another Creates an Invisible Return to You. When you speak to others about the good that you see in them, it communicates that you see value in them. When people sense you value them, they know you believe in them. Demonstrating belief in another is not only good for them and honoring to God; it creates confidence and influence in the atmosphere.

Add Value Before You Ask for Value. A hallmark of biblical communication is to create connection and relationship. To edify one another, you must first see the best in others. I have discovered that when I *look* for the best in others, I *find* the best in others. The opposite is true also. If I view someone through the lens of a critical spirit, then my perception of them is colored by my own filter. Here are three ways in which a person can add value before they ask for value. They start off by looking for the best in others and then speak to the best in others.

1. **AFFIRM** them. Each person carries within them a unique giftedness deposited in them by God. To recognize what God put in them and speak to that gift has the effect of drawing that giftedness out. Affirmation of another creates confidence in the receiving, and confidence neutralizes fear. People are more likely to move forward with you in decision-making when they feel strong in your presence.

2. **ACKNOWLEDGE** a past, present, or future decision. Joe Girard was recognized in the Guinness Book of World Records for selling over 13,000 automobiles. What was his secret to such extraordinary success? Joe was a relationship guru who always found something good to acknowledge in his customers. He would point to something special about the car they were currently driving or compliment a decision they were considering. Acknowledging another's decision communicates the confidence you have in them.

3. **ADMIRE** an accomplishment. Successes are sacred to the person who attained them. Honoring a pinnacle moment in a person's life, a threshold crossed, or praising a goal achieved signals that you hold them and what they achieved in the highest regard. When people feel honor from you, they will be drawn to you. Respecting and honoring another creates a magnetic pull between the giver and the receiver, and influence is increased.

REFLECT TO CONNECT

1. In what ways do you seek to edify people around you on a regular basis?
2. Within whom do you see greatness that others may be ignoring?
3. Whom can you affirm, acknowledge, or admire today?

Until you connect with people relationally,
they won't follow you financially.

THE EFFECTIVE EXECUTIVE

WEEK 1 | TUESDAY

Therefore, take up the full armor of God, so that you will be able to resist
in the evil day, and having done everything, to stand firm.
Ephesians 6:13

Every trade has a set of tools to create success. Today's marketplace is filled with apps to make people more productive. If you can think of it, there is an app for it. Paul uses the analogy of a soldier's armor to empower a Christian with the tools that a soldier of Christ can use on a daily basis. Some tools are offensive, and some are defensive, but each has a specific use. Before He entered His ministry, Jesus used the tools of a carpenter. Then He used tools of communication, compassion, mentoring, and more. What tools do you engage each day to leverage success?

6 SUCCESS TOOLS OF THE EFFECTIVE EXECUTIVE

FOCUS: Focus is the ability to work on one thing while eliminating all other distractions. By setting your focus, you are guaranteed to be productive on the "one thing" that is important. Multitasking is the enemy of focus. Paul said, "This one thing I do…" (Philippians 3:13 KJV)

TIME BLOCKING: Success is a scheduled event. By blocking out time on a calendar to accomplish the most important tasks, you are ensured progress. What events have you built a wall around on your calendar today?

EAT THE UGLY: Whatever is your most difficult task of the day, do it first. You'll be emotionally free to tackle easier tasks throughout the day. What have you been putting off that you know you must do?

PRIORITIZE: Spend the most time on the activities and events that produce the highest return on investment (ROI) in your day. Where possible, delegate tasks others can do so you have time to do what only you can do. What three things must you accomplish to be successful today?

GOAL SETTING: Creating short (1 year or less) and long-term goals (1 year+) will empower you to work on the future you want to create. When setting goals, keep them S.M.A.R.T. (Specific, Measurable, Actionable, Realistic, and Timebound). What goals create a motivational force in your life?

OPPORTUNITY ORIENTED: Someone somewhere has a problem. In my best-selling book *PERSUADE*, I discuss in "The Law of the Prospector" how successful people focus on discovering and solving problems. They've programmed their lens to see problems as opportunities to serve others and strengthen relationships. What problems may be around that you could solve for someone today?

REFLECT TO CONNECT

1. Whom do you know that is great at leveraging one or more of these skill sets?
2. Do you have a mentor you could ask to share their daily success system with you?
3. What tools do you use that are not on the list above that make you successful?

God built mental technologies into your brain
to help you run your race in life like the wind.

THE PUZZLE MASTER

WEEK 1 | WEDNESDAY

Now while Peter was greatly perplexed in mind as to what the vision
which he had seen might be, behold, the men who had been sent
by Cornelius, having asked directions for Simon's house,
appeared at the gate.
Acts 10:17

God often hides something from you so that you can find someone He wants to connect you with. God is the architect of partnerships. He will often give you only one half of what you need to be complete, so you will be driven to find the other half He has planted in someone close by. In Peter's vision, Peter did not receive its "understanding" until he spoke to Cornelius. *While they talked, Peter was able to put two and two together to discern what God was trying to communicate to him.* What piece of the puzzle is missing in your life? Where and within whom could God have placed it for you to find?

Whom has God designated as a missing piece to your puzzle? In my book *PERSUADE*, I discuss how "The Law of the Prospector" was birthed from the principle that God does everything through a person or place, and He always plants something in someone close by so you will be drawn to the right people on your path. This truth causes me to look around and within every time I have a need, knowing that while God is answering my prayer, He wants to put me together with someone so I, too, can be an answer to their prayer. It is up to you to discern where God has planted the solution to your problem. If you are unsure where to start, here are a few suggestions.

TALK IT OUT TO DRAW IT OUT

- Ask God for help, then wait to see what person He brings to mind. Don't discount anyone He flashes across the screen of your imagination. It may be someone from your past or present.
- Begin to share your need with those you come into contact with and see who engages you. You'll be surprised how solutions begin to emerge as you "talk it out" with someone God leads you to. Sometimes God will speak a solution to you in a seemingly unimportant conversation if you have your antenna up.
- Read Scripture with an open heart and, as you do, keep your query planted in the forefront of your mind: "God, what should I do about this?" Turn on your "seeker-sensitive antenna" to see what emerges.

REFLECT TO CONNECT

1. Whom do you feel led to share your problem with today as a way to "talk it out"?

2. What problem are you facing that someone close by may have some experience with?
3. Is it possible that someone in the last week has sought you out to be a "hearing ear" about something they are struggling with, and you dismissed them?

God's partnership plan includes giving one piece of the puzzle to you and another to someone else so you will be driven to "seek out the missing piece."

———————————◆◆◆———————————

GODLY GOAL SETTING

WEEK 1 | THURSDAY

Then the LORD answered me and said, "Record the vision And inscribe it on tablets, That the one who reads it may run. For the vision is yet for the appointed time; It hastens toward the goal and it will not fail. Though it tarries, wait for it; For it will certainly come, it will not delay."
Habakkuk 2:2-3

Have you asked God for a vision for your life? Not all visions come from God, but when God impregnates a vision within you, He does so on the tablet of your heart. Vision shows up as a picture or desire to move you in a specific direction. Once you commit to this vision, your reticular activator, better known as the "attention center of the brain," begins to capture and catalog all manner of information and inspiration to bring about what God has brought about. Like search results capturing relevant information, your mental neural net is now programmed to recognize and attract unseen forces to help you accomplish the desire that now burns within you from the vision God gave you. This is the built-in mental mechanism God has given you to become successful.

Incubate to impregnate yourself with vision until it is birthed in your life. If you behold the vision and do not let it fade, it will grow and become larger within you. As it grows, it takes shape, and as it does, you are compelled to act on it. Successfully pursuing a vision for your life will include goal setting. Submitting your goals to God will ensure they are healthy and balanced for the journey ahead.

When you write your goals, write them in pencil—
they will evolve as you pass through the seasons of life.

Below are a few areas of goal setting to consider. You will need to customize your list based on the area of your life you are working on in this season. Remember, it is not possible to work on ALL goals at the same time. If you chase two rabbits, both will get away.

1. **Spiritual**: Before you can learn God's purpose, He wants you to know Him as a person. Setting aside time each day to learn about Him and talk to Him is the most important goal you can set according to Matthew 6:33. Everything you put God first in, He will bless.

2. **Social and Relational**: Whom do you need to attract to your inner circle, and who needs to be released from it? Ask God to give you discernment as to who belongs and who doesn't. Some people will empower your vision; others impede it.

3. **Emotional**: The key to feeling a certain way is to *think* a certain way. Controlling your emotions is central to success. Define how you want to feel and the successful ways of thinking you need to pursue. You can learn these from Scripture and people from whom you'd like to adopt behavior.

4. **Vocational**: In the lane of your assignment, what growth, positional, influential, and intentional steps will you measure your progress by?
5. **Financial**: There is an important link between finances and achieving one's life purpose. Money is a powerful tool in the hands of a giver. You've got to make enough to be generous. What income goals have you asked God's help with?
6. **Physical**: What regular exercise programs and eating disciplines will you put in place to ensure you have the strength and stamina to stay the course?

REFLECT TO CONNECT

1. Are there areas of your life that might be out of balance?
2. How can you help someone else accomplish their goals?
3. What goal or vision has God given to you for this season?

Incubate to impregnate yourself with God's vision until it is birthed in your life.

RISE

WEEK 1 | FRIDAY

For God has not given us a spirit of timidity, but of power and love and discipline. 2 Timothy 1:7

There is an acronym for F.E.A.R. that has helped me to choose faith over fear—well, two, actually. The acronym stands for two choices that we all have to make: "Forget Everything and Run" or "Face Everything and Rise!" I choose the latter. At some point or another, every saint will face fear with this decision: "Will I persevere and move forward, or will I shrink back and stay where I am comfortable?"

Fear can be facing an upcoming uncomfortable conversation, rejection, or a sense of impending doom from a performance expectation. We all must manage our F.E.A.R., and thus, you need a strategy for overcoming it in the moment of decision. That strategy includes reciting God's words aloud so you can feel what God feels, for faith comes by "hearing" the Word of God (Romans 10:17). Here are a few of God's words that empower me to move forward in the face of F.E.A.R.

It is written...

- "I can do all things through Him who strengthens me." (Philippians 4:13)
- "Greater is He who is in me than he who is in the world." (1 John 4:4)
- "God has not given us a spirit of timidity, but of power and love and discipline." (2 Timothy 1:7)
- "Your servant has killed both the lion and the bear; and this uncircumcised Philistine will be like one of them." (1 Samuel 17:36)
- "We overwhelmingly conqueror through Him who loved us." (Romans 8:37)

When you are facing fear, remember what faith stands for: F.A.I.T.H. = Forward Action Inspired Through Him.

REFLECT TO CONNECT

1. When was the last time you were paralyzed by fear?
2. Do you have a strategy for overcoming?

3. In what ways has God challenged you to leave your comfort zone and set sail for uncharted territory?

You are made to be a conqueror through His Word,
which gives you power to overcome.

THE FOUR VOICES

WEEK 2 | MONDAY

*Forsaking the right way, they have gone astray, having followed
the way of Balaam, the son of Beor, who loved the wages of
unrighteousness; but he received a rebuke for his own transgression,
for a mute donkey, speaking with a voice of a man, restrained the
madness of the prophet.* 2 Peter 2:15-16

Have you ever talked yourself into something you knew you shouldn't have? Balaam was an important prophet and a mouthpiece for God to the nation of Israel... until he wasn't. Balaam started off well, but things went south when he allowed his greed to override his good judgment. He fell prey to *listening to the wrong voice* when he put his desire above God's command. He was offered a bribe, but he knew better. Wanting to justify himself, he asked God, and God answered. Not liking God's answer, he allowed himself to be talked into asking God again.

Have you ever not liked an answer to prayer but kept asking? God steered Balaam away from making a bad decision, but Balaam persisted. The Apostle Paul describes our mechanism of right and wrong in Romans 2:15: Our conscience excuses or accuses us. Conscience can be bent and even broken if one is not careful. For example, if after knowing the "right" in a situation, one persists in doing wrong, the sensitivity which first made the conscience cry out will be quieted or silenced entirely, making it easier to ignore the conscience again in the future.

If you ask God for guidance but ignore His answer, often another voice will emerge, wanting to substitute itself for the voice of God. That is what happened to Eve when she put her desire above God's command. Failing to follow what you know is right opens the door to becoming self-deceived.

There are four voices you must learn to distinguish clearly:

YOUR VOICE: Your mind automatically and habitually feeds thoughts and impressions to you. It is important to distinguish between an "auto thought" or "auto suggestion," which requires processing and thinking through vs. that of a "knowing thought," which comes from God. Your brain was designed by God to be an internal supercomputer that serves you. You must direct your thoughts or become a slave to them.

GOD'S VOICE: God's voice is intuitively discerned. You may feel yourself thinking or processing in self-talk, but a sudden certainty of "knowing in your knower" what to do is the defining factor of knowing vs. thinking. For example, the voice of conscience tells you instantly what is right or wrong; you can rationalize all you want, but you know better. What does God's voice sound like? God's voice sounds like the Bible, always pointing us toward the higher and more difficult road. Learning His voice will help you distinguish between the four voices.

OTHER PEOPLE'S VOICES: This includes daily conversations, the Internet and media, people of influence speaking into your life, and past conversations remembering what others have said. It is important to differentiate outside influences from your inside thought life. How do you know if God is speaking through another to get a message to you? God asks us to "test the spirits" to make sure they are from Him. Specifically, testing any message from God will require that it line up with and not be in contradiction to Scripture. It points to those things that are God-honoring and edifying for others, not those things that are selfish and bring others down.

THE ENEMY: A demonic voice finds its entry into a person's subconscious as a suggestive thought that masquerades as one's own. How can you distinguish the enemy's voice from others? The suggestions or impressions you receive from the enemy will contradict the Bible and go against your conscience. The enemy's trap is to entice one with a sense of self-satisfaction or payoff at the expense of another or acting contrary to one's conscience. If you are ever feeling a certain way or attempting to change the subject of your own self-talk but feel resistance, be aware that this is one piece of evidence that the enemy is attempting to intrude and override your will.

REFLECT TO CONNECT

1. Can you recall a time when your conscience steered you away from a decision or course of action you were contemplating?
2. Which of the four voices within you is the loudest right now?
3. Have you ever found yourself "talking yourself into something" like Balaam did?

If you ignore the voice of God in your life,
another voice will step up to take its place.

STOP SELLING AFTER THE YES

WEEK 2 | TUESDAY

So David received from her hand what she had brought him,
and said to her, "Go up to your house in peace. See, I have listened
to you and granted your request." 1 Samuel 25:35

Don't talk past the sale. Once David agreed to and affirmed that Abigail had been successful in convincing him to follow her recommendation, Abigail stopped talking and went her way. Abigail was in a tense situation, yet she was wise enough to know when to end and exit the conversation. Have you ever been in a conversation with someone when they didn't know when to stop talking? People can get what they want in a conversation and then talk the other person out of it by continuing to talk when they should be listening or leaving.

In Abigail's case, she was standing before a king. Have you ever thought long and hard about how to make an "ask" of someone in authority? Maybe you had a conversation coming up with a spouse, a supervisor, a loan officer, or someone of great influence or authority. In that case, you likely thought through the conversation, prepared yourself mentally and emotionally, and knew what you would say and even how you would ask your request. Here are a few ways people sabotage themselves in a "selling situation" you can be on the lookout for the next time you are making a big "ask" of someone in your life or someone is making an "ask" of you.

- **Nervousness:** When people get nervous, they have a hard time not talking. Excessive talking in sales, negotiation, or high-stakes conversation will eventually make the other person nervous.
- **Hold Your Peace:** After making an "ask" (your request), be silent and let the other person answer. If you take the bait off the hook, you'll never catch a fish.
- **Professional vs. Causal Rapport:** It's not uncommon when a person receives a yes to their "ask" that their guard comes down, and they forget their surroundings and become too personal or too familiar when a professional rapport is more appropriate than a casual conversation.

1. As you reflect on requests (ASKS) you've made in the past, do you recall your emotional state and how you handled yourself during the meeting?
2. Is there a safeguard system or mental trigger you can put in place to alert you of when to further your argument or make your "ask" and leave the room?
3. Whom do you know that is good at getting what they want and then knowing when to exit?

It's self-sabotaging to make an "ask" and then keep talking without giving the other person time to answer.

GOD'S GPS

WEEK 2 | WEDNESDAY

Delight yourself in the LORD; And He will give you the desires of your heart. Psalm 37:4

Human nature is wired to pursue pleasure and avoid pain, to have peace when we make the right decision, and restlessness when we make the wrong one. The purpose God plants within us is like a tractor beam that causes us to find pleasure and peace when we stay on course or pain and restlessness when we drift off course. To be sure, these signals should always be tested against God's Word, but they are also God's "magnetic pull" within us, guiding us to His designed destination.

If there is a right place that we belong, that means every other place is wrong. The GPS (God Positioning System) that God often uses is our heart, guided by His Word to keep us or move us where we should be. C.S. Lewis said it this way: "God whispers to us in our pleasure, speaks to us in our conscience, but shouts at us in our pain." Is God using pleasure or pain to talk to you today?

Where is God's tractor beam leading you? Interrogative questions will unearth strong emotions that can act as clues to guide you through the present, then propel you into your future.

6 CLUES TO DISCOVER GOD'S GPS FOR YOUR LIFE

1. **What keeps me up at night?** Worry is a clue of something God wants you to break through and resolve or embrace and overcome.
2. **What burdens am I carrying?** What occupies your mind consistently is a clue to an assignment in that season.
3. **What brings me fulfillment?** What you are doing when you lose track of time is evidence that you are running in your lane of assignment.
4. **What is causing me pain?** Unless you are called to a season of brokenness, pain is a strong indicator of "where" you don't belong and "what" you don't belong doing.
5. **What frustrates me?** Anger and discontent are powerful emotions—until you learn to leverage negative energy to leave your present circumstance, you will never reach the future God intended.
6. **Where am I fruitful?** There is always provision and plenty in His presence. God always provides where He guides.

1. Whom do you know that has learned to discern God's direction in their life?
2. GPS: Where is your GPS, your "God Positioning System," guiding you?
3. What clues have you discovered God is using to communicate with you?

God communicates with you before He tries to move you.
What is He saying?

DIVINE INTERSECTIONS

WEEK 2 | THURSDAY

Do not neglect to show hospitality to strangers, for by this some
have entertained angels without knowing it. Hebrews 13:2

A few years back, on the way to Jerusalem, we stopped in Athens, Greece, for a few days. Leaving the airport at 2 a.m., it was difficult to find our flat in a neighborhood because the street signs were in another language. After two hours of wandering, we were lost. Those of us in the van began to pray because, for the first time, we realized what it meant to be reading "Greek." We saw a young girl walking along the road, and we stopped to ask her directions. To our surprise, she said, "I'll take you there," and she hopped into our van uninvited. Within a short period of time, we arrived at our destination. Before she left, we told her who we were and asked her name. "My name is Gabrielle," she said. Gabriel was known as the angel who gave directions and information in the Bible.

You can expect divine Providence for assistance at times in your life. For it is God who wills and works within you to accomplish His purposes (Philippians 2:13). Although you cannot spend your days looking for signs and angels (that would be highly unproductive), you *can* spend your day in an attitude of prayer looking to God for His guidance and direction. It is said that we "live our faith forward but see it played out in reverse." One day we will look back and see all the times God was there helping and directing us to find our way. Do you pay attention to strangers that appear on your path? What chance encounters have you encountered? When you become aware of God's hand of Providence, intentionally serving those within your reach will create tangible, recognizable God moments in the intersections of your life.

REFLECT TO CONNECT

1. When was the last time you recognized God helping you in the middle of your workday?
2. Did the "help" seem to emerge unexpectedly or follow a prayer request?
3. If you knew God had your back every step of the way, what would you attempt to do or achieve?

God walks around dressed in plain clothes every day—do you recognize His providential fingerprints in your life when He shows up?

THE BAR OF EXPECTATION

WEEK 2 | FRIDAY

Whoever forces you to go one mile, go with him two. Matthew 5:41

When Jesus walked the earth, the law stated that a Roman soldier could not compel a citizen to carry their gear more than one mile. Jesus used this as an example to challenge people's thinking to do more than settle for the least. This became known as "going the extra mile," or doing more than is expected of you.

If you were to outline expectations of what your customers, company, or supervisor might consider meeting expectations, what would that list look like? How would you judge if you were missing, meeting, or exceeding expectations? Consider grading yourself on a scale of 1-10 from the following list, which is taken from "The Law of Relationship" in my best-selling book *PERSUADE*. Customize the questions to whom you serve in your business and then grade yourself.

EXPECTATIONS

1-10

- Being late or unprepared   _____
- Letting problems go unresolved   _____
- Failing to notice signals of dissatisfaction   _____
- Forgetting to watch over the little things   _____
- Paying attention to details   _____
- Keeping your promises   _____
- Showing up on time, informed, and prepared   _____
- Calling back even if you don't have an answer   _____
- Uncovering their need before sharing your need   _____
- Listening, then following instructions   _____

- Making good (and then some) on mistakes that were made   _____
- Asking for feedback on how to improve   _____
- Surprising people with gestures of appreciation   _____
- Remembering what is important and acting on it   _____

REFLECT TO CONNECT

1. Whom do you need to over-deliver for this week?
2. What area of expectations do you need to improve upon?
3. How would those you serve grade you on your ability to meet and exceed expectations?

The bar of expectation is usually hidden within plain sight. Doing more than is expected causes people to think more of you.

THE BABY AND THE SWORD

WEEK 3 | MONDAY

"Get me a sword." So they brought a sword before the king.
The king said, "Divide the living child in two, and give half to the one
and half to the other." Then the woman whose child was the living one
spoke to the king, for she was deeply stirred over her son and said,
"Oh, my lord, give her the living child, and by no means kill him."
But the other said, "He shall be neither mine nor yours; divide him!"
Then the king said, "Give the first woman the living child,
and by no means kill him. She is his mother." 1 Kings 3:24-27

King Solomon had a dream where God asked him what he
wanted. When Solomon asked for understanding and good
judgment, God rewarded him with WISDOM.

What is wisdom? It is discernment—the ability to know what
to do, how to do it, and when to do it. Immediately following God's
gift of wisdom, God would arrange for a public demonstration. In
my book *PERSUADE*, "The Law of the Sixth Sense" will teach you
how to develop a sense of the T.I.E., *Timing, Intuition, and Emotion*. While emotional intelligence deals with reading emotions in
yourself and others, a leader leveraging their sixth sense brings timing and intuition into the equation. With a developed sixth sense,
you can read and lead a situation, assess the emotional environment,
and then use wisdom to create a productive outcome.

Emotional intelligence isn't enough. In a stunning demonstration of God's wisdom, Solomon ordered the dividing of the baby
with a sword as a way to *set the stage for the emotional reaction of*
both mothers to be observed. Solomon knew (intuition) that the true
mother would never allow the child to be killed. While one mother
spoke up to protect her son, the other showed indifference to the
child's life. In that moment (timing), while Solomon observed the

emotional reaction of both women, he was able to determine who the true mother was. Success in any field requires a degree of leveraging the sixth sense, knowing how to use Timing, Intuition, and Emotion to create a productive outcome for yourself and others.

What are you doing to increase your ability to grow the T.I.E. in your leadership?

REFLECT TO CONNECT

1. Whom do you know that has a sense for what to say, how to say it, and when to say it?
2. Can you recall a time when you were "out of sync" with something you said or "missed the moment"?
3. What steps can you take to become more aware of the sixth sense in operation during meetings and conversations you attend?

A highly trained Sixth Sense (T.I.E.) is the differentiator between the talented and uber-talented.

———————◆◆◆———————

THE A.R.T. OF CORRECTION

WEEK 3 | TUESDAY

A gentle answer turns away wrath, But a harsh word stirs up anger.
Proverbs 15:1

Have the right heart when correcting. Whether you are a parent, teacher, leader, or coach, correcting bad behavior or poor performance is never easy. Hebrews 12:6 says, "For whom the Lord loves He disciplines." If people know you care for them and they trust you, their hearts will be open to what you have to say. When people believe you have their best interest at heart, fear dissipates, walls go down, and you have a straight line to influence the heart.

Remember, when you are correcting someone, you are not only handling a problem; you are handling a person.

Correction is more art than science. While specifics can be boiled down to a multi-step approach, the A.R.T. of correction must be adapted to each person and set of circumstances. Your potential as a leader can skyrocket or sink based on your ability to help those around you to grow past their limitations. Here are a few simple steps to help you navigate the process of correcting poor performance and behavior.

THE A.R.T OF CORRECTION

A ffirm your appreciation for them by acknowledging their strengths and contribution to the organization.

- **Connect** to the heart. People consider themselves and their contributions valuable, even sacred. Verbalize your confidence in them by acknowledging specific ways their contributions benefit the team.
- **Speak** to their talent sets and strengths you have observed in operation using specific examples. People don't mind a little "buttering up" as long as it is sincere, meaningful, and from the heart.

R esist the temptation to communicate in anger or frustration; instead, correct in gentleness, confront with candor, and coach with clarity.

- **Correct** in gentleness. A meeting with a person in authority already carries a weight of heaviness and intimidation. For this reason, the leader may need to go the extra mile in disarming a defensive employee. Try to separate the person from the problem so you can speak to the issue while stewarding the heart that has been entrusted to you.

- **Confront** with candor. Addressing the issue head-on and not beating around the bush makes for a more productive meeting on a subject that is already difficult for the one being corrected. If you are not prepared with your talk track and the tone necessary to be effective, it is a form of emotional abuse to lead a person through a corridor of their failures or weaknesses without being able to close the meeting with them feeling as if a positive deposit in the relationship bank account has been made.
- **Coach** with clarity. Outline your expectations clearly, so the person being corrected knows where the goalposts are. It is disheartening to have a meeting with a supervisor where you walk away saying, "I don't know what they want." Communicate with specific examples of the behavior you've identified that needs changing while using examples, analogies, and simple metaphors for them to understand. It may be necessary to give examples of how the organization, culture, or people have been impacted by the behavior you are discussing.

T imeline and outline specific expectations, how progress will be measured, and reiterate your confidence in them to make the necessary improvements.

- **Give** the employee an opportunity to provide feedback, so they feel as if the discussion was collaborative and not dogmatic. Follow up on what was discussed and expected in writing with a memo that includes a "what, why, and by when."
- **Look** for improvements over time to catch them doing something right and look for subtle changes they need to course correct. If you don't follow up on the "meeting of correction," they will doubt your sincerity or, worse, feel you have abandoned their growth.
- **Be sure** to encourage with confidence and affirmation regularly. Consistent encouragement and affirmation will counterbalance any relational withdrawals you've made as a leader.

1. What has been your experience in being corrected or having to correct another?
2. What do you feel is the most important skill a leader must use when correcting behavior?
3. What advice would you give to the leaders in your circle about correcting performance and behavior?

Your potential as a leader can skyrocket or sink based on your ability to help those around you to grow past their limitations.

THE ART OF PERSUASION

WEEK 3 | WEDNESDAY

For a man named Demetrius, a silversmith, who made silver shrines of Artemis, was bringing no little business to the craftsmen; these he gathered together with the workmen of similar trades, and said, "Men, you know that our prosperity depends upon this business. You see and hear that not only in Ephesus, but in almost all of Asia, this Paul has persuaded and turned away a considerable number of people, saying that gods made with hands are no gods at all. Acts 19:24-26

Influence isn't enough. Everywhere the Apostle Paul went, he preached, reasoned, and persuaded people that Jesus was the Christ and that they should turn to Him to restore their relationship with God. "To influence" means to have an "effect" on someone or something. "Persuasion" means to "move" someone to do something. Paul's goal was not to merely influence people but to persuade them in order to *move them* from darkness into light. Influence can be a stepping stone along the way to closing the sale, but influence itself is not enough. To be successful in any endeavor, you must learn to PERSUADE.

TO PERSUADE PEOPLE, CONSIDER HOW PAUL WOULD SET THE TABLE

CONNECT: Whether speaking to Jews or Greeks, Paul would build rapport by finding commonality with something from their past or present to build a bridge between himself and them. Connection always precedes closing. People must buy into what you are saying before they buy what you are selling.

COMMUNICATE: Paul used facts, figures, and sometimes miracles to persuade people that he had authority in what he was saying. Paul was passionate about his message, and that passion was convincing. It is fair to say that he also received much of his strategy from the Holy Spirit in a practical, executable way—as he passionately proclaimed what he believed, the Holy Spirit provided the conviction to convince and then convert nonbelievers into believers. When you communicate with confidence, it neutralizes the "no" people often default to when unsure or afraid.

CLOSE: Paul called for the decision. He was not preaching just to get to the end of the meeting so they could have coffee and donuts. Paul wanted the win souls for the kingdom of God. He was called by Christ to be a closer and "MOVE" people from death to life with his words and the power of the Holy Spirit. His influence continues today because of his ability to sell a sinner on the idea that they need a Savior. The Gospel has a persuasive element to it, yet it requires a closer to consummate the new relationship between the sinner and a Savior.

People are paid for results, not best efforts. You'll never see a box on your W-2 at the end of the year for "influence." Your skill level to influence others is an important step to be effective, but it isn't enough. Whether your vocational lane is in ministry or the marketplace, following Paul's strategy to convince and convert will assist you greatly in fulfilling God's purposes in your life as you pursue the art of persuasion.

REFLECT TO CONNECT

1. How would you describe your skill level with influence and persuasion on a scale of 1-10?
2. Whom do you know that has the ability to "win with others" and persuade them?
3. What is your strategy to persuade others in the direction you want to move them?

Influence isn't enough. If you want to be successful,
you will need to persuade people to take action.

———————◆◆◆———————

THE DIVINE NATURE

WEEK 3 | THURSDAY

Being then the children of God, we ought not to think that the Divine Nature is like gold or silver or stone, an image formed by the art and thought of man. Acts 17:29

P aul, in his sermon on Mars Hill, connected with his audience by commending them on their pursuit of God. His purpose was to build rapport and then "compete for the truth" as he brought their attention to a stone statue dedicated to the "Unknown God." As Paul pointed to what they proclaimed in ignorance, he then proclaimed what he knew of God and His divine nature.

How does God's divine nature work in you as you go about your day? Your personal knowledge and experience of His divinity is a precursor to proclaiming His movements within you. Can you describe how the divine nature works in you practically and spiritually?

YOUR IDENTITY AS PART OF GOD'S NATURE DWELLING IN YOU:

- You are a child of God, forgiven, approved, adored, with an inheritance waiting for you. (Romans 8:17)
- You have the mind of Christ in you who knows "all things." (1 Corinthians 2:16)
- You are seated with Christ in heavenly realms, able to hear His voice, His direction, and advice for your life. (Ephesians 2:6)
- You are set apart for good works which He has prepared in advance for you to do. His plan is laid out for you to discover, like an invisible roadmap etched on your heart. (Ephesians 2:10)
- You have access to boldly walk into God's throne room in prayer and ask anything according to His will, knowing He will grant it. (Hebrews 4:16)
- You have access to wisdom, knowledge, and discernment for decision-making. (1 John 2:27)

Every promise in the Bible is now "yes and amen" for you. As you go through your day, consider asking God to show you one more way to reveal His divine nature through you. He delights to work in you and through you, but only to the degree you allow. Give God your permission.

REFLECT TO CONNECT

1. How would you describe God's nature at work in your life?
2. Do you believe God wants to interact with you daily?
3. Are there specific ways in which you can demonstrate the DIVINE NATURE?

*The divine nature deposited in you at salvation
must be drawn out and appropriated for you to be formed
into the image of Christ.*

BECOMING A MASTER ASKER
WEEK 3 | FRIDAY

*And Jesus said to them, "I will ask you one question, and you answer
Me, and then I will tell you by what authority I do these things.
Was the baptism of John from heaven, or from men? Answer Me."*
Mark 11:29-30

Jesus was a "Master Asker." In the book *Jesus is the Question,*
Martin Copenhagen noted that Jesus asked 307 questions of His
audiences, but only answered 3. Socrates, too, was known for his
ability to sit in the city square and teach by asking questions. Great
communicators know how to capture an audience's attention using
the powers inherent within a question. Whether you are speaking
to a large room or an audience of one, the use of a question at the
right time, asked in the right way, produces powerful results. In
my book *PERSUADE*, there is an entire chapter called "The Law of
Discovery" dedicated to questions. Here are a few powers inherent
within a question:

- Questions create the emotional impact of pulling people toward you during conversation; statements push them away.
- The person asking the questions sets the direction of the conversation.
- A question is like a spoon, able to dig deep into the heart of an issue and unearth that which is hidden.
- Good questions, when asked the right way, have the ability to create an atmosphere of discovery and a sense of wonder.
- Questions "make people think" and create a healthy "pause" in the conversation.
- Questions are a powerful tool when asking for feedback.

Leaders are Socratic in their communication. Try changing your "talk track" to more *asking* than *telling* and see what happens. When you want to impress someone, talk about yourself, but when you want to connect with them, ask about them. Whether you are leading a meeting, talking with a coworker, conducting a performance review, or speaking from a platform, questions, when used the right way, draw people toward you.

REFLECT TO CONNECT

1. Have you ever developed a series of questions in order to lead yourself to a decision?
2. Whom do you know that is a master at setting and directing a conversation; how do they do it?
3. Have you met the 5 "W Brothers": Who, What, When, Where, Why?

Influence is often created more by what you ask than what you say.

ANGELS ON ASSIGNMENT

WEEK 4 | MONDAY

Do not neglect hospitality to strangers, for by this some have entertained
angels without knowing it. Hebrews 13:2

Have you ever seen an angel before? In the Old Testament, people identified "God sightings" as angels and sometimes even identified them with God Himself. Imagine the lengths God will go to in order to assist someone, to save them from danger, to save them for an eternity with Him vs. without Him. Jesus said He would leave the 99 to find the one (Luke 15:4). Now imagine God at a five-way stop intersection whereby He is orchestrating traffic flow for the Father, Son, Holy Spirit, angels, and people on your path conspiring to bring you into alignment with His plan so you can receive all He has preordained for you. If you had to list the "God incidences" or intersections in your life, what does that list look like?

Ask God to show you the miracles in your life. While you may not have seen an angel before, you can metaphorically be one today for someone else by being God's hands and feet in service to someone. I know God is always at work doing miracles behind the scenes, so I asked Him to show me examples of miracles He was doing in my life. Within a week or two, things happened I would not have been aware of unless I was "watching and praying," being alert in my spirit for His answer.

The first instance involved finding an envelope outside of Longs Drugs without postage on it addressed to a credit card company. It had been dropped on the ground by its owner, who was likely unaware it was lost. I took it to the person's house and dropped it off (they were not home). As I drove away, God pointed out to me that they would see the envelope on their front doorstep and think they dropped it there, grateful they had now found it but unaware it was God's invisible hand saving them from an unfortunate event. That was miracle number one behind the scenes.

The second took place the morning I was weed whacking. I always use open-toed flip-flop slippers but couldn't find them that morning, which had never happened before as I am a creature of habit. While I was fiddling with the weed whacker, the power engaged. The high-speed string swiped my foot, which I felt but without injury as I was wearing closed-toed shoes. If I had had my flip-flops on like the thousand times before while weed whacking, I would have gone to the emergency room, likely with one less toe. This was invisible miracle number two. One was done by God for me, and the other through me for another.

REFLECT TO CONNECT

1. What was the last miracle you experienced?
2. Have you ever suspected an "angel's" intervention in your life?
3. What would you do if you asked God to show you the miracles in your life today, and then you saw them?

While you are waiting for God to show you an angel,
you may be the angel God is calling into service
to help the person in need right next to you.

———————◆◆◆———————

THE POWER OF MOTIVATING RELATIONSHIPS

WEEK 4 | TUESDAY

But they shook off the dust of their feet in protest against them and went to Iconium. And the disciples were continually filled with joy and with the Holy Spirit. In Iconium they entered the synagogue of the Jews together, and spoke in such a manner that a large number of people believed, both of Jews and of Greeks. Acts 13:51-14:1

Know when it's time to move on. **Paul and Barnabas knew** when it was time to cut their losses and move on to more fertile ground. There will be relationships, jobs, and temporary situations that have beginnings and ends. You will also experience rejection and doors slamming in your face. Developing the ability to discern where you belong and where you don't can save you a lot of pain. Even Jesus told His disciples to depart and shake the dust off their feet when rejected.

If God is prompting you to move on, it's because He has something better planned for you. Not everyone will accept you. In my best-selling book *PERSUADE*, I discuss how you can discern between what a "right fit" looks like and what a "wrong fit" feels like. It takes self-honesty to admit that you can't win everyone over, so you will know when it is time to cut your losses and move on; get used to it. Consider the contrast between the right and wrong relationships:

Motivating Relationships Will:	Demotivating Relationships Will:
• Energize you	• Drain you
• Perceive you can meet their need	• Tell you they have no need
• Welcome and receive you	• Reject you, and then forget you
• Put you off only temporarily	• Put you off indefinitely

- Signal a connection with you
- Be accepting of your presence
- See value in you
- View you as a solution to a problem

- Show contempt toward you
- Resent your presence
- Devalue you
- Perceive your presence as a problem

REFLECT TO CONNECT

1. Whom in your life do you feel fits perfectly in relationship with you and why?
2. Are there unhealthy relationships or situations you need to eliminate from your life or team?
3. Can you give an example of a relationship you stayed in too long?

If Jesus didn't stay in a place He wasn't wanted, why would you? Shake the dust off your feet and go where you are celebrated, not tolerated.

————————◆————————

SHAMED FOR SUCCESS

WEEK 4 | WEDNESDAY

But those who want to get rich fall into temptation and a trap, and many foolish and harmful desires which plunge people into ruin and destruction. For the love of money is a root of all sorts of evil, and some by longing for it have wandered away from the faith and pierced themselves with many griefs.
1 Timothy 6:9-10

Money is good! Pursuing money is not evil, but money as the only pursuit leads one astray. The currencies of this life are temporary, yet even Jesus said they could be converted into eternal purposes. Money, when used for eternal purposes, is godly steward-ship. Money can be a powerful weapon when stewarded for God's purposes in the fight against the kingdom of darkness. Don't ever let anyone shame you for your success or level of financial prosper-ity. Instead, turn your thoughts of money toward stewarding your resources for God's purposes. It's okay to handsomely provide for yourself, too, if your work warrants it. Even David was conscious of a reward when he asked, "What will be done for the man who kills this Goliath?"

Many people are compensated through salary and bonuses. Their job is to serve employees and customers, generate revenue for their company, and earn a well-deserved income for their fami-lies—the worker is worthy of his wages. It is NOT a sin to pursue prosperity or provision—there is a reward system in the heavenly realm *and* earthly realm. While salvation is free, rewards are earned. However, putting the pursuit of prosperity above God's purposes will lead one astray. Consider a heavenly vs. worldly mindset toward money:

SAINT'S VIEW OF MONEY	SINFUL VIEW OF MONEY
• Trusts in God	• Trusts in wealth
• Focused on earning and providing	• Focused on accumulating and keeping
• Uses money to fulfill assignments	• Uses money to attain security
• Invests money for eternal purposes	• Protects for personal purposes
• Receives money and rejoices	• Receives money but can't enjoy it

REFLECT TO CONNECT

1. What is your opinion on the use of money for worldly vs. heavenly purposes?
2. Who in your universe uses money in a way that represents godly stewardship?
3. Do you believe today's topic should focus more on an "amount" of money or the "use" of money?

God doesn't mind buttering your bread with
"more than enough"—God loves to see you do well.

----◆----

THE WORTHLESS BOSS

WEEK 4 | THURSDAY

"Now therefore, know and consider what you should do, for evil is
plotted against our master and against all his household; and he is such
a worthless man that no one can speak to him." 1 Samuel 25:17

What does a fool look like? How does one go about getting that reputation? Do you know someone who is considered unreachable and unteachable like Nabal was to his staff?

People stop talking when leaders stop listening. In the story of David, Nabal, and Nabal's wife, Abigail, Nabal is referred to as a "worthless man" by both his staff and Abigail. Why was Nabal regarded as a fool and a worthless man? Because he had a reputation for not listening to anyone, even when people were trying to warn him that his arrogant behavior was going to cost him. Nabal was unteachable and unreachable. His wife Abigail, on the other hand, was considered wise because she could learn and discern what was happening in an environment and in the moment and then adapt. How did she do this? By listening to what others had to say. Leaders listen with their eyes, ears, and heart.

My wife will bring to my attention my behavior if I talk to her with the wrong words or a harsh tone. I have learned over the years that the wounds of a friend are better than the kisses of an enemy (Proverbs 27:6). When she is correcting me (respectfully), that is my cue to listen. I want to be teachable and reachable so when these conversations pop up, I regard them as my cue to sit up and listen up. The next time you sense someone is getting frustrated with you, consider going into "listening and learning" mode. You can always disagree at a later date. However, if you develop the habit of defending yourself and not discerning the moment, you, too, could one day be remembered as unteachable and unreachable like Nabal.

REFLECT TO CONNECT

1. What reputation do you have among those you are closest to?
2. Why are those in charge sometimes unreachable?
3. How do you respond when someone is trying to correct you?

Leaders listen to learn, then adapt and in so doing,
earn the respect of those around them.

GOD'S ALLEY-OOP

WEEK 4 | FRIDAY

*Then Pharaoh said to his servants, "Can we find a man like this,
in whom is a divine spirit?"* Genesis 41:38

What's your secret weapon in serving others? God taught Joseph how to advance using this specialized approach that increased his ability to persuade wherever he went. From the pit to the palace, Joseph spent 13 years in Egypt as a slave. Starting at the age of 17, Joseph consistently proved himself. He worked his way up while increasing influence and garnering favor with both God and man along the way. What secret skill did Joseph possess that kept getting him noticed for his performance? He was focused on solving problems for those around him. Joseph solved problems for Potiphar, the prison warden, and even Pharaoh, which led him to become the governor of Egypt. Whether you are working for a boss, a customer, or trying to increase your relationship equity in the marketplace, finding a problem and solving it for another will unlock currents of favor in your direction.

As people pray to God to solve their problem, God sends you! Leaders are problem solvers. God will often place a problem on your path like an "alley-oop" in basketball to help you score. When God passes you a problem to solve for another, He is opening a door for you. For Joseph, God gave him the gift of dreams and wisdom to solve problems in the marketplace. What God-given talent are you using?

TEN PROBLEM-SOLVING QUESTIONS
THAT CREATE SUCCESS

In *PERSUADE: The 7 Empowering LAWS of the SalesMaker*, people grow in their powers of persuasion by asking themselves and others

"Problem-Solving Questions." Here are a few questions that can help you uncover golden opportunities hidden within a problem. Consider adapting these problem-solving questions so they fit you.

1. What other options do you have?
2. What problem are you trying to solve?
3. What does the perfect purchase look like?
4. What is the biggest challenge you are facing?
5. What made you want to meet with me today?
6. If I could solve any problem for you, what would it be?
7. Of all your priorities and pain points, what is at the top of the list?
8. What will be the outcome if you are not able to get what you need?
9. If you could change anything about your situation, what would it be?
10. Did something recently happen that caused you to consider buying now?

REFLECT TO CONNECT

1. What problem is God passing you the ball on?
2. What solutions do you see that no one else sees?
3. What strategy is God sharing with you that will equip you to solve someone's problem today?

Problem-solving is the golden ticket that creates currents of favor, influence, and relationship equity for your life.

STORY INVENTORY

And He answered and said to them, "Go and report to John what you have seen and heard: the BLIND RECEIVE SIGHT, the lame walk, the lepers are cleansed, and the deaf hear, the dead are raised up, and the POOR HAVE THE GOSPEL PREACHED TO THEM." Luke 7:22

I n *Persuade,* I discuss how a SalesMaker can "connect on credible ground" as a way of building rapport with others.

We've all seen TV reporters who go onsite to report on an epic event taking place. But why do news organizations bear the expense of sending someone in person when we have the technology to avoid it? Because there is no substitute for sharing—up close and personal—what you have seen and heard. Firsthand testimony carries a credibility that is hard to argue with.

Your Testimony Carries Authority. An eyewitness account is personal, powerful, and communicates a persuasive story. Articulating what you've been through, what you've experienced, and the conclusions you've come to that led you to do what you've done and feel the way you do influences people to do the same. A leader's ability to tell a story that includes a personal testimony goes a long way in gathering people to them.

What stories from your life have impacted you? Consider developing a "story inventory" you can use to connect with others. Here are a few ideas to get you started:

1. If an experience impacted you, it will impact others.
2. Talking about how the turning points in your life changed you will change others.
3. Being vulnerable and willing to share your struggles, not just successes, will connect you to others quickly.

REFLECT TO CONNECT

1. What is the testimony behind that of your product, your company, or your vision?
2. What personal experience can you share with people that persuades them to feel what you feel?
3. When have you experienced a time when it was your "conviction" that convinced another?

Witnessing is telling them what you've seen
and heard and how it changed you—nothing more,
nothing less.

DEVELOPING THE PAUL WITHIN

WEEK 5 | TUESDAY

That which is known about God is evident within them;
for God made it evident to them. For since the creation of the world
His invisible attributes, His eternal power and divine nature, have been
clearly seen, being understood through what has been made,
so that they are without excuse. Romans 1:19-20

Everybody has sensed God at some point on their journey. After all, there is an awareness of God within every person. God's life force resides within each living being, and Romans points out that each person has encountered the spiritual side of their being. Whether they acknowledge God or not, acknowledging that there are life forces within (and out) that can't always be explained is common ground most people can agree on.

Develop thick skin. Jesus said on more than one occasion, "Blessed is he who is not offended by Me." Jesus knew that once offense occurs, the heart shuts down and is no longer receptive to what a person has to say. The Apostle Paul became "all things to all men" that he might win some, which means he was flexible (1 Corinthians 9:22). Paul must have encountered many different belief systems in the marketplace, yet he made progress by identifying with them, not attacking them. In the same way, if a leader hopes to connect with everyone on spiritual ground, they must look for the thread of commonality to build a bridge that will lead to connection and relationship, as Paul did.

Until you uncover a person's "frame of reference" for why they believe what they believe, you can't connect on spiritual ground. "Connecting on spiritual ground" is one of ten different ways in which a person can build rapport and relationship from my best-selling book *PERSUADE.* Consider some of the ways in which to explore a path to building rapport on spiritual ground, and you will be well on your way to leading others to a newfound relationship with God.

THREE STRATEGIES OF THE APOLOGIST

1. **Worldview:** People define their beliefs by the experiences which shaped their past. Asking about a person's past will eventually uncover mountaintop and valley experiences, and knowing the events that shaped them can help you to understand why they believe the way they believe.

2. **Beliefs:** People can often trace their beliefs back to a parent's faith or a spiritual encounter along the way. Finding out about a person's church or religious background or asking why they believe what they believe can often uncover an area of commonality you can connect with.

3. **Pursuits:** Asking about a person's goals will uncover what they are focused on today and are hoping for tomorrow. This direction of discussion can open doors to belief, faith, and underlying motive for what is driving someone from the inside out.

REFLECT TO CONNECT

1. Regarding how you came to God, how did the person lead the conversation with you in the beginning?
2. What advice would you give to someone who wants to share their faith; how should they start?
3. Will you have more success connecting on spiritual ground by telling a person what you believe or asking them what *they* believe?

> *Until you uncover a person's frame of reference*
> *for why they believe what they believe,*
> *you can't connect on spiritual ground.*

THE KING AND THE FOOL

WEEK 5 | WEDNESDAY

"Now let this gift which your maidservant has brought to my lord be given to the young men who accompany my lord. Please forgive the transgression of your maidservant; for the LORD will certainly make for my lord an enduring house, because my lord is fighting the battles of the LORD, and evil will not be found in you all your days. Should anyone rise up to pursue you and to seek your life, then the life of my

lord shall be bound in the bundle of the living with the LORD
your God; but the lives of your enemies He will sling out
as from the hollow of a sling." 1 Samuel 25:27-29

The wisest woman in the Bible. Abigail is regarded as a woman
of wisdom in the Bible, described as someone of intelligence and
kindness. Upon hearing that her unwise husband had just rejected
and rebuffed David's request for a little consideration after protect-
ing his cattle, she quickly got into action upon hearing that David
was on his way to exact retribution against Nabal. What did she do?

Wisdom is known by her children. Abigail quickly recognized
what was about to happen and made a plan. How could a woman capture a man's attention and redirect his focus to sparing her husband's
life when he was bent on shedding blood? She appealed to the greatness
within him. It is said, "There is a king and fool in each of us. The one that
you speak to comes out." Abigail spoke to the king in David. If you need
to turn a volatile situation around, consider the strategy Abigail used.

1. Abigail got David's attention by coming into agreement with
   him about Nabal's behavior. She didn't disagree.
2. Abigail accepted responsibility for Nabal's actions and asked
   for forgiveness, even though she was not to blame. She took
   the bullet for another—this got David's attention.
3. Abigail met David's immediate need with provisions she prepared for him and his men.
4. Abigail spoke to David about an area of his strength, his
   skill with his slingshot. When you speak to someone about
   their gift, they feel enlarged, and you capture their attention
   because you are speaking to their focus.
5. Abigail spoke to David about his future and God's promise
   to make him king. By bringing something sacred into the
   conversation (someone you both respect), she appealed to

his sense of reason and the bigger picture. Talking to people about vision always moves them.

Most people are consumed with something. When you know what is on someone's mind and speak to their focus, you will gain their attention.

REFLECT TO CONNECT

1. How do you win others over?
2. What tactics do you use to calm people when they are out of control?
3. Is there a time you saw someone succeed in the way Abigail did?

When you speak to a person about their giftedness,
you have captured their attention.

THE HALO EFFECT

WEEK 5 | THURSDAY

The LORD was with Joseph, so he became a successful man. And he was in the house of his master, the Egyptian. Now his master saw that the LORD was with him and that the LORD caused all that he did prosper in his hand. So Joseph found favor in his sight and became his personal servant; and he made him overseer over his house, and all that he owned he put in his charge. It came about that from the time he made him overseer in his house and over all that he owned, the LORD blessed the Egyptian's house on account of Joseph; thus the LORD'S blessing was upon all that he owned, in the house and in the field. So he left

everything he owned in Joseph's charge; and with him there he did not
concern himself with anything except the food which he ate.
Genesis 39:2-6

G od is looking for problem solvers. Leaders in the marketplace are in the business of meeting needs and solving problems. God often advances His purposes by giving a saint the power to
solve a problem for an authority in their world. In the very position,
company, or calling you find yourself in today, God has purposes
He wants to fulfill, but He is looking for a person to fulfill them
through. God will help you to solve problems *as a way to increase
your influence and position you for His purposes.* Joseph solved a
dream problem for Pharoah and a food problem for Egypt, David
solved a Goliath problem for Saul, and Esther was positioned in
government to save her people.

You have a kingdom assignment in the marketplace. When God
opens your eyes to a unique problem or need only you see or can solve,
get excited. He is setting you up for a kingdom assignment. When God
gives you access to a king, queen, prince, or princess in the marketplace (people in high authority), look for His insight on how to serve
them by solving a problem for them. By Him blessing the work of your
hands, success in the marketplace creates a halo effect of favor around
you, and your influence grows. This is the way of the Lord to create
success for those called to the marketplace. Learn it, look for it, and
leverage it to fulfill God's purposes in your life and in the marketplace.

REFLECT TO CONNECT

1. What problems are you facing in your position today?
2. God has a strategy to successfully navigate every marketplace
   mission; have you asked Him for his strategy for you?

3. What doors of service to "high authority" has God opened for you?

Seeing a problem in the marketplace is God's way of tapping you on the shoulder and showing you the back door to success.

———————◆———————

LOOKING FOR THE NEXT DAVID
WEEK 5 | FRIDAY

For when Solomon was old, his wives turned his heart away to follow other gods; and his heart was not wholly devoted to the LORD his God, as the heart of David his father had been ... Now the LORD was angry with Solomon because his heart was turned away from the LORD, the God of Israel, who had appeared to him twice, and had commanded him regarding this thing, that he should not go after other gods; but he did not observe what the LORD had commanded. 1 Kings 11:4, 9-10

Legacy fractures if it is not built on a firm foundation. Solomon would choose a path that led to the success of Israel with temporal wealth and success but, in so doing, would sacrifice the principles his father spent a lifetime living by. Solomon would use all God gave him to create a worldly legacy that would last for one generation but be remembered for all generations. What led to Solomon building a successful worldly legacy but ended in shuttering a spiritual legacy left by his father David?

The ones being succeeded are not responsible for the decisions made by the next generation, but they *are* accountable for how they prepare the people who follow after them. Consider some of the "lessons of leadership" earned by one king vs. the gifted entitlements granted to the next king.

PICKED AND PROVEN
VS. ANOINTED AND APPOINTED

1. **David sang songs to God.** David was a worshiper who lived in the wilderness for years before becoming a king, while Solomon was raised a prince who inherited a crown. There is no shortcut to success; the stripes earned that define a person's character come from struggle, not inheritance.
2. **Knowledge isn't necessarily knowing.** David wrote to God, while Solomon wrote about God. It's possible to have great knowledge of someone and still not know them. It's possible to know the Bible cover to cover and still not *know* God.
3. **David embraced what was in God's heart, not just what was in his hand.** David followed God's heart and inherited everything, while Solomon received the gift of wisdom from God's hand and eventually lost the most precious thing. If you only seek what's in a person's hand but not their heart, mentorship has little value.
4. **God's will happens in your life only if you want it to.** David's sense of wellbeing and emotional equilibrium was dependent on what God thought, while Solomon's was on what the people wanted. David was steadfast not only in devotion but in keeping God's ways; Solomon was quick to intermarry with other nations and succumb to spousal pressure to set up places for idol worship.
5. **God gravitates to seekers.** David sought God's strategy when fighting wars and won; he grew up a "seeker" who learned to PURSUE AND LISTEN. Solomon had God's wisdom granted to him and eventually would use it to serve

himself, but David pursued God's direction and followed it to serve *the people.*

6. **God observes when you are tempted to see if you will choose your desires over His way.** David was watchful on the drift of his heart and quick to repent when he went off course. Solomon allowed, observed, and was fascinated by the seduction of his heart. While David was aware of God's opinion and adjusted himself, Solomon was sensitive to his feelings and explored the depths of pleasure until they consumed him.

7. **God has a "wilderness training program" for you; what is it?** David paid his dues learning to lead people and lean on God during his wilderness years before and after he met King Saul. Solomon walked into kingship after growing up in the pleasures of the palace. One builds character; the other, a comfort zone that is hard to leave.

8. **God watches to see if you will choose His commands over your own comfort.** David honored the role of the priest, while Solomon grew dismissive of spiritual leadership when they conflicted with his desires. It's possible to mistake the blessing of God in your life with the approval of God as both Solomon and Balaam did.

There is danger in pursuing the prosperity that comes from the hand of God while leaving the heart of God behind.

REFLECT TO CONNECT

1. Why did the Apostle Paul say in 1 Corinthians 15:33, "Bad company corrupts good morals"?
2. What are some of the "trappings" that have led you off track before?

3. What safeguards can a leader put in place to ensure they are not seduced away from pursuing God?

*Successful succession planning must include
a transfer of the heart, not just the wallet.*

THE COURAGE TO CONFRONT

WEEK 6 | MONDAY

*But when Cephas came to Antioch, I opposed him to his face, because he
stood condemned. For prior to the coming of certain men from James, he
used to eat with the Gentiles; but when they came, he began to withdraw
and hold himself aloof, fearing the party of the circumcision. The rest
of the Jews joined him in hypocrisy, with the result that even Barnabas
was carried away by their hypocrisy. But when I saw that they were not
straightforward about the truth of the gospel, I said to Cephas in the
presence of all, "If you, being a Jew, live like the Gentiles and not like the
Jews, how is it that you compel the Gentiles to live like Jews?"*
Galatians 2:11-14

It takes courage to correct a person of influence. **Just before**
Paul is about to correct the Galatians for following the law vs.
grace, he shares that he once had to correct the Apostle Peter, the
head of the Jerusalem church. Correcting behavior requires finesse
and people skills.

Correcting, like coaching, is an art form because it requires cus-
tomization based on the person and circumstance. Confrontation is
not comfortable yet is necessary for a leader to grow the organization
and those in it to higher performance levels. Whether you are correcting bad behavior, addressing a low-performance issue, or coaching
someone in people skills, learning the art of correction is necessary
for the success to continue. Here is a simple acronym I use to remind
me to *care* for the person while I am *confronting* the behavior:

A.C.T.

A: AFFIRM the person by acknowledging their contribution to the
organization, the talents/strengths they possess, and why you view
them as a valued member of the team.

C: CONFRONT the behavior that needs changing with candor, then set specific expectations moving forward so the other person knows what you EXPECT of them. Do not correct out of anger or frustration. If you successfully deliver the message but damage the person, fixing the problem while creating fear will cause you to forfeit your influence.

T: TRACK progress over time, provide feedback, and reaffirm your confidence in them to correct the behavior and make the turn.

REFLECT TO CONNECT

1. What has been your experience when someone has corrected you; did you feel condemned or empowered?
2. When you have had to bring correction into someone's life, what was the outcome?
3. How is the approach to correcting different when correcting someone who is a peer, a subordinate, or a supervisor?

Bad behavior left unchecked is considered approved by those in the organization.

———————◆◆————————

SEVEN CHARACTERISTICS OF GOD'S GIFTS

WEEK 6 | TUESDAY

Fan into flame the gift of God, which is in you through the laying on of my hands. 2 Timothy 1:6 (ESV)

A ll gifts are given by God through the Holy Spirit and meant to flow through us, not just to us. While they benefit us, they are intended to be used in service to *others*. God has made you to be a river, not a reservoir. He desires to flow through you. Like a muscle, if gifts are not used, they will atrophy and eventually become useless. Gifts that God gives to you have potential that lies dormant unless developed. When they are fed, they expand; when they get used, they strengthen. Consider the following seven characteristics of God's gifts. The Apostle Paul reminds us that "use it or lose it" also applies to giftings of the Holy Spirit when he encourages us to activate them by "fanning" them.

1. **ASSIGNMENT ORIENTED:** Gifts are given in service for a specific purpose. What gifts has God given to you, and for which vocational lane?

2. **CALLING ACTIVATED:** Gifts begin to enlarge when used for God's purposes. How have you seen your gifts expand with use?

3. **OTHERS FOCUSED:** Gifts are given in service to serve others that God puts on our path. Who is it within your power to help today?

4. **STRENGTH:** Gifts become stronger as they get used. Which gifts have you been able to strengthen through use?

5. **MULTIPLICATION:** Gifts, when exercised, multiply into other areas of giftings as they are used in different situations. How have you seen God's gift multiply to serve in new areas of need?

6. **UNLOCKED IN SEASON:** Gifts will emerge in different seasons of life, maturity, and environments. What new areas of giftedness is God unlocking in you this year?

7. **STEWARDSHIP:** Gifts are entrusted to us for service to a cause greater than ourselves. Is there a gift God has given to you that is not being put to use properly?

Kingdom leaders grow intentionally, not accidentally. Growth of our gifts comes through use and intentional personal development. Whatever you do daily will expand in your life.

REFLECT TO CONNECT

1. What gifts (talents or strengths) has God given to you?
2. Whom are you assigned to serve with those gifts?
3. What is your growth plan for strengthening your gifts?

Motivation may get you going,
but intentional learning keeps you growing.

GENUINE VS. COUNTERFEIT FRIENDSHIPS

WEEK 6 | WEDNESDAY

... flattering people for the sake of gaining an advantage. Jude 1:16

We all know them. **Friends who befriend us for what they** can get out of us. In the marketplace, sellers, in a friendly attempt to win over buyers, can give off a BFF (best friends forever) vibe. However, seasoned buyers can sense this a mile off. Using emotional currencies to win friends is normal, but falsifying friendship by misrepresenting motives is sinful. Here are a few ways to judge motives in relationships:

Pretending Friendships	Genuine Friendships
• Only want something from you.	• Always want the best for you.
• Prioritize profit ahead of people.	• Put people ahead of profit.
• Focused on adding value to self.	• Focused on adding value to others.
• Manipulates for personal benefit.	• Acts for mutual benefit.

REFLECT TO CONNECT

1. Who in your business world falls into the pretending vs. genuine friendship category?
2. Have you ever fallen prey to misrepresenting your motives for the sake of a deal?
3. Does your "integrity monitor" go off when someone untrustworthy crosses your path in business?

Manipulators maneuver to get something from you; friends look for ways to serve you.

ABCS OF CORRECTION

WEEK 6 | THURSDAY

Do not sharply rebuke an older man, but rather appeal to him as a father, to the younger men as brothers. 1 Timothy 5:1

Have you ever had to confront or correct a parent, supervisor, elder, a person twice your age, a friend, or peer? It can be intimidating and difficult to be put in a position to "speak truth to power." Bad behavior is not limited to youth only; it shows up in adults, too. My father used to say, "Adults are nothing more than children with wrinkles."

At some point, it will fall to you to have a meeting where it is necessary to confront someone you care about. It could be someone who has authority over you or a situation where there is a good chance the meeting will cost you financially, emotionally, or professionally. The stakes get higher when confronting behavior in the workplace with a coworker or supervisor or in the marketplace with a customer. Whether correcting vertically or horizontally, caring for the person should be at the forefront of your mind when confronting them.

1. **Care to confront.** Correct as you would want to be corrected, with gentleness and understanding, in an atmosphere of hope for the future of the relationship.

2. **Emotionally compartmentalize.** Get "emotionally right" before you enter the conversation. God has given each person the ability to emotionally compartmentalize personal feelings when necessary. If you are not in the right space emotionally or suffer from being wounded, frustrated, or injured by the person you are confronting, you may want to consider delaying the meeting or take in another person with you.

3. Following the simple **A-B-C Coaching Plan** to confront ensures a process that rehabilitates the behavior while caring for the person.

Affirmation: Start the conversation by acknowledging how much you value the person. You can do this by showing appreciation for their contribution to you personally or the organization. Another way to affirm is to acknowledge a person's strengths, areas of giftedness, and how they add value to you and others.

Behavior: Correct the behavior by stating what is happening, how it is affecting others, and what the expectation is for a change moving forward. Be brief, and if others are in the meeting with you, be careful not to "pile on." It is important to allow for feedback and discussion after the confrontation to ensure understanding on the issues. **Confidence:** Wrap up the meeting by encouraging the person you have just confronted. Assert your confidence in them to turn things around and reaffirm the future ahead for them and the potential you see in them. Schedule a follow-up meeting to check in where appropriate. It is important that people feel your confidence in them, especially after correcting them.

REFLECT TO CONNECT

1. When was the last time you had to correct someone?
2. What was your experience during the conversation?
3. What advice would you give to someone in your shoes?

The ability to biblically confront and correct others enters you into God's higher-calling rehabilitation and reconciliation program; not everyone can do it.

———————————◆◆◆———————————

THE DIVINE LOVE AFFAIR

WEEK 6 | FRIDAY

I will dwell among the sons of Israel. 1 Kings 6:13

How does it feel to fall in love? When I first met my wife, one of the early indications that she was "the one" was that we could spend hours together in each other's presence without talking. We were content with or without words, and we simply enjoyed "just being together." One day, I realized I didn't want to spend the rest of my life without her.

God made you to walk with Him into eternity. Imagine a love that knows your every need, desire, thought, inclination, and good and bad sides, and this love wants to be with you more than anything. Imagine there is nothing you can do to dissuade or diminish this love for you. Imagine that this love doesn't want to only be *with* you but live *in* you. This is how God feels about you; it's why He has made you His dwelling place to abide with you forever. Although He lives in you, He won't intrude, He won't ever crowd you or overstep His bounds; He wants to be invited into deeper relationship but waits on you. He's waiting for you to discover the next level of intimacy with Him. The Apostle Paul tells us that nothing can separate us from the love of God. Won't you draw near to Him now so He may reach out to you?

REFLECT TO CONNECT

1. How is God drawing you in right now?
2. What is the evidence that God is waiting on you?
3. Do you wait for a sign to draw near to God or initiate contact every day?

God desires reciprocation in the relationship so
He can draw you closer.

FORGIVENESS AT WORK

WEEK 7 | MONDAY

Straightening up, Jesus said to her, "Woman, where are they?
Did no one condemn you?" She said, "No one, Lord." And Jesus said,
"I do not condemn you, either. Go. From now on sin no more."
John 8:10-11

When the woman caught in adultery was thrown at Jesus' feet, some wanted to know why He didn't condemn her. Others wanted to know what He was writing in the sand that caused the religious leaders of the day to walk away when He said that those without sin should cast the first stone. But more important is what Jesus' response was to her sin. He let her off the hook and told her not to do it again.

Forgive means to forget. I remember saying something I shouldn't have to a boss one day, only later to come and ask for forgiveness. He accepted my apology, but I was still concerned my inappropriate comment might come back to me. When I apologized a second time, he forgave me a second time and said, "We're adults; I forgive you, let's move on." His words did more than clear my debt; they set me free. We never forget when someone lets us off the hook when we don't deserve it. To let someone off the hook when they've done wrong is just as important as forgiveness. Isn't that what we want as much as forgiveness, to know that the debt isn't just paid but that we are okay in the eyes of the one we transgressed? Mistakes are made every day in the marketplace by what people do and say. Unforgiveness can manifest as frustration goes unresolved. Whether mistakes are made out of ignorance, anger, or lack of experience, everybody deserves a second chance, including you and those around you. When you get in the habit of extending forgiveness, you get better at receiving it. Often the most important person to forgive is yourself. If God has forgiven us, who are we to withhold forgiveness from ourselves or those around us?

REFLECT TO CONNECT

1. Whom do you need to let off the hook?
2. Why is feeling free as important as feeling forgiven?
3. Have you ever done something bad on purpose and still received forgiveness for it?

When you set someone free with forgiveness,
the prisoner that is freed is you.

SELF-IMAGE BY GOD

WEEK 7 | TUESDAY

Then I said, "Alas, Lord GOD! Behold, I do not know how to speak, Because I am a youth." But the LORD said to me, "Do not say, 'I am a youth,' Because everywhere I send you, you shall go, And all that I command you, you shall speak. Do not be afraid of them, For I am with you to deliver you," declares the LORD. Then the LORD stretched out His hand and touched my mouth, and the LORD said to me, "Behold, I have put My words in your mouth." Jeremiah 1:6-9

Y ou will handicap God's ability to bring you into your potential if you choose your self-image over the way God sees you. Successful saints set aside their emotions so they can embrace His eternal assignment, which He's prepared before the foundation of the WORLD.

Trust what God says about you above what you feel about yourself. Consider what God provided to Jeremiah; He wants to provide for you, too, in the journey ahead.

1. **CORRECTION:** God corrected Jeremiah's mindset so he would see himself as God saw him and not through the limiting self-image of his youth. Jeremiah said, "I am but a youth," and God rebuked him. It's common for God to see more in us than we see in ourselves. Just as Jeremiah was immature and undeveloped in his mindset, so are we—until we learn to see ourselves as God sees us. When you feel corrected by God, get excited; He's about to move a mountain and use you to be the mountain mover.

2. **COURAGE:** God gave Jeremiah courage by putting "His words" in his mouth. When we say what God said to us, we feel the way God feels toward us. What has God said to you before? What is God saying to you today? If you are unsure, open His Word and see which verses He may highlight as you read. When you sense the weight of a verse hitting you in the heart, that's God. Stop reading and wait on God. As you meditate on what gripped your heart, write what you hear, and courage will come.

3. **COMMAND:** God gave Jeremiah a command. When you come to God, sometimes He will give you options; other times He will give you advice, and yet other times, He will tell you what to do. If God has given you an instruction, follow it. If God has not given you a new idea or instruction for a while, it's possible He is waiting for you to act on the last command He gave you. What was the last thing God told you to do? If you've been away for a while, grab a blank tablet and a pen, write down your questions for God (not your shopping list or today's to-do list), and then listen.

4. **CONFIDENCE:** Confidence to carry out a call comes from the One who called you. God's assignments in your life cannot

be accomplished through mental assent, meaning you can't THINK your way to reaching your potential apart from hearing God's voice. God's confidence comes from inward revelation. His voice is always inward because that is where He lives—in your heart.

REFLECT TO CONNECT

1. What misperceptions of your self-image do you imagine God wants to change in you?
2. Have you ever written out your questions for God and then waited for Him to answer?
3. How does the Bible say that God sees you?

When you see yourself as God sees you,
you will feel about yourself as God feels toward you.

THE DOOR OF GOD
WEEK 7 | WEDNESDAY

For thus says the LORD in regard to Shallum the son of Josiah, king
of Judah, who became king in the place of Josiah his father, who went
forth from this place, "He will never return there; but in the place where
they led him captive, there he will die and not see this land again."
Jeremiah 22:11-12

Sometimes a door closes, and there is no going back; the only way is forward. Sometimes our choices intentionally or unintentionally close a door to circumstances out of our control. Have you, God, or another closed a door for you? God often gets blamed for actions we initiated that close our doors of opportunity.

There are times I have had to pray through options, while other times, I have only had one choice in front of me. Some doors you may not want to walk through, but you know the only way forward is to walk by faith through the door right in front of you. It is only after walking through the door in front of you that God will show you the second and third doors. If your desire is to please God, you can't miss Him; He will be waiting for you on the other side of every door you walk through. Here are some questions to consider when making decisions about which doors to walk through:

1. What doors of opportunity has God opened for me in the past?
2. Whom has God put on my path in this season that could be a door opener?
3. Whom can I open a door for; what is God wanting to do in another's life through me?
4. What doors has God been prompting me to close in my life?

REFLECT TO CONNECT

1. What doors is God asking you to close from your past?
2. What doors might you be fearful of and not want to push on?
3. If God is prodding you to move forward, do you believe He won't let you fail?

On the other side of the door of faith,
God is waiting. Start walking.

THE SIXTH SENSE OF TIMING

WEEK 7 | THURSDAY

Like apples of gold in settings of silver Is a word spoken in right circumstances. Proverbs 25:11

Do you know how to read a moment? Timing is critical to success in every circumstance of life. If a stockbroker buys the right stock at the wrong time, they experience loss. If we go through a traffic light when it is red, we've advanced toward our destination but at the wrong time, and an accident might occur. Wisdom is the application of facts at the "right time." It is not enough to know what to do; you must know "when" to do it.

TIMING is a sixth sense issue. We live at the intersection of decision every day when speaking with a teacher, client, supervisor, and others in conversation. Our sense of timing leads to success or failure. If you've ever wished you would have said something when the time to say it had passed, you know what good vs. bad timing is. In my book *PERSUADE,* "The Law of the Sixth Sense" goes into detail on how to read and lead a conversation by recognizing good and bad timing. Consider the importance of timing in a profession where there is an instant reward or consequence for how we handle people's emotions, desires, and thought processes when considering a purchase:

1. Saying the right words at the wrong time = FEAR
2. Saying the wrong words at the right time = HESITATION
3. Saying the wrong words at the wrong time = STALL THE CONVERSATION
4. Saying the right words at the right time = ADVANCE THE CONVERSATION

REFLECT TO CONNECT

1. Can you think of an example of when you said the right thing at the wrong time with a coworker, friend, or supervisor?
2. Who in your circle of influence has a sense of good timing for saying the right thing at the right time?
3. What steps could you take to improve your timing during conversation?

Good timing requires one to read, lead,
and learn in the moment.

THE RELATIONSHIP EXAM

WEEK 7 | FRIDAY

Test yourselves to see if you are in the faith; examine yourselves!
2 Corinthians 13:5

Throughout Scripture, saints are encouraged to examine themselves. Ways in which to examine oneself may include:

- Evaluating your walk and the way with which you conduct yourself.
- Evaluating your thought life, feelings, and attitudes.
- Evaluating your relationship with God and others.

God's Priority is People. One of the chief roles of the Holy Spirit is to ready us for the day we will meet Jesus face to face. He readies us by transforming us day by day into the image God created us to mirror—that of His Son. Our day-to-day walk, vocational calling, challenges, and victories become the potter's wheel in which the Potter molds His clay, which is us. At the top of God's list of character traits to mold within us is the health of our relationship with others. God prioritizes healthy relationships to the degree that Jesus said that if we become aware of a relationship problem while worshiping, He'd rather we go repair it and be reconciled and then return to finish worshiping. Maintaining healthy relationships is critical to your success regardless of your chosen profession.

A theme in *PERSUADE* is "Relationship Selling," which prioritizes the relationship above revenue. In fact, I refer to the first three chapters as the "Relationship Chapters." One of the ways in which a person can examine the health of a relationship is to give themselves a "Relationship Check-Up." If you are struggling in a relationship, performing a Relationship Check-Up may reveal where the breakdown started or prevent a break before it occurs. Preparing to strengthen a relationship will always be easier than repairing one. Here are a few questions you can ask yourself about the health of your relationships. Consider adapting these questions specifically to your situation.

THE RELATIONSHIP CHECK-UP QUESTIONS   Y/N

R eliability!	Do people feel they can count on you?	____
E ngagement!	Do people feel you are engaged in meeting their needs?	____
L istening!	Do people feel you listen to them or just head-nod them?	____
A ction!	Do people see you taking steps to fulfill their needs?	____
T rust!	Do people feel they can trust you?	____
I nterest!	Do people feel you have their best interests at heart?	____
O pen!	Do people feel you are open to new ideas, input, criticism?	____
N earness!	Do people feel you are available when their need arises?	____

S ecurity!	Do people feel comfortable sharing private confidences?	___
H istorical!	Do people feel you have good or bad history together?	___
I ntegrity!	Do people feel you will always protect their interest?	___
P rincipled!	Do people perceive you as being principled?	___

REFLECT TO CONNECT

1. How do you build relationships?
2. What do people value most about working with you?
3. What one word would people use to describe you?

A "strengthening relationship" strategy
is a skill set every leader needs to learn.

SPEAK TRUTH TO POWER

WEEK 8 | MONDAY

"For you have shown today that princes and servants are nothing to you; for I know this day that if Absalom were alive and all of us were dead today, then you would be pleased. Now therefore arise, go out and speak kindly to your servants, for I swear by the LORD, if you do not go out, surely not a man will pass the night with you, and this will be worse for you than all the evil that has come upon you from your youth until now." 2 Samuel 19:6-7

C orrect authority carefully. David had successfully put down a mutiny by his son Absalom, but the price of victory was the death of his son. While David mourned his son publicly, he was inadvertently disrespecting his staff and servants privately. Joab, his commander, courageously spoke on behalf of the people and corrected his king for his behavior. Sometimes you will be required to speak into someone's life; however, do it carefully if they are an authority.

"Speaking truth to power" is often a scary and dangerous proposition. For most of us, going into our boss's office to request a raise is nerve-racking enough, but to rebuke, correct, or admonish a supervisor seems almost an impossible task. When correcting those in authority over you, pray it through, talk it through, then consider the following advice:

FIVE STEPS TO SPEAKING TRUTH TO POWER

Be Humble. If you were in that situation, how would you want to be approached? Remember that you, too, have blind spots. Put yourself in their shoes before you put them in their place. Identify with their situation emotionally before you communicate intellectually.

Be Careful. You are speaking to authority, so choose your words wisely before making your case. If you sense an open door, proceed. If you see a closed door to your input, then retreat and don't kick the door down—nothing good will come of it. Be courageous and willing to risk, but don't say something you will regret or make matters worse.

Be Brief. If you can't make your point in 3-5 sentences, you have not thought it through enough. You should be able to state the issues, how it's affecting others, and a potential solution in 1-2 minutes or less. Spending time personally emoting and not identifying with them backfires because you are focused on yourself and not them.

Be Gentle. "A gentle answer turns away wrath, But a harsh word stirs up anger." (Proverbs 15:1) If you speak out of frustration, your emotional response will be what is remembered over the importance of your argument.

Be Thankful. Thank your supervisor for their willingness to allow you to be heard and close the meeting compassionately and quickly— do not linger lest you say what shouldn't be said out of nervousness or frustration.

REFLECT TO CONNECT

1. When was the last time you encountered a scenario where speaking truth to power was required?
2. How can you mitigate the uncomfortableness that comes from dealing with difficult conversations?
3. What advice would you give to a friend who has to speak truth to power to a customer, coworker, a parent, or supervisor?

Those in authority can sense who is manipulating
them and who is looking out for them.

———————◆———————

THE SUICIDE OF
SELF-PROMOTION
WEEK 8 | TUESDAY

"Of all my sons (for the LORD has given me many sons),
He has chosen my son Solomon to sit on the throne of the kingdom
of the LORD over Israel. He said to me, 'Your son Solomon is the one
who shall build My house and My courts; for I have chosen him to be a
son to Me, and I will be a father to him. I will establish
his kingdom forever if he resolutely performs
My commandments and My ordinances, as is done now.'"
1 Chronicles 28:5-7

When it came time for the transfer of position and power of kingship, Adonijah, Solomon's brother, sought to assume the position of king. His choice to anoint himself led to his death. Consider the contrast between a vacancy being filled by a self-appointed king vs. a God-anointed king:

Self-Appointed	God-Anointed
• Decides the timing and terms of appointment	• Waits for the timing of God's appointment
• Is motivated by self-interest	• Is empowered by God's anointing
• Is moved by what others say	• Is moved by what God says
• Self-promotes their assignment	• Is promoted by others
• Selects their inner circle	• God reveals the inner circle

- Promotes their position

- Is positioned by God for favor with men

God won't allow your talent to take you to a place your character won't sustain you. Acting wisely requires positioning oneself in business, whether you are leading or following. There is nothing wrong with positioning oneself in a positive light when done with integrity. God promotes in His time, and after seasons of trying and testing, His promotions stand the test of time. Self-promoting only short-circuits God's development process of getting you ready for His greater purposes. The marketplace is the canvas with which He works His will to fashion you into the likeness of His Son. If you are not sure where you are in the cycle of testing and promoting, ask Him to show you His hand in your career.

REFLECT TO CONNECT

1. When you have to share the stage, are you ever tempted to self-promote or edge others out?
2. Whom do you know that raises their hand to put themselves in a place of prominence?
3. What do you feel are the "character qualifications" of the next rung up on God's ladder?

People promote you for performance,
but God promotes where character and
competence intersect, and performance follows.

———————————◆◆◆———————————

THE ART OF HONOR

WEEK 8 | WEDNESDAY

And He could do no miracle there except that He laid His hands
on a few sick people and healed them. And He wondered
at their unbelief. And He was going around the villages teaching.
Mark 6:5-6

Honor and faith must be in the atmosphere for God to perform a miracle. That's why Jesus so often asked prior to doing a miracle, "Do you believe I can do this," or "What do you want Me to do for you?" He was confirming honor and belief were present while building expectation with the audience surrounding him. If faith wasn't present, He would change his surroundings. While visiting His hometown, Jesus performed miracles that people saw with their own eyes, yet their unbelief and familiarity with Him eventually neutralized the power of God. Unbelief and dishonor are powerful forces that can cancel out the power of God to perform a miracle.

Go where you are celebrated, not tolerated. Whether you are a salesperson calling on a customer, an employee at a corporation, leading, or serving in the nonprofit or public sector, it's important to behave in such a way so that you practice the art of honoring. Leaders can create an atmosphere of honor by:

1. Celebrating the contributions, talents, or gifts of people by acknowledging the greatness in them. Doing this creates empowerment and appreciation in the atmosphere.
2. Contributing to others by serving their needs, asking for their input, and helping them to overcome weaknesses.
3. Communicating in words and actions that make deposits into the relationship bank account.

4. Caring and praying God's best for others, especially those who do not treat you well.

As you practice these godly qualities, you are creating an atmosphere around you where God can work miracles in and through you. If practicing the "Art of Honor" doesn't improve your environment, it is possible God is guiding you to leave one place for another, exit one relationship in exchange for another, or be moving you to a place or people group who will honor and celebrate your contribution. Even Jesus knew there were places He didn't belong. In some places, He sensed it was time to go; in others, He was asked to leave. Not everyone will celebrate and honor you. If you encounter this situation, get over it, shake the dust off your feet, and advance to where God is leading you. The place of your assignment has changed.

REFLECT TO CONNECT

1. Who honors your contribution at work, in your peer group, in your community?
2. Whom can you show more honor and respect to in relationships?
3. What is God showing you about how to give respect and honor to those around you?

The atmosphere of honor can be created, and it makes way for miracles.

———————————◆———————————

THE GOLIATH TRACK
TO ADVANCEMENT
WEEK 8 | THURSDAY

When all the men of Israel saw the man, they fled from him and were
greatly afraid. The men of Israel said, "Have you seen this man who is
coming up? Surely he is coming up to defy Israel. And it will be that the
king will enrich the man who kills him with great riches and will give
him his daughter and make his father's house free in Israel."
Then David spoke to the men who were standing by him, saying,
"What will be done for the man who kills this Philistine and takes away
the reproach from Israel?" 1 Samuel 17:24-26

What Goliath are you facing today? David was opportunity-oriented—he could sense a divine appointment when it showed up on his path. While visiting his brothers on Israel's battlefield, he noticed a reoccurring problem that no one could solve. The Philistine army taunted Israel daily by challenging their bravest to face Goliath, but no one had the courage to meet the challenge.

What do you see that no one else sees? Within your sphere of influence, there is someone who has a need you are uniquely equipped to meet. What problem has God given you a unique insight into? God will often arrange a public performance of your abilities like He did with David when He wants to advance you.

Opportunity is created through problem-solving. John W. Gardner, former Secretary of Health, Education, and Welfare, said, "We are all faced with a series of great opportunities brilliantly disguised as insolvable problems." Is there a king in the marketplace you work for that has a Goliath-sized problem?

In *PERSUADE*, I discuss the importance of meeting needs in business. Every person has visible and invisible needs. The visible need is why they meet with you, and the invisible need is why they will buy from you. When you become sensitive to discovering the needs around you and how to meet them, doors of opportunity swing open for you. Without a need to meet or a problem to solve, it will be difficult to make a sale, get promoted, get noticed, or increase your influence. Meeting needs and problem-solving is one of the greatest ways to add value to others and increase your influence with them. Zig Ziglar said, "You can have everything in life you want, if you will just help enough other people get what they want."

REFLECT TO CONNECT

1. What needs around you have you become sensitive to?
2. Is there a situation God has given you a unique insight to?
3. Whom do you feel an unction to call today and inquire as to what they are facing?

Every person carries within them visible and invisible needs.
The visible needs are why they are meeting with you.
The invisible needs, when met by you,
are why they will follow you.

———————◆———————

DEVELOP YOUR SAMSON STRENGTH

WEEK 8 | FRIDAY

Then the woman gave birth to a son, and named him Samson;
and the child grew up and the LORD blessed him.

And the Spirit of the LORD began to stir him in Mahaneh-dan,
between Zorah and Eshtaol. Judges 13:24-25

For much of his assignment, Samson was a great judge whom God worked through to bring justice to Israel against her enemies. God granted him great physical strength, and with it, he won many victories for his people. Whenever the Holy Spirit would come upon him, he would be supercharged to carry out the assignment of God for that day. In Old Testament times, God's power would come and go upon a person. Today, He lives within you, and the same power that raised Christ from the dead dwells in you.

Where is the energy in your assignment today? What goal or task does God want you to accomplish? God desires to partner with you today to accomplish His purposes. As you wait on God, submit your calendar of events to Him, and ask Him questions about your day. God loves when you ask Him questions to seek His advice. His preference is always for a dialogue, not a monologue. When you inquire of Him, He will begin to highlight what He is going to touch in your life. As you move toward what He is moving on, He will anoint the work of your hands. Follow His anointing and focus on what is creating energy in your life today. You will accomplish more with His help than without it. Projects, relationships, or sticking points in your life that you have struggled with for weeks can resolve themselves with one touch of His hand. As you focus on the works He is touching today, that anointing will spill over into the other areas of your life.

What strength has God given you? Like Samson, God will often work through something He has given you. In season, Moses had a rod, Paul a handkerchief, and Samson super strength. What are the strengths God has placed within you? Today, He wants to ignite within you the power to move you forward and to accomplish His purposes. Any gift God has given you is a supernatural talent that requires developing. What talent, when exercised, energizes you? Follow the energy moving you today and see what God can accomplish through you if you let Him guide you.

REFLECT TO CONNECT

1. What is God anointing in your life today?
2. What do you do better than anyone else—your Samson super strengths?
3. What is the dark side of your strengths?

Where the Holy Spirit moves, there is the energy and anointing to accomplish your assignment for the day.

PERSUADE LIKE PAUL (PART I)

WEEK 9 | MONDAY

When they had set a day for Paul, they came to him at his lodging in
large numbers; and he was explaining to them by solemnly testifying
about the kingdom of God and trying to persuade them concerning
Jesus, from both the Law of Moses and from the Prophets, from morning
until evening. Some were being persuaded by the things spoken,
but others would not believe. Acts 28:23-24

The Apostle Paul is the undisputed chief evangelist in the New Testament. Interestingly though, he was not an impressive man to look at. History records him as being short, squinty-eyed, and even bowlegged. However, even as an unimpressive man to look at, he would become the primary mouthpiece to bring the message of salvation to the Gentiles, become a father of New Testament doctrine, and the most prolific writer and evangelist in the New Testament. Paul said in 1 Corinthians 9:22 that he has learned to "become all things to all people" that he may win some.

Many things could be said about the world's greatest evangelist, but one thing is unmistakable: The Apostle Paul was persuasive. *Evangelism is sales,* and anyone who has attempted to make a persuasive argument can employ Paul's process for persuading. The principles of persuasion found in the Bible are timeless. Although Paul would describe his message as "simple" and not flashy, there were many occasions where his words and style of persuading and presenting moved audiences to believe using sophisticated selling skills. The Apostle Paul was a PERSUADER, a selling saint, and chief evangelist to the Gentiles. Here are a few of the ways in which a student of evangelism, communication, sales, presentation, leadership, and persuasion can learn from the Apostle Paul.

PAUL'S PROCESS FOR PERSUADING

1. **Pre-Sell the Presentation!** Paul called on the leading Jews in Rome to make his initial case. The goal of Paul's first meeting was to get a second meeting but with a larger audience. His goal was to make a small sale before a big sale by getting the "chief influencers" to get more influencers and decision-makers in the room. What small sale do you need to make before attempting a bigger sale?

2. **Prepare for the Presentation!** Paul knew he would have a large audience with many who lived in Rome. The stakes would be high, so he readied himself for his pitch. He had to make a positive impact if he was to garner momentum in getting the word out about the Gospel. Preparation for a presentation can include researching people and data points, thinking through problems and objections before they arise, and mentally role-playing an argument you will need to make. Paul was a master at all of these. How can you prepare for your next big meeting; whom can you ask to help you prepare?

3. **Pray Before the Presentation!** Prayer should always precede a presentation. God delights in giving His children success when they seek His guidance, favor, and grace for an upcoming meeting. Praying for favor with God and man can unleash early acceptance. Consider praying for wisdom, knowledge, discernment, and currents of favor that would flow to you in the direction of the decision you are seeking.

PERSUADE LIKE PAUL (PART II)

When you bring God into your work, He blows His inspiration upon you whether you are a leader, teacher, parent, seller, or singer. When persuading others to buy into you or your ideas, here are a few more ways in which the Apostle Paul became the Chief Persuader of the Gospel to the Gentiles:

1. **Persuade on Sacred Ground!** It was common for Paul to include tactical points of persuasion in his presentation. Paul would teach the Jews from the books of Moses and the prophets. Consider how Paul was able to leverage beliefs his audience held sacred as a way to identify with them on *common ground* and then connect on *sacred ground*. Acceleration in relationship building can take place by identifying shared beliefs and passions early on and then speaking to those. Knowing the Jews' convictions in the sacred text allowed him to tap into beliefs they already held dear.

2. **Connect the Dots!** Paul built a bridge by taking what they already knew in the Old Covenant and connecting it to the New Covenant, unpacking God's promises and explaining why Jesus was the Messiah. Leaders who touch on and honor the past have a better chance of persuading people to follow them into the future.

3. **Persuade with Character!** Central to a message is the messenger. Your background, credentials, and experiences all give credibility to you as a person. This is important because people must first buy into *you* before they will buy into what you are selling. Paul always started off his presentations by giving an elevator speech on who he was and why he

believed what he did. This gave weight to what he was about to say. Paul was a Pharisee of Pharisees, a Roman citizen, Greek educated, and he bore marks bearing rejection and imprisonment for what he believed in. This gave his message even more credibility when people realized the length of sacrifice and suffering he was willing to endure for what he believed in.

4. **Know Your Audience!** Paul knew how to adapt his message to his audience. He persuaded the Jews differently than the Gentiles. Paul also knew that the Pharisees would be more open than the Sadducees because they already had a foundational belief in the resurrection. Paul was adept at learning a culture, what they held sacred, and then speaking to what was important to them. *You must know your audience before you can sell your audience.*

5. **Persuade with Passion!** When delivering your message, an audience will respond to "how" you are saying what you are saying as much as "what" you are saying. A presenter must move people emotionally if they hope to persuade them logically. A passionate presentation goes a long way in converting beliefs because strong conviction in the story you tell convinces an audience. One of the best ways to convince is with personal testimony. *Telling others what you've been through, how you feel, and why you are "fully persuaded" moves people from indifference to decision.* People buy into passion when they see that it is lived outwardly, not just felt inwardly.

PERSUADE LIKE PAUL (PART III)

WEEK 9 | WEDNESDAY

1. **Be Bulletproof!** Paul was a seasoned evangelist, having persuaded people in The Way for years. He knew there would always be some who would accept his message while others would reject it. He knew he would have a failure rate; nonetheless, he never ceased to continue to persuade people wherever he went. Paul wasn't dissuaded by the nos. He always turned a *rejection* into a *redirection* for the Gospel by moving from one prospect to the next, one assignment to another, and finishing the task at hand. Paul embraced the Lord's next instruction and stayed focused on the long-term mission, not the temporary setbacks or failures.

2. **Persuade with Evidence!** As a Persuader, your tools of persuasion will not be unlike the tools the Apostle Paul used. All persuasive arguments must have a foundation in the truth if they are to be convincing. Using facts, figures, reason, and storytelling must all find their way into your toolbox. When persuading, consider the "Feature-Benefit" approach as a way of making your presentation relevant and well received by your audience.

PERSUADE WITH FEATURE-BENEFIT
POSITIONING

Answer "WII-FM," or they will tune you out! One of the ways in which you can successfully make an argument is to create relevancy with each statement you make. For example, each selling feature you share should be followed by how the other person would personally benefit. In your imagination, pretend that someone just gave you a key selling point, and as you heard it, you thought to yourself, "So what?" Often, what is meaningful for the presenter is meaningless to the receiver. For this reason, practicing the "so what" exercise will keep your presentation on track and your audience engaged.

Next time you want to share something with someone, say to yourself, "So what?" and then add a second statement on the back end of your selling statement that communicates what the major benefit to the other person is. This will help the other person answer WII-FM for themselves, which stands for "What's in it for me?" The best way to get and keep someone's attention is to speak to their interest in a way that is relevant to them.

REFLECT TO CONNECT

1. What do you have in common with how Paul positioned himself and his message?
2. What tactics can you employ from the Bible to become a skilled person of persuasion?
3. What is the most important lesson you learned from how the Apostle Paul persuaded others?

Evangelism is sales—the Apostle Paul was the chief sales officer for the Gospel.

EMOTIONAL INTELLIGENCE IN THE BIBLE

WEEK 9 | THURSDAY

*Now he had still another dream, and related it to his brothers,
and said, "Lo, I have had still another dream; and behold, the sun and
the moon and eleven stars were bowing down to me." He related it to his
father and to his brothers; and his father rebuked him and said to him,
"What is this dream that you have had? Shall I and your mother and
your brothers actually come to bow ourselves down before you to the
ground?" His brothers were jealous of him, but his father kept
the saying in mind.* Genesis 37:9-11

As a youth, Joseph had not yet learned how to discern the environment and atmosphere around him. He lacked emotional intelligence. While his dream was from God, he was unaware of the proper timing to reveal the dream and the emotional impact his behavior would have on his brothers and father. It would be only a few years later that Joseph, in order to survive, would learn to develop his ability to correctly read, react, and adapt in the moment.

In my best-selling book, *PERSUADE*, "The Law of the Sixth Sense" teaches how to read, react, and adapt to the T.I.E. Leveraging your sixth sense engages your senses so you can listen with your eyes, ears, and heart to all that is being communicated. You must train your sixth sense over time as Joseph did.

Timing: There is a time to speak and a time to hold your peace. There is a time to act and a time to be patient. The ability to discern a moment is critical for leaders, speakers, teachers, preachers, and leaders. What is your ability to know "right timing" during a conversation on a scale of 1-10? _____

Intuition: A bend in the road is not the end of the road unless you fail to make the turn. Intuition is a "knowing" which can be taught through experience and even intercepted when God downloads supernatural knowledge to you. How would you measure your ability to "know" what to do in the moment on a scale of 1-10? _____

Emotion: Emotional intelligence is the awareness of your emotions and those of people around you and how you direct those emotions to a productive end. The ability to read the emotional environment and the effect you have on others will feed your sense of intuition and timing so you know what to do and when to do it. What is your "E.Q." or "Emotional Quotient" on a scale of 1-10? _____

REFLECT TO CONNECT

1. Is there a time when you said the wrong thing at the wrong time? What was the outcome?
2. Whom do you know that always seems to "read the moment" correctly? What do they do that others don't?
3. What number did you give yourself for your 1-10 T.I.E. assessment? Explain each area.

Submit your situation to the Lord,
and He will give you the timing to read, react,
and adapt to the environment.

SIGNS OF A SUPERPOWER

WEEK 9 | FRIDAY

*So King Solomon became greater than all the kings of the earth in riches
and in wisdom. And all the earth was seeking the presence of Solomon,
to hear his wisdom.* 1 Kings 10:23-24

You must inventory the gifts God has given you, then develop them. He used 10 miraculous signs in the time of Moses, the gift of dream interpretation with Joseph, a slingshot with David, super strength with Samson, wisdom and wealth with Solomon, and the list goes on. When he sent Jesus, He sent a servant leader who said that He had not come to be served but to serve (Matthew 20:28). His super-power was a servant's heart willing to sacrifice for those He loved.

God deposits gifts that create success *for* you so people will be drawn to Christ *in* you. What gift has God given to you that He may display His power and personality through you? If you are unsure what part of the divine nature given to you in Christ God has gifted to you, consider a few clues to discover the greatness planted within.

SIX SIGNS OF A SUPERPOWER

1. What do you hunger for, think about day and night, dream about doing, and strongly desire? Desire and ambition are powerful positive drivers God will use to direct you.
2. What have you discovered that you do better than anyone else?
3. What have you experienced rapid learning of?
4. What are you occupied with when you lose track of time?
5. What do you have a passion for? Passion is what you are willing to "suffer and sacrifice" for.

6. Is there something that angers you that you have a powerful drive within you to correct? God often speaks through powerful negative emotions like anger, disgust, and so on.

You may not be good with a slingshot or dream very much, yet God has called you to a place of calling and people to serve. Your responsibility is to draw out and develop the God nature within you in the place of your assignment.

REFLECT TO CONNECT

1. Can you describe your purpose in a sentence or two?
2. What is your most dominant gift?
3. What gifts do you possess that you aren't actively developing?

The "God Nature" within you is His gift to you; developing it is your gift back to Him.

LEADERSHIP TALK TRACK

WEEK 10 | MONDAY

God said, "Ask what you wish Me to give you." Then Solomon said,
"You have shown great faithfulness to Your servant David my father,
according as he walked before You in truth and righteousness and
uprightness of heart toward You; and You have reserved for him this
great lovingkindness, that You have given him a son to sit on his throne,
as it is this day. Now, O LORD my God, You have made Your servant
king in place of my father David, yet I am but a little child;
I do not know how to go out or come in. 1 Kings 3:5-7

God likes to feel appreciated; do you? When God reached out to Solomon to offer him anything he wanted, Solomon did not give an answer immediately. Instead, he showed appreciation by acknowledging the "lovingkindness" God had shown to his father—and now to him. David undoubtedly coached his son on the right heart posture to have when communicating with God, to always be thankful and demonstrate gratitude. But often, kids forget that their parents appreciate being appreciated. God, too, encourages His children to "appreciate Him." David mentioned in Psalm 100:4 that we are to "enter His gates with THANKSGIVING and His courts with PRAISE" [emphasis added by author].

Leaders appreciate being appreciated. Everyone reports to someone. It's easy to forget that leaders have feelings, too. While many followers may focus on how they look to leadership, the ones who show appreciation to those they serve stand out in a positive way. Showing appreciation to leaders for what they have done for you or the organization sets you apart. On the flip side, leaders who show appreciation to their people engender loyalty and higher levels of commitment. When showing appreciation for those you are leading, remember this:

The single most important word is "We."

The two most important words are "Thank you."

The three most important words are "I appreciate you."

The four most important words are "You make a difference."

The five most important words are "I can count on you."

The six most important words are "You always do a great job."

The seven most important words are "I truly can't do it without you."

REFLECT TO CONNECT

1. To whom can you expression appreciation today?
2. How did you feel the last time someone expressed appreciation to you?
3. How does depositing value into another increase your influence with them?

Leaders look for value in people,
then find what they seek.

———————◆———————

THE RAVEN OF REVENUE

WEEK 10 | TUESDAY

The word of the LORD came to him, saying, "Go away from here and turn eastward, and hide yourself by the brook Cherith, which is east of the Jordan. It shall be that you will drink of the brook, and I have commanded the ravens to provide for you there." So he went and did according to the word of the LORD, for he went and lived by the brook Cherith, which is east of the Jordan. The ravens brought him bread and meat in the morning and bread and meat in the evening, and he would drink from the brook. 1 Kings 17:2-6

Provision is waiting in the place of assignment. Leaders look to God for direction as followers look to them to provide vision and resources for the journey ahead. As you make big decisions for yourself, your family, or your team, consider how God guided and then provided for Elijah.

- Elijah was directed to go to a specific place. In each season, you may feel a pull toward a person or place. If you are seeking God, the magnetic pulls He puts in your heart get stronger over time. Follow them.
- Elijah was obedient to go where God told him to go. He didn't know the second step, only the first. Every assignment is connected to a person whom you are drawn to work for or serve.
- Elijah was provided for *in the place* God told him to go. There is provision for the vision God gives to you. As opportunities emerge to serve, don't be picky. Compensation eventually follows servanthood in the marketplace.
- Elijah had to TRUST God's word that He would provide. Provision came from a supernatural source, seemingly out of the sky through a raven. In 1 Kings 17, God "commanded" a raven and then a widow to provide for Elijah. Elijah had probably never been fed from a bird before. How has God chosen to feed you in this season? Be careful not to shoo away the birds of provision.

REFLECT TO CONNECT

1. Have you had to trust God to provide for you supernaturally before?

2. In what ways has God provided for you in the past?
3. Are you in the right place for God to provide?

Provision awaits you in the PLACE of obedience,
often with a creative compensation package
where God provides in unique ways.

———————◆———————

PERSUASIVE LEADERSHIP
WEEK 10 | WEDNESDAY

Then the king said to me, "What would you request?" So I prayed to
the God of heaven. I said to the king, "If it please the king, and if your
servant has found favor before you, send me to Judah, to the city of my
fathers' tombs, that I may rebuild it." Nehemiah 2:4-5

Good leadership can't exist without strong salesmanship. Leadership is an exercise in persuasion. Persuasion is to salesmanship as influence is to leadership; leadership requires both. Whether you are leading one or leading many, you must develop the skills of salesmanship if you are to become an effective leader. For Nehemiah, he first set up the sale by preparing and positioning before he could close the sale. How did he do this? By leading King Artaxerxes in a way that would give him a favorable response to the requests he would make after the king said "yes" to his first "ask." Whether you believe God used Nehemiah or Nehemiah on his own used leadership and salesmanship to accomplish God's plans, both were necessary.

Nehemiah led the king using persuasive leadership. Many things God wants to do through you have a timing element to them, just like opportunities in life. Having emotional intelligence gives you the ability to recognize what is happening in you and around you so you can leverage the feelings in the atmosphere to move people. Taking it a step further, persuasion is the art of moving people from point A to B in a conversation or their behavior. But successfully using emotional intelligence requires the gift of discernment so you can act when prompted to. Engaging God in your plans invites Him to prompt you when it is time to influence and persuade. Consider some of the seasons of persuasive leadership Nehemiah had to discern to be successful.

SEASONS OF PERSUASIVE LEADERSHIP

There is a time to sell yourself and a time to sell others.
There is a time to share the vision and a time to keep it quiet.
There is a time to seek God for strategy and a time to execute.
There is a time to make an "ask" and a time to refrain from asking.
There is a time for allowing buy-in and a time for leaving naysayers behind.
There is a time to pray and wait and a time to stop praying and start acting.
There is a time for pushing your team and a time for celebrating with them.

REFLECT TO CONNECT

1. How do you use persuasive leadership (sales and leadership skills) in your day-to-day?
2. What do you view as the most important skill when leading others?
3. Of the leaders you know that successfully blend sales and leadership skills in their profession, how do they do it?

There must be a persuasive element to your leadership
if you want people to follow you. Without sales skills,
a leader's potential is limited.

———————————◆◆◆———————————

SEASONAL ASSIGNMENTS

WEEK 10 | THURSDAY

The word of the LORD came to Jonah the son of Amittai saying,
"Arise, go to Nineveh the great city and cry against it,
for their wickedness has come up before Me." Jonah 1:1-2

Assignments come from God in three discernible ways. They can all be "callings" bucketed for your benefit and God's purposes. Assignments by nature are bound by time and with windows of opportunity that open and close. If you miss an opportunity, fail to walk through a door God has opened, or refuse it, it likely goes to someone else. Yet there are still examples where God pursued his prophet Jonah until he relented from running away from his office of prophet.

The Lifelong Assignment: While God's calling and gifts are without repentance, the one called *can* refuse the calling. Moses, King Saul, and Gideon were all reluctant at first. You can receive a lifelong assignment that comes from a clear word of direction from God, a specific place and time the assignment was given, even an unavoidable apprehension where God intersects and then alters your trajectory like Paul the Apostle experienced. The honor of being handpicked by God for a lifelong office or lane of assignment requires your acceptance.

The Seasonal Assignment: Purpose discovered based on your geography, vocation, and station in life will always come with assignments that seem "present" to you in the form of a need, desire, or sense of duty as part of fulfilling a greater plan. Seasonal assignments can go on for months; they can also turn into permanent posts in serving God's purposes not yet discovered.

The Micro-Assignment: These assignments may be for the day or hour and are more fleeting. They are time-sensitive where you may feel prompted to call someone, do something, act upon an idea, or more. Answering these callings or promptings appropriately qualifies you for greater assignments. Some assignments come by invitation, others by command. They all require cooperation and being obedient to the voice of "Christ in you."

REFLECT TO CONNECT

1. Have you passed or missed out on a God opportunity before?
2. What category of assignments are you aware of in your life? Explain.
3. Have you ever "pulled a Jonah" before and run away from what God asked you to do?

> *God's assignment tells us what we must do,*
> *but not all of His "whys" behind His ask.*

———————————◆◆◆———————————

IMAGINATE WITH GOD

WEEK 10 | FRIDAY

And I said to the king, "If it please the king, let letters be given me for the governors of the provinces beyond the River, that they may allow me to pass through until I come to Judah, and a letter to Asaph the keeper of the king's forest, that he may give me timber to make beams for the gates of the fortress which is by the temple, for the wall of the city and for the house to which I will go." And the king granted them to me because the good hand of my God was on me. Nehemiah 2:7-8

Meditate to create. Your spirit is a "creation chamber." Whatever you put in it grows. When God said, "Let Us make man in Our image," one of the many qualities He gave you was an imagination. But it works best when you use it to create with the Creator. Your imagination gives you the ability to rewind the tape playing in your mind and visit your past or fast forward it to peer into a potential future. Nehemiah, in preparing for his big "ask" to the king, prayed to God for help. This invited God to strategically speak into his plans. Bringing God into your planning allows you to see what God foresees so you can be ready to capture the future as God creates it.

Meditate + Incubate = Imaginate. One quality of all successful leaders, whether they are athletes, business owners, people in ministry, or moguls in the marketplace, is they all leverage their imagination in a productive way. How do they do this? By bringing God into their planning process through prayer and meditation. This allows Him to "download" His thoughts and His "creative process" into your plans for you to accept or reject. In any new venture you are beginning, bringing your plans and putting them before God during prayer invites Him to touch, increase, and multiply your efforts. As you bring God into your plans, insights for the journey ahead will spring alive in your heart that come with His foresight and favor. Whether I am preparing to speak to a large group, sell a big client, or lead a new team, I enter my meditative planning state with an invitation to God to breathe on me. With paper and pen handy, I document what I hear and perceive, for God has chosen journaling to clarify through the pen what the Spirit has spoken. By "imaginating" with God, He will show you what to anticipate on the road ahead and how to plan for the unplannable.

REFLECT TO CONNECT

1. What would be a productive vs. destructive use of your imagination?
2. What project could you bring God into so He can co-create with you in your imagination?
3. What does it mean to "see yourself doing it" before you do it? What did Jesus mean when He said that He could only do what He saw the Father doing? Did He see the future in prayer?

   Bringing God into your planning allows you to see what God foresees. When you see it, you can seize it.

STRATEGIC SILENCE

WEEK 11 | MONDAY

*On that day King Ahasuerus gave the house of Haman, the enemy of
the Jews, to Queen Esther; and Mordecai came before the king, because
Esther had disclosed what he was to her. The king took off his signet
ring, which he had taken away from Haman, and gave it to Mordecai.
And Esther set Mordecai over the house of Haman ... In each and every
province and in each and every city, wherever the king's commandment
and his decree arrived, there was joy and jubilation for the Jews, a feast
and a holiday. And many among the peoples of the land became Jews
because the dread of the Jews had fallen on them.* Esther 8:1-2, 17

Everything God does has strategy to it; part of it is silence.
The story of Esther had a happy ending. God reversed the plot
to exterminate the Jews using King Ahasuerus. He rewarded Esther
and Mordecai and removed Haman, the enemy of the Jews, from
the equation. For God's plans to work, Esther and Mordecai had to
be careful whom to talk to, what to say, what not to say, when and
when NOT to reveal how they were related, and when to mention
or not mention or even hide their relationship with God when they
sought Him in fasting and prayer.

Don't blow your cover. There are places it would be dangerous and unwise to share with others your race, religion, plans, etc.
Evangelizing in the work environment or anti-Christian countries
unwisely would put your career, life, or mission in jeopardy. You
have to know when to button your lips. Knowing when to be covert
or overt in your place of work is an important skill set you need
to develop so as not to blow your assignment or ruin God's plans.
Even Jesus said there are some with whom sharing "good news" is
as "pearls before swine" and to "shake the dust off your feet" and
get out of there. Jesus knew during His three-year mission that He

was not to preach to the Gentiles, but to reach the lost sheep of Israel. God had the Gentile assignment planned for another time and another person, named Paul. Do you know to whom you are called?

REFLECT TO CONNECT

1. What advice would you give to someone to gauge when to share their faith and when to be silent?
2. How do you know when a door to witness is open vs. closed?
3. In what ways does a marketplace believer have a "cold start" to a conversation about Christ that a pastor doesn't in a Sunday morning service?

At times, evangelists are like CIA operatives working undercover; they need to know how to hide in plain sight yet be ready to act on a moment's notice.

WORDS THAT CREATE MAGNETISM
WEEK 11 | TUESDAY

And all the people were speaking well of Him, and admiring the gracious words which were coming from His lips; and yet they were saying, "Is this not Joseph's son?" Luke 4:22

Wherever Jesus went, He used words that created healing, magnetism, inspiration, empowerment, teaching, truth, and more. In my best-selling book, *PERSUADE*, I talk about the power of words: "With words the world was created; with words she will say 'I do'; with words you can make or break someone's day." Solomon said in Proverbs 15:1, "A gentle answer turns away wrath, But a harsh word stirs up anger." Words have the power to bring people together or break them apart. It's been said that 90% of arguments start from the tone we use when talking to people.

How you see them is how you will speak to them. With our words, we cannot strengthen and weaken at the same time; we cannot encourage and discourage at the same time. We must be intentional in the atmosphere we want to create. With words, deposits or withdrawals are being made in the relationship bank account in every conversation. The words we choose have the power to draw people toward us or make them want to retreat from us. Words have the power to create the emotional environment around us. With our words, we can choose to create an atmosphere of warmth or coldness, acceptance or rejection, distance or closeness.

Leaders use the power of words to increase their influence, empower people, and move their organization forward. Speaking words of affirmation, with warmth in tonality and with a positive "posture of the heart" toward others has the ability to create a magnetic pull between you and others. How do leaders do this using the power of words? Leaders view people in a positive light so they can speak to them in a way that creates empowering relationships.

LEADERS:
- Want the best for others.
- Think the best of others.
- Speak kindly to others.
- Plant words of hope in others.
- See and believe the best about others.
- Intentionally encourage others so they feel built up while they are with them.

1. How would people describe the way in which you communicate?
2. Regarding those who are especially loyal to you, what creates this magnetism toward you?
3. Who is a master of using words to create motivation, magnetism, and a positive environment that you could model your leadership after; how do they do it?

Words are like keys that can open or close the door to the heart; use them wisely.

SERVE JESUS BY SERVING PEOPLE

WEEK 11 | WEDNESDAY

If anyone serves Me, he must follow Me; and where I am, there My servant will be also; if anyone serves Me, the Father will honor him. John 12:26

What does it mean to serve Jesus? To serve Jesus is to serve whom Jesus loves. God often spoke of looking out for the orphans, the widows, the homeless, and those who are less fortunate or defenseless. Jesus went as far as to say that if you visit a prisoner in jail, it is as if you had visited Jesus Himself. Is Jesus saying that when we serve others, He credits it to our account as performing the same service directly to Him? Absolutely. When we look out for what Jesus keeps His eye on, He credits these good deeds to a heavenly account with your name on it where moth and rust can't destroy.

Whether you are focusing on serving God or serving those God has given to you, consider some of the ways in which you might best serve both God and others. The service-oriented person is:

- **SEEKING:** They keep their antenna up, looking for ways to serve and exceed expectations.
- **COMPASSIONATE:** They are sensitive to picking up signals that point the way to helping and adding value to others. Jesus served the Father and models for us how to serve Him by serving those He puts on our path.
- **DISCERNING:** They are aware of dynamic environments so they can anticipate future needs and act accordingly by planning ahead to meet a need before it arises.

By serving customers, coworkers, or supervisors, God uses your struggle along the road to success to shape your character as a way to position and prepare you for future success. What is the open door God puts before you to act as an invitation to partner with Him? The door to service.

REFLECT TO CONNECT

1. Whom do you feel compassion toward that you could reach out to?
2. What areas of service has God made your heart sensitive to?
3. In what ways could you provide an act of service or kindness?

When you serve people as "unto the Lord,"
it is as if you are serving Jesus directly,
and God receives your gift of service.

THE FOCUS FACTOR

WEEK 11 | THURSDAY

Finally, brothers and sisters, whatever is true, whatever is honorable,
whatever is right, whatever is pure, whatever is lovely,
whatever is commendable, if there is any excellence and if anything
worthy of praise, think about these things. As for the things you have
learned and received and heard and seen in me, practice these things,
and the God of peace will be with you. Philippians 4:8-9

W hat you feed (think on) grows in your thought life. What you starve (do not think on) dies. Why is that? Because the human heart is an incubator. Whatever you put in it and *keep in it* grows. Paul knew that "thinking on something specific" would yield a specific fruit in our lives. If you are feeling one way and want to feel another, you must begin by changing your thoughts.

You must pick a track for your mind to run on to keep it focused. The most important quality that differentiates someone successful from someone who is not is how they think. Paul was a disciplined thinker and advised us on what to think on when it comes to our spiritual life. His advice can be applied to the practical task of creating deliberate outcomes in our lives. Here are a few productive subjects by way of example you can focus your mind on:

PROSPECTING: If you set your mind to look for opportunity all the time, you will see ideas begin to emerge everywhere. This is how one leverages their God-given reticular activator, the focus center of the brain.

SERVING: If your focus is set on ways to serve and exceed people's expectations, you will find opportunities all around you.

WISDOM: If you program your mindset to think more in questions than in statements, your thought life will become Socratic.

REFLECT TO CONNECT

1. What is your mental strategy for what you will think on today?
2. If you were to inventory your thoughts, what would you discover?
3. What can you co-create with God today by focusing your thought life?

Successful people "reprogram" their minds to think successfully by renewing their thought life to see life through the eyes of Scripture. That's a God Mindset.

WIELDING THE SWORD OF PERSUASION

WEEK 11 | FRIDAY

We know that the Law is good, if one uses it lawfully. 1 Timothy 1:8

By pointing out the "good use" of the law, Paul also suggests that there is a "bad use" of the law. Since the beginning of time, God's ways, words, and wisdom have been used to take advantage of others. Incorrect use can include misapplying biblical principles to fit a situation or twisting them to suit one's own purpose. The twisting of God's Word is everywhere. Satan started twisting and misapplying God's Word in the garden and also when he tempted Jesus in the wilderness. He continues to manipulate people today with tools of truth God intended to be used to help people.

Saints like Paul wielded the sword of truth to bring instruction, correction, and closer connection to God. They also check themselves to ensure they are using their sword correctly and not coercing others inappropriately. Leaders wield the principles in the sword of truth to move people toward a decision. But while a person may work to make a sale, satisfy a customer, and provide for their family, their craft can be wielded for good or bad. What holds true in the pulpit holds true in the marketplace: You should only ever wield the sword of persuasion to serve others and honor God—this is the honorable and correct application of your saintly superpowers. If you are ever unsure of whether you are wielding the sword of persuasion for selfish reasons, ask yourself these questions: "Who is helped and who is hurt by this transaction?" and "Does it honor God?" and then make an adjustment if necessary.

Your gift and powers of communication can be used to move people, so move them appropriately.

REFLECT TO CONNECT

1. Have you ever used your influence in the wrong way?
2. How do you go about persuading others to your viewpoint?
3. Have you ever sensed God advising you in the middle of a conversation?

Great evangelistic communicators wield the sword of persuasion nobly, honorably, and biblically.

THE WALK INTO MATURITY

WEEK 12 | MONDAY

Therefore leaving the elementary teaching about the Christ,
let us press on to maturity, not laying again a foundation of repentance
from dead works and of faith toward God, of instruction about washings
and laying on of hands, and the resurrection of the dead
and eternal judgment. Hebrews 6:1-2

There are three positions we can find ourselves in: standing still, slipping backward, or moving forward. It is said that some people have ten years of experience while others have one year ten times over. Time may pass, but progress is not guaranteed. Progress happens when we make the choice to leave where we are: to trade our comfort zone for the transformative lifestyle that leads to maturity. This is true spiritually, and it is true vocationally.

So, what about you? Have you been moving forward toward maturity or going in the other direction? Here are a couple of questions to test whether you are moving forward or backward.

- Am I struggling with the same things today I was a year ago, or am I facing new challenges?
- Are the people in my inner circle challenging me to get better or stay the same?
- Am I willing to convert my TV time into growing time?

The choice to stretch, improve, and grow into maturity begins with a single step. What three things are within your power to change?

1. _____
2. _____
3. _____

1. Whom do you know that is making progress daily?
2. Do you have a daily growth plan that includes reading, reflecting, and learning?
3. What can you do differently today to make a change for the better?

Successful saints prepare for the future
by growing themselves in the present.

———————◆———————

THE REFINER'S SANDPAPER
WEEK 12 | TUESDAY

Servants, be subject to your masters with all respect, not only to those
who are good and gentle, but also to those who are harsh. For this finds
favor, if for the sake of conscience toward God a person endures grief
when suffering unjustly. For what credit is there if, when you sin and are
harshly treated, you endure it with patience? But if when you do what is
right and suffer for it you patiently endure it, this finds favor with God.
1 Peter 2:18-20

At some point in your career, you will be treated unfairly by a supervisor, a coworker, a customer, or maybe even a friend or family member—nevertheless, God sees. With Christ as our example of what it means to suffer for what is right, saints are instructed to endure unfair and harsh treatment. This is easier said than done. When one is on the "right side of right," it is difficult to endure unjust treatment with grace, yet we are told that God is watching and that enduring with a heart of submission (not lip service) finds favor with God.

Thankfully, the call to endure is to a specific end. That end includes your maturity and your advancement in earthly and kingdom affairs. God uses our struggles as sandpaper to smooth out our rough edges. Here are a few questions that can help give you perspective and shift the optics of your situation to how God may want to use it:

- How might God use this situation for my good and the good of those involved?
- Is God using my example to sow the seed of the Gospel into this person's life?
- What is the other person going through that may be driving their behavior?
- If suffering for what is right is short-term, how will God use the fruit of my submission long-term?
- With God watching as I endure, what is His opinion of how I am enduring under this unjust treatment?

REFLECT TO CONNECT

1. Whom do you know that submits to authority when treated unjustly?
2. In what ways can you help another who is enduring a difficult situation?
3. If you shift your focus from your suffering to God's pleasure, what comes to mind?

Seasoned saints see past harsh treatment,
knowing that God uses difficult circumstances
as sandpaper to smooth out rough edges.

GOD'S BREADCRUMBS

WEEK 12 | WEDNESDAY

"He made from one man every nation of mankind to live on all the face of the earth, having determined their appointed times and the boundaries of their habitation, that they would seek God, if perhaps they might feel around for Him and find Him, though He is not far from each one of us; for in Him we live and move and exist, as even some of your own poets have said, 'For we also are His descendants.'"
Acts 17:26-28

Assignments are to people and places for a season (time), and everything God does is through a person or place. When He wants to bring something to you, He will bring someone to you. Here are some ways you can discern whom God has assigned to you or whom you have been assigned to:

- **Whom do I feel a burden toward?** When I sense God's compassion toward someone, I know God is sharing His heart with me because He has an assignment for me. This assignment may be short-term (for someone He wants to touch) or long-term (for something He wants to change). This is how God gives us opportunities to serve Him. He places people on our path and a pain or desire in our heart for someone and credits our account as if it were Jesus Himself we were serving. ("Truly, truly, I say to you, he who receives whomever I send receives Me; and he who receives Me receives Him who sent Me." John 13:20)

- **Whom do I feel drawn to?** When God shares His heart with me (Psalm 37:4), it may take the form of a person whom I have a desire to see, call, or write to. I want to be obedient to where He is drawing me, and I want to be swift to act, knowing His assignments are time-sensitive.

- **Whom am I called to?** There are some people I feel protective of or think about often. I may even feel their pain. I may have a desire to serve them. Some assignments are obvious: family, friends, and some in the work environment. If God is putting me together with someone or wants me to do something, a prompting desire will build within me that I can't shake.
- **What place am I called to in this season?** When I am where I belong, I have a peace and a sense of being settled, even in difficult circumstances. When I am not where I belong, I am uncomfortable as if I am out of place or out of season. When you feel pushed, it is often from below; when you feel pulled, it is from above. When God calls you to a new place, He always calls you to a person, too. God likes the waiting season because it is during such seasons that He births something new in us.
- **Where am I feeling pain?** This is an area that God wants me to resolve. When my bell is getting rung on the inside, this is God's alarm to wake me to action.

REFLECT TO CONNECT

1. Where has God been leading you?
2. Whom has God put on your heart to engage?
3. In what ways is God getting your attention lately?

God is Spirit, and so it is within the depth of your being that you will find Him nudging you.

STAGES OF AN ASSIGNMENT

WEEK 12 | THURSDAY

"But I tell you the truth: it is to your advantage that I am leaving;
for if I do not leave, the Helper will not come to you; but if I go,
I will send Him to you." John 16:7

Jesus came to launch His God-given mission on Earth. He left so you could be empowered to complete your God-given mission. Fifty days after Jesus was raised, He gave the Holy Spirit so that every believer could have the power of God in them, not just with them. As you journey from the temporal to the eternal, you will walk through many seasons. Consider the stages within a given assignment. Consider the following stages of a season God may use to move you.

1. **Announcement:** You have a strong sense and subsequent realization that God is calling you to a person, place, or both.

2. **Excitement:** You know what to do, and a door of opportunity opens. You are ready to launch into action. A holy energy and determination enter and propel you.

3. **Equipping:** God provides for a given mission with resources, revelation, and co-laborers. He may put you under authority to test you and train you. This is part of equipping.

4. **Decision:** Every piece for the journey won't be provided— you will be faced with a choice to either trust God and keep moving or turn back. Your decision will involve settling inward doubts, fears, and making sacrifices.

5. **Divine Assistance:** If you could do it alone, God's partnership wouldn't be necessary. He will show up in miraculous ways to assist you. As you move forward, you will know and feel the Holy Spirit working alongside you as He nudges you, readies you, and helps you along the way.

In God's eyes, your vocational calling and ministry are one and the same. As you are serving God in all that you do, He considers and counts your motives and mission as service to Him.

REFLECT TO CONNECT

1. How would you describe the stages of an assignment you have experienced?
2. What advice do you envision God would give you about the stage you are in?
3. Why is it important to identify the stages of an assignment?

The recognition of a stage within an assignment enables you to see the ending of one stage and the beginning of another.

———◆◆◆———

THE MASTER ASKER
WEEK 12 | FRIDAY

*A plan in the heart of a man is like deep water,
But a man of understanding draws it out.* Proverbs 20:5

Every person carries within them unexplored questions, uncharted territory, undiscovered potential, and so much more that is hidden and tucked away within the human heart. Day-to-day responsibilities bury many of these mysteries, yet getting access to them is the key to helping unlock hidden treasures. What is the tool of the trade for gaining understanding? A question. A question has the ability to unearth hidden knowledge, buried memories, wisdom, and the ability to get someone talking who might otherwise be locked up or labeled a "quiet type." We all need someone to ask us deep, insightful, penetrating questions that capture our hearts.

A question within the hands of a good listener can set the direction of the discussion, create positive emotions within the conversation, set the mood of the atmosphere, create desire, and so much more. Questions can be used to:

- Show you care by the areas you probe and how you listen.
- Plant seeds of thought for future discussion.
- Make a point with a rhetorical question.
- Get a person thinking in a specific direction.

Next time you are in conversation, consider spending most of your time listening and the rest asking questions. Start your sentences with one of the 5 W-Brothers: Who, What, Where, When, Why. With every question you ask, you are one step closer to gaining the wisdom and understanding that Solomon often wrote about in Proverbs. Like a ladle in a pan of soup, a question can draw out understanding, experience, and hidden wisdom from deep within.

REFLECT TO CONNECT

1. How often do you ask questions vs. make statements during discussions?
2. Have you developed a questioning roadmap that leads a conversation to the desired destination?
3. What important questions come to mind that you should be asking yourself about your own life?

Asking the right questions can be more important than knowing the answers.

THE HALL OF FAVOR

A good name is to be more desired than great wealth;
Favor is better than silver and gold. Proverbs 22:1

A good name is the result of having a good reputation, and favor can be the byproduct of reputation. Favor is not a mystery. It is the result of following the instructions God gives us, either through His own direct speech or indirectly through a delegated authority. Delegated authorities from God in our lives can be a family member, a mentor, a supervisor, a pastor—anybody God chooses. If you have great favor, you have stewarded well the responsibilities given to you and have submitted to the authorities in your life. If you resist authority or are lackadaisical, spend your time giving lip service to game authority, your favor will be reduced.

Hebrews chapter 11 is known as the "Hall of Faith." But there is also a "Hall of Favor." Joseph gained favor with Potiphar and Pharaoh by submitting to God's plan and the earthly authorities he was subject to. Joshua obtained favor with Moses and the people by faithfully fulfilling all he was asked to do. And it is said of David that he was a "man after God's own heart" because he did whatever God asked him to do. When we submit to God and honor those He has put over us, we are granted ears to hear God's wisdom, discernment, and knowledge. If you have fallen out of favor with a supervisor, a client, a coworker, or a family member, you can course-correct your steps today and get onto a path of increasing your favor by submitting to God and doing what He tells you to do. The Hall of Favor is filled with saints submitted to earthly and heavenly authority.

1. Whom has God assigned to raise you up in your current station in life?
2. In what ways could you increase favor with an authority in your life?
3. What has God asked you to do that you could take action on today?

Finding FAVOR is not hard to do: Submit to authority, do more than is asked, and be excellent at what you do, and those in high positions will find you.

THE POWER OF ASSOCIATION

WEEK 13 | TUESDAY

Do not make friends with a person given to anger,
Or go with a hot-tempered person, Or you will learn his ways
And find a snare for yourself.
Proverbs 22:24-25

The power of association is a double-edged sword. God knew this and shared this timeless truth with Solomon. Over time, we pick up the characteristics of the people and circumstances we associate with. As Paul told the Corinthians, "Bad company corrupts good morals." If you hang around negative, unmotivated people, they will rub off on you. The reverse is also true. If you invest your time developing friends, mentors, and associations of people you aspire to be like, they will rub off on you, too.

Consider making a list of the five people you spend the most time with; these are the people who imprint on you. Now, make a list of the five you wish could be the inner circle of your work world and make a plan to create the relationships. These will be your future.

REFLECT TO CONNECT

1. Whose inner circle do you wish you were included in?
2. What steps could you take to level up in the area of your associations?
3. Is there anyone in your life that it is time to say goodbye to?

Successful people sink or swim based on whom they run with.
If you are going to hang out at the water cooler,
hang out with winners.

———————————◆———————————

PAULINE PIONEERING
WEEK 13 | WEDNESDAY

For we are not overextending ourselves, as if we did not reach to you,
for we were the first to come even as far as you in the gospel of Christ;
not boasting beyond our measure, that is, in other men's labors,
but with the hope that as your faith grows, we will be, within our sphere,
enlarged even more by you, so as to preach the gospel even to the regions
beyond you, and not to boast in what has been accomplished
in the sphere of another. 2 Corinthians 10:14-16

From the beginning of Paul's ministry, his goal was to, as the TV show Star Trek proclaimed, "To go where no man has gone before." Paul did not want to "build" upon another man's work; instead, he wanted to pioneer a new work and preach Christ where Christ had not been preached before. His ambition was for the gospel, and he took a holy pride in taking ground for the Kingdom. In Paul's letter to the Corinthians, he touches on this ambition again, saying that his ultimate goal was to reach the Corinthians, then go beyond them and expand the sphere of Christ's influence.

To pioneer means to be among the first to explore a territory or settle an area. Here are some "Pauline Style" pioneering questions to consider:

TAKING TERRITORY FOR CHRIST

1. What territory would you like to take for Christ, your family, in your career?
2. What territory would you like to take that no one has ever taken before?
3. Is there an area or uncharted territory God would like you to pioneer?

REFLECT TO CONNECT

1. From where you are at, what is your launching pad?
2. Who can help you jump-start your dream for the marketplace and ministry?
3. What has God called you to pioneer, to be the first in your family to do for him?

Pioneering a new work is risky, messy,
and requires the courage of Christ when taking territory.

OPEN TO INPUT

WEEK 13 | THURSDAY

Like an earring of gold and a jewelry piece of fine gold
Is a wise person who offers rebukes to a listening ear. Proverbs 25:12

J esus said, "Blessed is he who does not take offense at me."
(Matthew 11:6) He knew that when a person feels offended, their
heart closes, and they can no longer hear what is being said. So it is
with the one who puts emotional comfort above professional progress. For leaders to continue improving each day, they must cultivate
a listening ear, and that means being open to feedback.

1. **Be Correctable:** A listening ear has a healthy appetite for
   course correction. Having a "correctable spirit" ensures others feel welcome and safe to tell you when you are drifting.
2. **Be Coachable:** A listening ear ensures that you are open and
   willing to receive advice.
3. **Be Thankful:** The evidence of a listening ear is feedback in
   the form of gratitude toward one who takes the time to invest
   in your development.

It's more work to give feedback than it is to let it slide. Candid feedback is difficult for most people because it risks the relationship.
Receiving correction is also difficult because it often involves pain.
In either case, instructing others and maintaining a "teachable attitude" requires consistent "open-mindedness." Saints who maintain
an attitude of openness to correction, coaching, and thankfulness
position themselves as team members whom others want to work
with. It also communicates to God that you are moldable.

REFLECT TO CONNECT

1. Whom do you know that has a teachable spirit?
2. What steps could you take to position yourself as coachable?
3. Is there someone whom you should approach to provide candid feedback?

People who remain open to feedback may feel stretched to straighten out but, in the process, are also strengthened.

ASK—DON'T TELL
WEEK 13 | FRIDAY

Do you see a person who is hasty with his words?
There is more hope for a fool than for him. Proverbs 29:20

God has given us two ears and one mouth, and we should use them in that proportion. The wise person is more inclined to ask questions than to make statements. They have trained their minds to think in questions. In this way, they develop a bent toward becoming "Socratic" in their communication. Whether we are drawing near to God or sitting in front of a supervisor or customer, learning to think in questions rather than statements can yield many benefits. When communicating:

1. Consider your options before making a recommendation. Your first thought will rarely be your best. Pausing before presenting produces a better idea. Then, present it as a question vs. a statement.

2. Consider the potential outcomes before suggesting a course of action. By "playing the tape to the end" in your mind's eye, you can begin to experience the emotional benefits of being on the other side of the decision. Armed with more intelligence, you may reconsider your options, then ask a question.

3. Consider the consequences of your words before they leave your lips. Like toothpaste out of a tube, you won't be able to put them back. Counting the cost before the spoken transaction takes place can save you a lot of unnecessary pain. Posing questions vs. positioning a statement has the emotional effect in conversation of pulling people toward you. Statements push; questions pull.

4. Consider how you might say what you are going to say before you say it. Words *reflect* feelings in the one saying them and *produce* feelings in the one hearing them. Over 90% of communication is nonverbal, so consider the kinds of feelings you are about to reflect and then ask them, "How would you feel if…"

REFLECT TO CONNECT

1. Have you ever tried to have a conversation using only questions?
2. What percentage of your typical conversation is in questions vs. statements?
3. Whom do you know that exercises mastery using the questioning techniques?

Right questions precede right answers.
Learning to think in questions will make one a better thinker
and will get the focus off oneself and onto others.

THE TWO-SECOND RULE

WEEK 14 | MONDAY

One who withholds his words has knowledge, And one who has a cool spirit is a person of understanding. Even a fool, when he keeps silent, is considered wise; When he closes his lips, he is considered prudent.
Proverbs 17:27-28

The best way to defuse a conflict is by asking a question. Responding with statements when under fire throws fuel on the fire, whereas the right question can neutralize and redirect the emotion of the moment.

Have you ever said something you wish you had not said? A lot of times, we respond hastily with words we know we would not have said if we had thought them through before speaking. The words we speak don't always represent our position but only how we feel in the moment. They may be a first response, but that doesn't mean they are the right response. As a safeguard to ensure you mean what you say and say what you mean, practice the two-second rule. The next time you are in conversation and it is your turn to speak, take two seconds for a long breath to consider what an appropriate response should be. If you make the two-second rule a habit, you will rarely regret what you say.

REFLECT TO CONNECT

1. Whom do you know that does a good job of "thinking before speaking"?
2. How will practicing the two-second rule help you in your communication?
3. Can you describe how you go about reading a situation before speaking into it?

It is in the "pause" between thinking and speaking
that you make room to hear what God has to say.

THE GIFT SET

WEEK 14 | TUESDAY

A person's gift makes room for him And brings him before great people.
Proverbs 18:16

Your job is what you are paid for, but your purpose is what you were made for. When you discover the gifts God has placed in you, you will uncover the plans He has designed for you.

Do you know the greatness God has placed in you? God has given every person a part of Himself. You are made in His image, and His greatness has been deposited into you. The gift set given to you by your Creator has specifically designed you for success in achieving His purposes and your success. Your gift back to Him is to discover the combination of gifts He has placed in you, develop them, and wield them to win favor with God and with men. Here are a few clues that can help you discern what some of your gifts may be:

TIMELESSNESS: What are you doing when you lose track of time?
OBSESSION: What are you always thinking about, dreaming about, or wanting to learn about?
PASSION: What would you do for free if you could?
NATURAL BENT: What are your natural thinking tendencies or habitual patterns?
MAGNETISM: What are you drawn to?

TALENT: What do others acknowledge you for or point to when speaking of your talents and successes?

A strong "tendency" or combination of tendencies that work together to help a person create high performance and accelerate in their field is a **gift set** in operation. Here are a few examples of behavioral tendencies that work in combination to create consistent success in the life of a person in the profession of sales:

1. The desire to serve and care for a customer. (Serving gift)
2. The desire to pursue and close a sale. (Conquering gift)
3. The desire to strategize the future. (Planning gift)
4. The desire to seek out opportunity. (Ambition, prospecting gift)
5. The desire for new relationships. (Cold calling gift)

REFLECT TO CONNECT

1. What have others said about your talents before?
2. Do you have gifts you are not using?
3. In what ways is God asking you to use your gifts?

Your job is what you are paid for, but your purpose is what you were made for. When you discover the gifts God has placed in you, you will uncover the plans He has designed for you.

SET YOUR COMPASS

WEEK 14 | WEDNESDAY

The mind of the discerning acquires knowledge,
And the ear of the wise seeks knowledge. Proverbs 18:15

"Seek, and you will find; knock, and it will be opened to you."
(Matthew 7:7) These were the words spoken by God's Son,
Jesus. At face value, these words suggest that we shall receive whatever we pursue, seek, or ask for. What did He mean? Why would God make such an outrageous promise? As most commentators recognize, Jesus's point here is that if we seek the things of God, we will receive the things of God. But there is an earthly application to what He is saying as well.

Engineered within the mind map of every human being at birth is the reticular activator, otherwise known as the "attention center" of the brain. Whatever a person sets their will to focus on, that is what their brain begins to notice. Have you ever set your mind on something you strongly desired and noticed that it started to show up on your path? It's not mystical or magical; it's the attention center of your brain gathering relevant data and experiences to come into agreement with what you are focused on. This automatic power can be set to create, destroy, build, tear down, or work to our benefit or harm.

Work with the hardwiring God engineered in your nature.
The reticular activator is at work within everyone. All anyone needs to do is to set their compass on a definitive objective, and they will begin to see all manner of help and input appear on their path to assist them. It is in fragmented focus that plans are buried and not put into action. Focus on what you want, submit your plans to God's will, and let God's nature implanted within you do the rest.

REFLECT TO CONNECT

1. Are you aware of the purposes and plans God has put in you?
2. In what way can you direct the reticular activator's activity in your life?
3. Do you recognize the power of the reticular activator at work as you reflect on your past?

Saints who set their mental compass on fulfilling
God's will in their work will find themselves
finding God as they work.

NEGOTIATE YOUR POSITION
WEEK 14 | THURSDAY

The cast lot puts an end to quarrels,
And decides between the mighty ones. Proverbs 18:18

The casting of lots in the Old Testament was to decide a matter when human wisdom had reached its limit. The last time casting of lots happened in the Bible was when the 12th disciple was chosen in the book of Acts. After that, Pentecost happened, and it became common practice to be able to hear and discern the will of God within the inner man. You are meant to hear God guide and direct you on a regular basis.

When a disagreement arises between two people, it can be difficult to yield when you feel you are on the "right side of right." The flipping of a coin, although not conventional, could put both in a position to accept an outcome and "go with it" even if they don't agree. In a business situation, we go along with decisions we may not agree with but find it harder to do that personally at times. What is the solution? Consider the following criteria before deciding to fight for your position.

PUT YOUR POSITION TO THE TEST

1. If you get your way, who is helped and who is hurt?
2. Would God be pleased with your victory or your yielding?
3. What is the worst that could happen if you yield your position, and what is the best that could happen?

Decision-making isn't easy for anyone when they feel they must compromise their point of view, yet sometimes you can lose with the person even if you win with your position. Always remember to count the cost and weigh your position as God would. Sometimes it's better to take the high road instead of taking a stand.

REFLECT TO CONNECT

1. Have you ever asked yourself "What would Jesus do" when in conflict?
2. Whom do you admire as a peacemaker?
3. What are the merits of compromising and living to fight another day?

Sometimes the quickest way to the "high road"
is on your knees in prayer.

FOLLOW THE RETURNEES

WEEK 14 | FRIDAY

Prepare plans by consultation,
And make war by wise guidance.
Proverbs 20:18

An ancient Chinese proverb says, "If you want to know the way, ask someone on the way back." The Bible is filled with mentors pointing the way of what to do and what not to do. Scripture is filled with stories of success and failure. God wants you to have the best chance for success, so He's given you examples of the good, the bad, and the ugly.

Wherever you want to go and whatever you want to do, someone else has done something similar before. Sometimes you can find examples in the Bible, but sometimes you can find examples in your own life. If your ambition is from the Lord and your desire is for the purposes of God, He will prosper your way by placing you in contact with those who can give you the experience you need. This is God's mentorship plan.

A wise person seeks out wise counsel, not from those professing to know the way, but from those who have *gone* the way. Many talk about success, but wise people follow those who have attained success. Tom Hopkins, America's #1 sales trainer, once said, "Never take advice from anyone more messed up than you." When making plans and coordinating your attack in the marketplace, seek advice from those who have accomplished what you want to accomplish.

REFLECT TO CONNECT

1. Whom do you know either from the Bible or from your circle of influence that has achieved success similar to what you are pursuing?
2. What kind of behaviors and habits can you acquire that will make you successful?
3. Whom is God telling you to seek out and approach as a mentor?

The wise follow the path of those who have succeeded where they want to succeed until God shows them their own trail to blaze.

NEGOTIATE LIKE GOD

WEEK 15 | MONDAY

"Bad, bad," says the buyer,
But when he goes his way, then he boasts. Proverbs 20:14

G od once said, "This people honors Me with their lips, but their heart is far from Me." (Matthew 15:8) The disingenuous worshiper is like the disingenuous buyer. God knows the heart behind every word and the motive behind every deed. In business, God always knows what is fair or unfair, and He sees where there is transparency or someone is hiding. There are always two sides of a negotiation, yet in kingdom negotiation, both sides should win. The differentiator in what separates one negotiator from another is skill level. As far as it depends on you, negotiating in a godly way ensures you remain right with God and man. When you are in the right, God rewards. But this is different than simply "winning." When you win, do you consider who else might have won or lost at your hand? To whom might that person take their loss to? God?

If God was negotiating with you, how would He negotiate? Consider the heart of a godly negotiator and its opposite.

Godly Negotiator	Ungodly Negotiator
• Genuine	• Disingenuous
• Wants what is best for both sides	• Wins at cost to your side
• Positions facts in positive light	• Repositions your points in the worst light
• Vocalizes the value of both sides	• Devalues your side to increase their value
• Wants what is equitable for both sides	• Cares only for what they receive on their side
• Wants a win-win outcome	• Will win at your expense

1. What other contrasts in godly vs. ungodly negotiators can you think of?
2. In what circumstances have you seen both versions modeled?
3. Have you ever found yourself on the winning side of a negotiation but then on the wrong side of the person?

God measures a win by our motive to serve others over self.

———————————◆———————————

"10S" SERVE THE KING

WEEK 15 | TUESDAY

Do you see a man skilled in his work?
He will stand before kings;
He will not stand before obscure people. Proverbs 22:29

The world pays well for talent, high performers, and problem solvers. God gives talent to each individual, but the responsibility for discovering what those talents are and developing them is yours and yours alone. No one can do that for you. However, as you work to develop the gifts God has given you, you will also begin to discover areas of excellence within yourself. He has made you to excel in certain areas! In what areas are you currently a 10? Discerning not only what you are good at but what you are superb at will lead to confidence, and that can open doors for you to serve higher-ups in an organization. These higher-ups are the kings within a company, and the talent they value the most is competence. Now is the time to prepare, practice, and grow yourself into a 10 in your area of giftedness. Start today and watch the doors of opportunity open up for you. Your area of "10" is the gift God will use to advance you in your career.

Ecclesiastes 3:1 (ESV) says, "For everything there is a season," but talents can be unlocked in any season. Putting yourself in a consistent personal development plan will ensure you are always raising the lid on your talents, ready in season and out of season.

REFLECT TO CONNECT

1. In what areas are you a 10?
2. Who in your circle of influence is a 10?
3. Do you have a peer group that is growing or stagnating?

God is looking for progress, not perfection.

———————————◆◆◆———————————

WATER COOLER INNOCENCE
WEEK 15 | WEDNESDAY

"Allow the children to come to Me, and do not forbid them,
for the kingdom of God belongs to such as these. Truly I say to you,
whoever does not receive the kingdom of God
like a child will not enter it at all." Luke 18:16-17

In an unplanned moment, Jesus corrects the disciples who were preventing children from getting close. In this scene, we get an insight into what Jesus values: innocence. In contrast to the hardness of heart that sin creates, maintaining innocence is not just an avoidance of sin, but a refusal to become worldly wise by means of it. Here are a few mindsets that will help you maintain the right attitude:

1. Positive by choice or negative by choice.
2. Open-minded or closed-minded.
3. Curious at heart and adventurous.
4. Looking for God's perspective when challenges emerge.
5. Naïve of evil by choice, even if it is in your environment.
6. Trusting of others even if you've been betrayed.
7. Simple-hearted even if you are smart-minded.

Whom have you decided to become? In your work environment, you will choose whom to hang around and whom to avoid. Remember that if you hang around five people who are positive, good-hearted, and committed, you will be the sixth. If you hang out at the water cooler with five people who are negative, complain all the time, and are unkind, you will become the sixth. Are there conversations you should close your ears to at work so as to maintain your innocence?

REFLECT TO CONNECT

1. In what area do you desire to be innocent in?
2. Whom do you know that is good at maintaining their innocence?
3. What area does God desire you to return to innocence in?

Coming to God with a childlike heart doesn't happen
by accident but by choice.

IN THE SCHOOL OF GOD'S LEADERSHIP

WEEK 15 | THURSDAY

The king also allotted for them a daily ration from the king's choice food and from the wine which he drank, and ordered that they be educated for three years, at the end of which they were to enter the king's personal service. Daniel 1:5

D ifficulty in your circumstance is the backdrop by which the Potter refashions your clay into a masterpiece. Be moldable. For every work, whether in the marketplace or the ministry, God has a training program for it. When it becomes time for your promotion, God will assign you to serve someone to learn from. You may or may not like them but stick with them; it's not uncommon for God to put a person He is developing under subjection to a harsh ruler.

Jesus's training program lasted 30 years before His 3 years of ministry began. Moses spent 40 years in the plains of Moab, David was 15 when anointed by Samuel but 30 when he became king, Joseph's time of preparation was 13 years between the pit and the palace, and even Joshua was mentored under Moses for decades (40 years) before he led Israel into the Promised Land. How might God be using your present circumstances and the authorities over you to train you for bigger responsibilities in your future? Here are a few tests you will be required to pass in the marketplace for God *and* those He puts in authority over you.

FIVE TESTS OF GOD'S TRAINING PROGRAM

1. **SUBJECTION:** God will test your fitness to lead based on your ability to follow authority.

2. **SPIRIT:** Your attitude is the thoughts, feelings, and words you are projecting to authorities—they can tell if you are serving wholeheartedly without grumbling or with eye and lip service only.

3. **SPEED:** Your rate of responsiveness communicates to higher authorities the importance and sense of urgency you place on their requests.

4. **SUBMISSION:** Your ability to follow an instruction will set you apart from those who don't.

5. **SACRIFICE:** Your willingness to set aside your needs for the greater good shows you to be a worthy member of the team and not a self-serving employee.

Whether in captivity like Joseph and Daniel, on the front line of leadership like David and Moses, or moving through the world like Job and Jesus, if you see the above trials and tests on your path, you are likely being presented with an opportunity to participate in God's mentorship program.

REFLECT TO CONNECT

1. Whom in authority has God given you access to?
2. In what ways is God using "trials and testings" in the marketplace to train you?
3. Which area of God's training program are you struggling with?

You were designed to be a leader in the world,
an apprentice in the kingdom, and a child of a loving Father.

❖

THE PLACE OF PROVISION

WEEK 15 | FRIDAY

Now it came about in the days when the judges governed, that there
was a famine in the land. And a certain man of Bethlehem in Judah
went to reside in the land of Moab with his wife and his two sons.
The name of the man was Elimelech, and the name of his wife, Naomi;
and the names of his two sons where Mahlon and Chilion,
Ephrathites of Bethlehem in Judah. Ruth 1:1-2

G od may use lack of provision in one place to get you moving
to a new place. When provision dries up in one place, God
may move you to another. Yet that does not mean that everything
that happens in the new place is the providential hand of God. In
the story of Ruth and her husband Elimelech, while their problem
of provision was solved by traveling to Moab, there were great consequences to their family. These included their sons marrying foreign idol worshipers and, eventually, the deaths of Naomi's husband
and sons. Yet God had a plan to restore them to their people, His
purposes, and His way of providing back in Bethlehem. In fact, a
stunning turn of events was about to unfold as God would choose a
Moabite daughter-in-law who would cleave to Naomi and eventually
find herself placed in the lineage of Jesus Christ.

- Has God used "dried-up provision" in one place to move you to
  another before?
- What could God's purposes be for you to remain or leave your
  place?
- How can you discern if God wants you to stick it out or start
  packing?

There are other examples of God moving people to a new place
to unlock a new purpose and season. Jacob sent his sons to Egypt

to seek provision, where he was then later reunited with Joseph. The greatest story unfolded whereby God stationed a man (Joseph) in the marketplace to provide for the world during a famine. The raven stopped feeding Elijah, who knew it was time to leave the brook because God had changed his place of provision. God speaks and guides using provision consistently. What is He saying to you?

REFLECT TO CONNECT

1. What are the cultural dangers in the place you work or live?
2. How are the temptations of the place you are currently different from other places you have been?
3. Why do you suppose God might use "lack of provision" to move someone?

When provision dries up, that's a clue that your "place"
of assignment has changed.

I SUPPORT YOU

WEEK 16 | MONDAY

*King Jehoram left Samaria for battle at that time and mustered
all Israel. Then he went and sent word to Jehoshaphat the king of Judah,
saying, "The king of Moab has broken away from me.
Will you go with me to fight against Moab?" And he said,
"I will go up. Consider me yours, my people as your people,
my horses as your horses."* 2 Kings 3:6-7

Giving unconditional commitment to a leader is like giving unconditional love to a friend; it creates loyalty for life. When the king of Israel asked if the king of Judah would support him, he received a very affirming answer of "I support you; my resources are your resources." Has anyone ever thanked you for your support before? Have you ever vocalized your support for your leader?

When you know you have someone watching your back, there is a confidence in your leadership because of it. Smart leaders know whom they can count on and whom they can't. Consider reaffirming your unwavering commitment to someone today and watch how they react to you. As you commit and demonstrate loyalty to others, they, in turn, will do the same for you. Your alliance of commitment to someone will cause you (and them) to be:

STRENGTHENED: Knowing you have someone else's strength or resources to back you makes you stronger, confident, and more courageous. Isn't it true you are stronger together than apart?

SMARTER: Receiving the input of another gives you twice the brainpower and creativity you can then build upon. As I share my ideas with others, often, better ideas bubble up.

SECURE: Leaders who have the support of their people, their peers, and leaders outside of their organization create a sense of security that everyone needs in order to function without fear, take risks, and be bold in their leadership decisions.

REFLECT TO CONNECT

1. Whom can you verbalize your support and loyalty to today?
2. Is there someone you should ask for their support?
3. Is there a battle you will be facing that is driving you to form an alliance with someone you may not have otherwise considered?

Unconditional commitment is like unconditional love—it creates loyalty for life.

CAN YOU HEAR ME NOW?
WEEK 16 | TUESDAY

The hand of the Lord was on me there, and He said to me,
"Get up, go out to the plain, and there I will speak to you."
Ezekiel 3:22

There are times God will move us by moving His voice to a different location so we will follow. God sometimes moves us by moving provision, favor, and other things we seek as a way to get our attention to go in a new direction. Like the cloud by day and the pillar of fire by night God led Israel with, God gives us signs to know when we are geographically in the right place at the right time. Although it is impossible to be separated from the love of God, it is possible to not "feel" His presence all the time as we might want to. Where was the last spot you felt the presence of God? Where is the "spot" He may be moving you to? Go to that place; it's possible He's waiting for you there! This could look like a:

- Place of obedience
- Place of provision
- Place of favor
- Place of your geographical assignment

REFLECT TO CONNECT

1. Where do you best hear direction from God?
2. Have you found a "place" in the middle of your workday to spend time with God?
3. Has God ever asked you to change your geographical location, as He did with Moses, Elijah, Joshua, and Paul, so you could receive from Him?

Followers are sensitive to God's presence
so they can always be in proximity to the power.

SLINGSHOT SUCCESS

WEEK 16 | WEDNESDAY

Blessed be the LORD, my rock, Who trains my hands for war,
And my fingers for battle. Psalm 144:1

Whom do you learn from? God Himself was David's master mentor in the art of warfare. As God trained the Apostle Paul in the desert, He was with David in the field when he fought the lion and the bear. In the quiet times while David was tending his father's sheep, David honed his skill with his slingshot. It was his skill using the slingshot that catapulted David to national stardom while King Saul and the Israeli army looked on. What is the "slingshot" or super skill God has given you to empower your calling in the marketplace? What tools in your tool belt require developing? What has God gifted you to learn and pick up quickly?

God has put His potential in you, but you will play a role in your success. How are you developing what is within your power to improve? If you are a teacher, maybe you can work on holding the attention of students for longer periods of time. If you are a manager, maybe you have systems to improve. If you are a leader, working on your people skills will grow your influence. As David was in the wilderness before he met Goliath, so are you in the marketplace. What is it you are working on to develop your gift set?

As God trained David's hands for war, He will train your hands to create success. While David tended sheep in the wilderness, he looked after a flock with a heavy anointing given to him by Samuel. While he thought nothing was happening, God was preparing him in the times of silence and stillness.

To Moses He gave a staff, to David a slingshot, to Joseph He gave dreams, to Samson He gave super strength, to Solomon He gave wisdom, and to Elijah He gave a mantle that eventually would pass to Elisha.

WHAT HAS GOD GIVEN TO YOU?

_____

_____

_____

REFLECT TO CONNECT

1. What skill could you develop that would serve you in your vocational calling?
2. Is there a "Goliath" you could be facing this year that God wants to help you prepare for?
3. In your downtime, do you invest into honing your skill or entertaining your mind?

God trains the teachable in the classroom of life.
What slingshot skill are you developing?

———————————◆———————————

CHILDHOOD MEMORIES

WEEK 16 | THURSDAY

Beloved, do not imitate what is evil, but what is good. 3 John 1:11

Influence creates imprinting. From the cradle to the grave, we learn through modeling and mimicry. John Maxwell says it this way in *The 21 Irrefutable Laws of Leadership*: "People do what people see"; that is why example is so important. The Apostle Paul said, "Be imitators of me, just as I also am of Christ." (1 Corinthians 11:1)

The most powerful call Jesus gave to us started with the words "Follow Me." Whom are you following and imitating? Consider that as you follow others, someone is following you.

One of the most impactful ways of the example we set for others is found in my favorite poem. Mary Rita Schilke Sill prayed for the words to express her gratitude to her mom one day in a poem, and God answered her prayer. What you are about to read are the words given to her. As you read it, consider the impact and imprint your example makes on others and who you, too, might want to thank for their example to you.

When You Thought I Wasn't Looking
by Mary Rita Schilke Sill (C)1980

When you thought I wasn't looking,
I saw you hang my first painting on the refrigerator,
and I immediately wanted to paint another one.

When you thought I wasn't looking,
I saw you feed a stray cat,
and I learned that it was good to be kind to animals.

When you thought I wasn't looking,
I saw you make my favorite cake for me,
and I learned that the little things can be the special things
    in life.

When you thought I wasn't looking,
I heard you say a prayer,
and I knew there is a God I could always talk to, and I learned
    to trust God.

When you thought I wasn't looking,
I saw you make a meal and take it to a friend who was sick,
and I learned that we all have to help take care of each other.

When you thought I wasn't looking,
I saw you give of your time and money to help people who
    had nothing,
and I learned that those who have something should give to
    those who don't.

When you thought I wasn't looking,
I saw how you handled your responsibilities, even when you
    didn't feel good,

and I learned that I would have to be responsible when
I grow up.

When you thought I wasn't looking,
I saw tears come from your eyes,
and I learned that sometimes it's alright to cry.

When you thought I wasn't looking, I saw that you cared,
and I wanted to be everything that I could be.

When you thought I wasn't looking,
I learned most of life's lessons that I need to know to be a good
and productive person when I grow up.

When you thought I wasn't looking,
I looked at you and wanted to say, "Thanks for all the things
I saw when you thought I wasn't looking."

(www.whenyouthoughtiwasntlooking.com)

REFLECT TO CONNECT

1. Whom do you admire that you want to become like? This is whom you follow.
2. Whom have you noticed you have an influence over to the degree that they imitate you in words and actions?
3. What one quality of God's do you admire most? This is what He is asking you to model.

**The more influence you have with a person,
the more you imprint on their heart.**

THE OVERCOMER'S MINDSET

WEEK 16 | FRIDAY

For greater is He who is in you than he who is in the world. 1 John 4:4

There is an "overcomer" within you that is capable of succeeding in EVERY circumstance. With God, there is always a way to win and a plan to succeed. The mystery which was hidden through the ages has been revealed in these last times, and that mystery is that God is not just *with* you but *in* you, working *through* you. "[God's] power is perfected in weakness," said the Apostle Paul in 2 Corinthians 12:9. Whatever you are facing, remember that Jesus lives inside of you, and He shows those who seek Him what to do. When you feel weak, He can strengthen you. When you feel discouraged, He will encourage you. When you don't know where to go, He always knows what to do. Before you begin to pray, He already knows what you need.

Turn to the Strengthener who lives within you. You were made to be more than a conqueror. There is nothing He won't bring you to that He has not already decided to lead you through. Whatever you are facing today, turn to the overcomer inside of you, for "greater is He who is in you than he who is in the world." When needing a dose of the Savior's strength, repeat His words as they were given by the Holy Spirit and penned by the saints of old:

> *"All things are possible for the one who believes." Mark 9:23*
> *"No weapon that is formed against you will succeed."*
>   *Isaiah 54:17*
> *"For [God's] power is perfected in weakness." 2 Corinthians 12:9*
> *"[God] calls into being things that do not exist." Romans 4:17*
> *"I can do all things through Him who strengthens me."*
>   *Philippians 4:13*

"The steadfast of mind You will keep in perfect peace."
  Isaiah 26:3
"We overwhelmingly conquer through Him who loved us."
  Romans 8:37
"Now to Him who is able to do far more abundantly beyond all that we can ask or think." Ephesians 3:20

REFLECT TO CONNECT

1. Are you prone to doing life on your own or leaning on God?
2. What is your sense as to how God wants to help you problem solve today?
3. Just because you don't feel it, does that mean God won't do it on your behalf?

The problem you cannot solve, God has already solved.
While you only see your side, God sees all sides.

SEEK FIRST TO UNDERSTAND

WEEK 17 | MONDAY

Then the Lord said to me, "What do you see, Jeremiah?" Jeremiah 24:3

How can two people witness the same event yet have a different perspective? Throughout the book of Jeremiah, God is showing Jeremiah what is to come. God does this by showing Jeremiah what He sees, then asks him, "What do you see?" Sometimes to connect with others, we have to walk the proverbial "mile in their shoes" to see what they see and feel what they feel. God provides the perfect example of how to communicate and connect by asking questions.

"Seek first to understand, then to be understood."
Stephen Covey, *The 7 Habits of Highly Effective People*

Ask them questions to see what they see. An important skill of a successful leader is to be able to ask questions so they can see through the eyes of others. You don't need to share the same perspective, opinion, or conclusion as the other person; however, being able to empathize will allow you to disagree when necessary without being disagreeable. Next time you are struggling to connect with someone, ask them the following questions:

- What do you see that I am not seeing?
- What do you feel that I may be missing?
- What do you want me to know that I may not know?

REFLECT TO CONNECT

1. What perspective has God shown you in the last week that He wants you to see differently?

2. What has God said to you that He wants you to hear and heed?
3. Who are you struggling to connect with you can now reach out to?

When people want to impress you,
they will talk about themselves.
When they want to connect with you,
they will ask about you.

HOLLYWOOD PERSUASION
WEEK 17 | TUESDAY

What we have heard, what we have seen with our eyes,
what we have looked at and touched with our hands,
concerning the Word of Life—and the life was revealed, and we have
seen and testify and proclaim to you the eternal life, which was with
the Father and was revealed to us—what we have seen and
heard we proclaim to you also. 1 John 1:1-3

Personal experience is the birthplace of testimony, and there is no more credible witness than one who has been there, done that, and lived to tell the story. In my book *PERSUADE*, I discuss the principle "FACTS TELL—STORIES SELL." Hollywood knows this. Storytelling is how one captures the imagination of the mind. Stories enter through the side door of the brain, bypassing the judgment center and going straight to our heart. Next time you are struggling to connect with someone, start the conversation off with a personal story and watch how they engage.

Leaders persuade with storytelling by connecting their story with the story their audience is living. Since the beginning of time, there has never been a more powerful storyteller than "testimony." Sharing a personal story can create emotional impact that can defy logic and reason and can even be sensational simply because it is told from personal experience. When you read the Bible, which is easier to remember: a story or a list of facts and figures? With which do you spend more time in the Bible, genealogies or the inspired stories of how God is working in and through people's lives? When people hear about something that inspired you, they get inspired. Whether you work in the ministry or marketplace, one of the best ways to connect with your audience is to share your story. When developing your personal "story inventory," ask yourself:

- How did this experience impact me?
- What did I learn from it?
- How did it change me?

When you can answer these questions for yourself, you are ready to share your story with another.

REFLECT TO CONNECT

1. Why are the most successful leaders good storytellers?
2. What powerful experiences have you walked through in the last year that you could turn into a story?
3. Whose story do you need to listen to today?

The most powerful story is to tell them what you've seen and heard, then let God do the rest.

———————————◆———————————

THE SOUND OF STRENGTH

For greater is He who is in you than he who is in the world. 1 John 4:4

The number one requirement for access to God is belief. Faith is simply confidence in God. In fact, without faith, the Bible says it is impossible to please God (Hebrews 11:6). I have never met a Christian who didn't believe God could do anything; however, I *have* met many who didn't believe God could do anything through them.

Robert Schuller once asked, "What would you attempt to do if you knew you could not fail?" That question is pregnant with faith. Our self-talk has the same force. We can fill our self-talk with faith-producing questions and statements, or we can fill it with internal conversation that creates fear, doubt, and insecurity. Without confidence in yourself, it's impossible to be successful in life. But without confidence or "belief" in God, it is impossible to please God.

The next time you are feeling down, consider reading the Psalms OUT LOUD as a way of feeding God's confidence about you into you. For we are promised in Romans 10:17, "Faith comes from hearing, and hearing by the word of Christ." When you read what God wrote out loud, your inner spirit "hears" God's word, causing confidence to rise up in you. It is then that you will be able to do ALL things through Christ according to the supply of the Spirit that already resides within you.

1. Which voices do you put more weight on, voices of faith or fear?
2. Do you tend to believe your self-talk or "God-talk"—what God has to say about you in His Word?
3. Do you rely on others to build your confidence, or do you count on God and His Word to give you your daily dose?

Faith is voice-activated; when you say what God says about you out loud, you will feel how God feels toward you.

UPSIDES CREATE DOWNSIDES

WEEK 17 | THURSDAY

Now he [Elisha] went up from there to Bethel; and as he was going up by the road, some young boys came out from the city and ridiculed him and said to him, "Go up, you baldhead; go up, you baldhead!" When he looked behind him and saw them, he cursed them in the name of the LORD. Then two female bears came out of the woods and tore up forty-two of the boys. He then went on from there to Mount Carmel, and from there he returned to Samaria. 2 Kings 2:23-25

Problem-solving in the marketplace creates profits, but not all profits are God's hand of provision. God had just healed the water supply in a town through Elisha, and Elisha became the town hero. Shortly thereafter, a large group of young men verbally attacked him. Why? One suggestion is that prior to the polluted waters being healed, these young men had created an income stream by selling water they brought in from far away. God's miracle for some can create a revenue loss for others.

God's priority is people, not profit. It's only a matter of time before you witness God's goodness toward people negatively impacting someone else's ability to generate money. Jesus experienced this, too, when the demon He cast out of one man entered a school of swine that then ran off a cliff. While the town was happy for the man who was delivered from a demon, after seeing how much money the loss of the pigs cost, they asked Jesus to leave.

A problem in the marketplace is an opportunity to create provision, but know that if God's actions dry up one lane of provision, He can create another. If anything you do helps one while hurting another, know that you may create enemies.

REFLECT TO CONNECT

1. Do you have the ability to see the upside and downside of solutions?
2. What examples can you give where a problem solved resulted in financial prosperity?
3. Have you ever fixed one problem but then broke something else?

One lane of provision drying up is often a clue that another is about to open up.

FROM SILENCE TO SIGNIFICANCE, PART I

WEEK 17 | FRIDAY

When he knocked at the door of the gate, a servant-girl named Rhoda
came to answer. When she recognized Peter's voice, because of her joy
she did not open the gate, but ran in and announced that Peter was
standing in front of the gate. They said to her, "You are out of your
mind!" But she kept insisting that it was so. Acts 12:13-15

Serving well gets you promoted to higher levels of service. If
you've never heard of Rhoda before, you are in good company.
She is briefly mentioned in Scripture and easily dismissed. Yet the
Holy Spirit felt she was important enough to include in a story following a divine prison break of the Apostle Peter. WHY? Those
whom the world might label as insignificant, God calls significant.
Significance is serving a purpose and a person greater than yourself.

CHRISTLIKE CHARACTERISTICS
FROM THE LIFE OF RHODA

Rhoda was a SERVANT, even referred to as a maid. She practiced
sacrificing self-interest and putting others' interests ahead of her own.
Jesus said that He came to serve, not to be served (Matthew 20:28).
The front door to prominence in the world is through success, but
the first step to serving in the kingdom of God is through the servants' entrance. A servant's heart often requires one to "relinquish
their rights." It will always be in the service to others that Christ can
work most powerfully in your life. Servanthood is the DNA of God.

Joshua served Moses, Joseph served Potiphar, Timothy served
Paul—the list of the prominent figures all started in service to

someone and something greater than themselves. Hebrews 11 is often referred to as the "Hall of Faith." Notice that every saint mentioned in God's Hall of Faith was in service to someone and something greater than themselves. Even Rahab, a harlot, was considered great in the kingdom of Heaven and was mentioned with the saints of significance because she served a people and purpose greater than herself.

REFLECT TO CONNECT

1. What needs of others do you observe around you?
2. Whom might God be asking you to serve?
3. Why is suffering often linked to servanthood?

Success starts around back at the servants' entrance.

FROM SILENCE TO SIGNIFICANCE, PART II

WEEK 18 | MONDAY

Success and significance come through serving someone
and something bigger than yourself.

Acts 12:13-15: **Rhoda is rarely talked about, yet her service** to the early church is remembered. Rhoda was a servant girl, and her willingness to serve gave her access to leadership. It will always be through service to another that you are recognized, remembered, and even promoted. You can't be promoted by someone you don't serve. So next time a door of opportunity to serve opens before you, be the first through the door. It is through the door of service that those in authority are able to observe you and your gifts in operation.

When you serve others as "unto the Lord," God Himself receives your service and credits it to your account. God's measuring stick for greatness is often countercultural to that of the marketplace. His steps toward success differ from the ways of the world. In the eyes of the marketplace, it is your success that creates your significance. In the eyes of God, it is your significance that creates success, measured by how and whom you serve.

The secret to every good leader's success is that they were first a good follower. Rhoda was a good FOLLOWER. Rhoda had spent many hours listening to Peter in the past and knew the sound of his voice, even through a closed door. Jesus says in John 10 that His sheep know His voice and another they will not follow. All great leaders started by learning to become good followers first. Whom are you learning from in this season of your development? Whose voice do you know so well that when they speak, you immediately go into "receiving mode," knowing that God has caused you to sit at their feet to learn by serving them?

When God wants to promote you or advance you in His kingdom, He will often assign a mentor for you to serve. The clue that God is moving you up or out of your present season is that He will give you someone to serve and put it on your heart to do so. Their voice will carry weight when they speak, and as they speak, you will hear the "whispers of God" in your life. The invitation to follow requires one to bow their heart and reach out their hand to RECEIVE. God brings not only people on your path to serve, but people on your path to serve you. Let them.

REFLECT TO CONNECT

1. Who has been dismissive of you in your life, yet God may be calling you to serve them?
2. Those who serve the most are trusted the most. Why?
3. What "service opportunities" could give you access to people of influence?

You can't be promoted by someone you don't serve.

———◆———

FROM SILENCE TO SIGNIFICANCE, PART III

WEEK 18 | TUESDAY

God isn't giving up on you; don't give up on whom
God has called you to serve.

Acts 12:13-15: Rhoda was PERSISTENT. She lacked the influence and authority to persuade those in the house that Peter was at the door. Even while they dismissed her, she persisted in convincing them to listen to her. At some point, each of us gets dismissed by someone we deem important, and it hurts. There is a time to step up and a time to sit down, a time to speak up and a time to listen, and in Rhoda's case, a time to wait your turn and a time to push through and be persistent in an important moment. When you are dismissed, remember that Christ was dismissed by the movers and shakers of this world, yet when asked to speak, He persisted through rejection to fulfill His purpose by saying what needed to be said when the time came. Trials and tribulation are the proving ground for building your "persistence muscle." As you persevere, God's purposes will birth new opportunities where you are no longer dismissed but instead promoted to serve those with greater responsibility.

God isn't giving up on you—don't dismiss the opportunities to serve God has given to you.

When you persist through difficulty, you will eventually find yourself in the right place at the right time for what God has prepared for you. What season does God have you in right now in which He may be preparing you to receive an "opportune knock" at the door of service? If your persistence muscle isn't built before opportunity strikes, you will lack the strength to finish your race. It is through the struggle and sacrifice of serving others that God builds your persistence muscle. Let Him.

REFLECT TO CONNECT

1. Why is personal sacrifice an important piece to servanthood?
2. Why is Jesus the perfect picture of servanthood?
3. In what ways do you sacrifice so that others are served?

Embracing the struggle that accompanies service guarantees the reward God hides within servanthood.

FRAGMENTS OF WEALTH

WEEK 18 | WEDNESDAY

Jesus then took the loaves, and giving thanks He distributed them to those who were reclining; likewise also of the fish, as much as they wanted. And when they had eaten their fill, He said to His disciples, "Gather up the leftover pieces so that nothing will be lost." So they gathered them up, and filled twelve baskets with pieces from the five barley loaves which were left over by those who had eaten. John 6:11-13

While you are waiting on God to provide, He's waiting on you to see what He's already provided. Wherever Jesus is, there is provision, peace, and an answer to every prayer you pray. Jesus didn't just provide for the feeding of the 5,000; He provided until they had had their fill and then commanded that the fragments be gathered up so nothing would be lost. Is there provision within your reach you may be missing? Maybe something appearing to be insignificant (fragments) to you may be a seed of significance God is trying to point out to you. What are the fragments in your life that may be stewarded for better use?

According to author Gary Keesee of *Fixing the Money Thing*, "Small fragments can become a big part of your business." Fragments are what is left behind and ignored by others. They can show up in many areas of life. When you come to Jesus with a need, He provides ideas of how to meet that need. While many pray for a miracle of money to show up, God could be pointing to a source of saving He wants you to see. Provision in the form of fragments can show up in many different ways. Ask God today to show you where the fragments are in your life.

Here are a few examples of income-producing and cost-saving "fragments":

- Maximize credit card miles to purchase nontaxable deductible items.
- Savings in utilities, fuel, transportation, man-hours, online education vs. onsite, etc.
- Minimize interest payments to the bank by paying off credit cards, cars, and houses early. Interest paid on these items equates to well over $10,000 per year for most Americans.
- Identify something someone is paying for in your neighborhood and provide a service to make extra money (rideshare services, admin work, dog walking, housesitting, window cleaning).

REFLECT TO CONNECT

1. What income-producing ideas may be coming to mind?
2. There is always something you are missing; what is it with regard to provision?
3. What fragments do you imagine God would show you if you asked to see your circumstance through His eyes?

*Stop focusing on what you don't have
and start using what you do.*

WARNINGS AND WHISPERS
WEEK 18 | THURSDAY

The Lord spoke to Manasseh and his people, but they paid no attention. Therefore the LORD brought the commanders of the army of the king of Assyria against them, and they captured Manasseh with hooks, bound him with bronze chains and took him to Babylon. When he was in distress, he appeased the LORD his God and humbled himself greatly before the God of his fathers. When he prayed to Him, He was moved by him and heard his pleading, and brought him back to Jerusalem to his kingdom. Then Manasseh knew that the LORD alone is God. 2 Chronicles 33:10-13

The ability to self-correct is a sign of maturity. God often whispers to us, but if we ignore those whispers, they show up as pain. Consider the series of events in Manasseh coming full circle from ignoring God to following Him:

1. God speaks to Manasseh.
2. Manasseh ignores God.

3. God punishes Manasseh.
4. Manasseh humbles himself and comes to God.
5. God forgives Manasseh and restores him.

God sends us whispers and warnings to position us for success *and* to help us avoid pain.

God's got your back in every way. Is He trying to steer you away from something or toward something He sees in your future that you don't see? If God is whispering to you or nudging you in a certain direction, then it's because He's got something good He doesn't want you to miss. These warnings or whispers come to us in our conscience, events, or things people say, and they are always confirmed. You have an intuitive knowledge of God where He confirms within you what is right or wrong. Taking a lesson from Manasseh's life by heeding the warnings and whispers can lead to self-correcting long before it becomes necessary for God to do the correcting. Hasn't it been your experience that consequences rarely show up as a surprise?

REFLECT TO CONNECT

1. When was the last time you ignored God's prompting?
2. Did you eventually self-correct, or did God need to ratchet up the pain to get your attention?
3. Is there anything unresolved in your conscience today you need to discuss with God?

They who correct themselves will avoid being corrected by another.

MIRACLES IN THE MARKETPLACE
WEEK 18 | FRIDAY

[Jesus'] mother said to the servants,
"Whatever He tells you, do it." John 2:5

Divine assistance is available to you at work. A big majority of the miracles in the Bible happened in the marketplace, not the synagogue. This includes Jesus turning water into wine, healing the blind, cleansing the lepers, the walls of Jericho falling, and Elijah bringing rain to end a drought. There is nothing too difficult for God. Whether you need a miracle with your business, favor with customers or supervisors, or a lower price on something, it is a small thing for God to make the impossible possible. Working "at work" is His specialty when He has you to work through.

When you ask God for something, He will often ask you to do something. God gives instructions not to "get something" from you but to position you to receive from Him. Sometimes divine instructions won't make sense and may even seem foolish, but don't discount intuitive senses. Be careful not to discount the method or manner in how God wants to answer your prayer request. Answers to prayer often come disguised in unwanted packages. Here are a few common ways in which God answers prayer:

IDEA: As you pray to God and listen for an answer, a nudging, hint of direction, or sudden suggestion may come to mind. "God ideas" can come out of the blue or get sparked while you are in conversation with someone. Sometimes they come instantly, and sometimes it is a slower process. As an idea resonates with you, think on it, process it out loud with others, and see how God expands it. Even an old idea can be given new life when God's finger touches it.

Remember that miracles have a timing element to them, so act when prompted.

INSTRUCTION: For a specific action you know you are delaying, delay no longer. Following through on what you can do unlocks what you can't do. Like in a chess game, until you move, God cannot move. You have to "move" when it is your turn.

INSPIRATION: An unction can be an unexplainable motivation to do something, go somewhere, or meet with someone. When you experience this, follow the wind of inspiration. God may put you together with someone that provides a piece to your puzzle.

IMPARTATION: An answer sometimes shows up in your "knower." When you have the faith or the full assurance that your request has been granted, act to receive.

REFLECT TO CONNECT

1. Do you know what the favor of God operating at your work-place and in your work looks like?
2. What is the last instruction God gave you? Have you executed it?
3. What might you ask God's assistance with today?

If God can turn water into wine at a wedding,
helping you with your work problem is a piece of cake for Him.

SACRED MISSION, SECRET STRATEGY

WEEK 19 | MONDAY

"I did not recognize Him, but He who sent me to baptize in water said to me, 'He upon whom you see the Spirit descending and remaining upon Him, this is the One who baptizes in the Holy Spirit.'" John 1:33

Did you know that it's possible to meet God and not know it? The disciples did not recognize Jesus on the road to Emmaus, Samuel could not discern God's voice the first time God spoke to him, and the Apostle Paul said that "some have entertained angels without knowing it." God knew that John the Baptist was about to meet Jesus but would not recognize who He was, so He gave him a "clue" so he would know what to look for. At times, God will need to open your eyes in order for you to see what He wants you to see. God has a strategy for everything He does; sometimes He makes it known, but other times He keeps it hidden until the time is right. God may keep something from you so that you, others, or the enemy don't mess it up. When I am unsure of how to handle a situation or I am sensing a "divine pause" in my heart, I will ask God a few questions "in faith," believing He will reveal to me what I need to know:

- Lord, please show me what is hidden.
- Lord, can You show me a strategy for my situation?
- Lord, what other purposes might You want to accomplish in this circumstance?

Everything you hear from God is not meant to be shared. When God begins to speak to you about your life, His plans, or your future, write down what you hear and keep it to yourself until He gives you permission to share it. God is always doing multiple things at once, so waiting on Him and moving when He tells you to move is imperative if you are to cooperate with and not hinder the strategy He wants to execute with you.

REFLECT TO CONNECT

1. Have you ever passed through a moment and then realized you "missed" what was right in front of you?
2. What secrets has God shared with you?
3. Have you ever repeated something you should not have and later felt convicted that you let the "cat out of the bag"?

God impregnates His plans with timing, purpose, and divine strategy. His secrets are for a season and for a reason.

——————————————◆————————————————

THE ARCHITECT'S TIMELINE
WEEK 19 | TUESDAY

The Spirit of the Lord God is upon me, Because the LORD anointed me To bring good news to the humble; He has sent me to bind up the brokenhearted, To proclaim liberty to captives And freedom to prisoners. Isaiah 61:1

J esus had a specific mission to fulfill, and so do you. Your calling has a spiritual GPS to guide you toward God's higher purposes for your life, but it requires your submission and cooperation. **God can't fulfill His purposes in you without you.** While a saint may be preoccupied with what God is doing *for* them, He is always more concerned about what is being accomplished *in* them. While we may be impatient, remember God is creating His masterpiece in you, and He has eternity in His hands.

Jesus's ministry lasted 3 1/2 years, but God's preparation time before Jesus went into public ministry was 30 years. God invested 40 years readying Moses in the wilderness before he led Israel out of Egypt. Joseph spent 13 years in God's training program between the pit and the palace before he became governor of Egypt. And Noah took architectural instructions from God to build the ark over 100 years. The Apostle Paul spent three years in Arabia before starting his first missionary journey. God prepares leaders today for pressures they will face tomorrow.

Seeds for success are planted in the background of preparation where no one can see. It is not uncommon for a season of obscurity to precede a season of assignment. Consider God's training program for assignment.

PURSUIT: You don't go until God calls. If you are not sure what your assignment is in this season, consider a time of seeking, prayer, and fasting. Seeking precedes seeing what God has planned for you.

PREPARATION: God knows what you will face in the future, so He designs an environment for you to learn what you will need for what lies ahead. At times, the place of your preparation will have difficult people and problems you will need to navigate. However, navigating difficult situations is God's primary training program for developing problem-solving skills.

PEOPLE: Every assignment involves people, and every training program comes with coaches. Whom has God assigned to you—whom are you assigned to? The people in authority God has over or under you will sometimes be the sandpaper by which He smooths out your rough edges.

PROCEED: Whether years in the making or months in waiting, when it comes time to move forward, get into action. Like a door opening and closing, assignments are time-sensitive, with a beginning and an end. If you miss your window to step up, another will step forward and take your place.

REFLECT TO CONNECT

1. What is God preparing you for in this season?
2. Are you able to identify His training program and the mentors He's assigned to you?
3. How can you tell when God is moving you to a new place of purpose?

It is not uncommon for a season of obscurity
to precede a season of assignment.

BUILDING BLOCKS OF A LEADER
WEEK 19 | WEDNESDAY

The Lord is not slow about His promise, as some count slowness,
but is patient toward you, not wishing for any to perish
but for all to come to repentance. 2 Peter 3:9

D oes God believe in your potential more than you do? Transformation takes time. God doesn't see us on only one point on a timeline in history; He also sees who we can become in the future. God is the builder of the worlds that are and the worlds that are to come. He is also a builder of people, and that takes time, too. His patience is part of His process designed to form the image of Christ in you. Like a caterpillar that transforms over time into a beautiful butterfly, so is God transforming you into a son or daughter who shares the similarities and likeness of His Son. Jesus is the image of the invisible God, and transformation from where you are to where you could be is His greatest work. Developing you into a mature leader that models Christlikeness in your vocational calling is how He brings His rule from Heaven to Earth.

Leaders submit to God's ways and process for transformation, knowing that God can only do with them what they allow Him to do through them. God doesn't force His will on you. Instead, His desire is that you will see what He is building in you and become a co-laborer in the transforming of who you are to who you can become. What are the steps to getting into the transformation business with God?

WILLINGNESS: Attitude carries a scent. People can instinctively tell if you are with them or not. Without the right attitude, even God will struggle to wrestle you into submission.

COOPERATION: Hallmarks of cooperation include give and take, submission, going along to get along, and so on. Are you aware of your role and responsibility so that you can cooperate with God's plan and do your part?

RELATIONSHIP: Leaning into God each day by spending time with Him is what will shed light and provide insight into successful daily living. Without relationship, revelation is impossible. What you water grows; what you starve dies.

PARTNERSHIP: God is not a dictator; He also does not run a democracy from Heaven. There are times to weigh in with an opinion, and there are times to get into action and do what you are told. God desires to build your life with you, not tell you what to do every minute. That's no fun for you or God. We recognize this dynamic with earthly authorities; should we not afford it to God? Are God's goals your goals?

REFLECT TO CONNECT

1. Is there anything left undone that God is waiting on you to complete?
2. What has God had to be patient with you in?
3. Do you find that you struggle building your career more with God or without Him?

Christian leaders ask, "Am I building or blocking the work of God in my life?"

------◆◆------

YOUR CONTACT POINT WITH GOD
WEEK 19 | THURSDAY

But his delight is in the law of the LORD, and on His Law he meditates day and night. He will be like a tree planted by streams of water, Which yields its fruit in its season, And its leaf does not wither; And in whatever he does, he prospers. Psalm 1:2-3

What is the secret to success? David tells us in this Psalm that success is tied to staying connected to God throughout our day. Anything you do daily grows in your life. God reveals the secret to letting His wisdom infiltrate your day, which guarantees prosperity in whatever you do. How can God make this promise? Because meditating on His Word throughout the day keeps you in His presence and Him involved in your micro-decisions. With the Holy Spirit at your side providing wisdom, a guiding hand, and a nudge here and there, whatever you do prospers because it is influenced by God.

Like an IV at the doctor's office, you are fed spiritual food that, through meditation, is digested and developed into both eternal returns and temporal rewards. Consider starting on a Bible reading plan today and plugging into God's divine intelligence for your life. A simple formula for plugging into God's word and taking action on what you read can be found in my best-selling book *PERSUADE* in the C.I.A. section.

The Scripture that resonates with you as you read it is your contact point with God that day.

C = Connection: What resonated with you as you read? When a Scripture seems to illuminate itself or jump off the page at you, STOP reading and remain where you are. This is your contact point today with the Divine. As you remain, write down what you hear and write down the questions that come to you as you sit in God's presence. In this way, you will learn to hear and respond to the voice of the Spirit in your life.

I = Insight: As you meditate on what connected with you, what insight is coming to mind from what you read? With you and your circumstance as the context for the text, what "God insight" is God sharing with you? Inscribe the word God is sharing with you in your journal and return to it throughout the day and watch Him add to it. Meditating on the Scripture that resonates with you while reading the Bible is a key to abiding in Him.

A = Action: The seed of change is taking action on what you've heard. The changes God wants to bring into your life will take place when you take action on what God directs you to do.

REFLECT TO CONNECT

1. What is your current daily routine whereby you meet with God each day?
2. Is there someone you can invite to do daily devotions with?
3. Whom can you share with today what God has shared with you?

The Scripture that resonates with you as you read
is your contact point with God that day.

DISCOVER THE DAVID WITHIN
WEEK 19 | FRIDAY

For we are His workmanship, created in Christ Jesus
for good works, which God prepared beforehand so
that we would walk in them.
Ephesians 2:10

The legend is told of an artist in the 1400s who came across a large, discarded block of marble. Tossed aside and written off, Michelangelo saw what no one else could see. That block of marble later became the world-renowned sculpture known as *David*. Michelangelo was uncommonly equipped to do what no one else was capable of doing. Once he began to exercise his giftedness, it continued to expand, and the creative genius that God deposited in him began to emerge.

What has God gifted you to do? And what are you doing to expand your area of giftedness?

Where does vision to see future potential come from? Jesus said that He could only do what He saw the Father doing (John 5:19). Like a movie playing on the screen of your mind, a picture planted in your heart, or a word you keep returning to, God is the designer of the dreams within us. What recurring tape, idea, or picture do you catch repeating on the screen of your mind? This could be a clue to the gift God wants to unlock.

God's matrix of gifts was embedded within your spiritual DNA before you were born. Your unique gift matrix was determined by God but must be discovered and developed by you. In their undeveloped form, gifts may be hidden at times. Some gifts are unlocked early in life; others unlock later as you progress through the seasons of life and mature spiritually. Layered within your spiritual DNA is an invisible map that holds clues to your destiny. This map has many features only known to you, and they can include:

Likes and Dislikes: There is a reason why you enjoy some things and some types of people and others you clearly dislike. You will share commonalities with the people or people groups you are assigned to, and you will have likes and dislikes for a reason. Desire is like a magnet that pulls or repels you to where you belong.

Genius: God has perfectly designed a life of success for you. In your area of assignment, you will experience rapid learning, an intuitive sense that others won't have, and early success. You will see what others don't see. What is difficult for most will come easily to you. In your area of assignment, God has gifted you with talents to make you successful. This genius isn't just for your enjoyment and success, but for God's purposes.

Passion: There are things that motivate and inspire you that are unique to you. In your area of assignment, you will have the ability to run faster, work longer, and outperform those around you because you are running in your lane of strength which God has engineered you for. What is drudgery for others, you will find delight in because God has fashioned you for that lane. When you feel like you have hit your "second wind" as a marathon runner would, know that you are running in your lane under a power granted to you from Heaven. It's your gift matrix given by God and discovered by you that makes acceleration possible.

REFLECT TO CONNECT

1. What picture (emotional pull/desire) has God planted within you?
2. Do you have counselors or coaches you can discuss your gift matrix with?
3. What have you experienced rapid learning and early success in?

Your purpose is decided by God but discovered by you.
Your job is what you are paid for; your purpose
is what you were made for.

LEADERSHIP RESTORATION

WEEK 20 | MONDAY

Hezekiah did this throughout Judah; and he did what was good, right, and true before the LORD his God. Every work which he began in the service of the house of God in Law and in commandment, seeking his God, he did with all his heart and prospered. 2 Chronicles 31:20-21

The longer a leader waits to "right a wrong course," the harder it is to change direction. The image of a successful leader conjures images of influence, wealth, vision, loyalty, commitment, and more. Have you ever had to risk the benefits of leadership in order to apologize publicly (repent), make an unpopular reverse course in an organization, or lead by example when you knew what was right would cost you influence and key relationships? Reversals in leadership that change culture and set expectations and new rules are very difficult.

Do you desire God's influence to flourish in your leadership? At the young age of 35, Hezekiah became king and, upon taking the throne, rallied the priests, messengers, and all who were willing to return to the Lord. A return, repentance, and sacrifice of this size had not occurred since the time of Solomon. Upon seeing Hezekiah move with all his heart in doing what was right, God came alongside him and blessed the work of his hands, healed the people, and most importantly, received His children back into His presence.

Consider the way back to restoring relationship with God, which is always a precursor to success with people. The following always causes God to turn toward and restore a leader and their leadership potential.

1. <u>Repenting</u> from doing what is wrong.
2. <u>Returning</u> to do what is right.

3. <u>Reinstating</u> God's ways.
4. <u>Recommitting</u> to serving Him and His purposes in your life.

REFLECT TO CONNECT

1. Is there anything in your "relationship account" with God that needs to be dealt with?
2. What, in your opinion, could stop the flow of favor in your life from God?
3. If God has all of you, what could God accomplish through you?

When leaders release what they are keeping from God,
God is authorized to release what He is holding for them.

------------◆------------

THE WISDOM FORMULA

WEEK 20 | TUESDAY

But if any of you lacks wisdom, let him ask of God, who gives to all
generously and without reproach, and it will be given to him.
But he must ask in faith without any doubting, for the one who doubts
is like the surf of the sea, driven and tossed by the wind. James 1:5-6

Wisdom is knowing what God would do in your situation. Successfully following God in the marketplace requires the wisdom of God. For every situation you face, God has a strategy to help you become more successful with Him than without Him. The wisdom of God is part of your inheritance and is guaranteed to you.

Scripture describes wisdom as a person, not a possession. Jesus is God's wisdom, and when we are in His presence, we are with wisdom. Yet, it is possible to have God with us but not exercise the wisdom He makes available to us. What is God's formula for obtaining wisdom for an issue you are facing? Simply to ask. God promises to give generously to you but with a few caveats. Here is a simple A.S.K. formula to help yourself access Heaven's storehouse of wisdom for your life.

A. Ask God humbly for His help to grant you wisdom for your situation. If you don't ask, you won't receive. And when you ask, ask specifically for that which you are seeking; vague prayers create their own difficulty for you and the one desiring to answer them.

S. Seek God with your WHOLE heart, without doubting. If you make a request but, the moment you leave your prayer time, become lazy in your thinking and allow doubt to creep in, God hears the prayer of faith and the prayer of doubt simultaneously. *Doubt neutralizes faith.* In fact, the Apostle James goes as far as to say that if you make a request and then doubt, you shouldn't expect God to even answer. Even Jesus's ability to do miracles in Nazareth was thwarted because of unbelief.

K. Knock once and be on your way. It is not necessary to keep praying (begging) the same prayer time and again. If you "know" that God heard you (and He did), and you believe that God loves you (and He does), and you know that He is working out a solution to your request (and He is), give God time to work. Some answers will come quickly; some will take time. Take comfort that your prayer requests are precious in God's sight to the degree that He writes every word down that you pray. Knocking once is all that is required. The answer to your request may be revealed directly to you or may come through another person, so be on the lookout. The law of answered prayer states there is seed, time, and then harvest. There is always time between the "amen" and "there it is."

REFLECT TO CONNECT

1. How can you tell God's wisdom apart from your own?
2. When you find yourself in over your head, do you call a friend or bend a knee to talk to God?
3. What do you believe about your relationship with God—is God desiring involvement in your daily life or just the big decisions you make?

Greater than the wisdom of Solomon is Christ in you.

————————————————————

THE TEST OF A LEADER'S INFLUENCE

WEEK 20 | WEDNESDAY

*Do not become teachers in large numbers, my brothers, since you know that we who are teachers will incur a stricter judgment.
For we all stumble in many ways. If anyone does not stumble in what he says, he is a perfect man, able to rein in the whole body as well.
Now if we put the bits into the horses' mouths so that they will obey us, we direct their entire body as well.* James 3:1-3

There is accountability for how leaders use what they've been given. The influence of a master leader is not too different than that of a master communicator, seller, preacher, or motivational speaker. Powerful communicators know how to wield their gifts in a way that will move and motivate their audiences to action. They possess the ability to change people's beliefs, as well as move people emotionally, intellectually, physically, and financially. Scripture reminds us that our message and motive is naked in God's sight, so we should consider who and how we are moving people with our knowledge, gifts, and passions.

Powers of persuasion can be used for right or wrong purposes. For millennia, God has gifted people of the earth with the "secrets" of success, but many have misused His knowledge. Even Paul said in 1 Timothy 1:8, "The Law is good, if one uses it lawfully." Consider the following checklist as a guide to holding yourself accountable in how you use your gifts to move people to decision:

1. Does this decision add value to the other person in a meaningful way?
2. Will the outcome of this decision produce mutual benefit or satisfy selfish benefit?
3. Do my powers of persuasion advance God's kingdom or only *my* kingdom?
4. Am I persuading others as God would, knowing that He knows all things?
5. Do I lead others through discussion before making a skip the process and move them to see things my way?
6. Would Jesus applaud my way of using my gifts as works that serve others and glorify God?

REFLECT TO CONNECT

1. In what ways do you hold yourself accountable?
2. Have you ever persuaded someone in a way that you wish you had not? Why?
3. How do you handle someone that is pushing you to move you in the wrong direction?

Leaders negotiate decisions but never principles.

BOOMERANG BLESSINGS

WEEK 20 | THURSDAY

*...knowing that whatever good thing each one does, this he will receive
back from the Lord, whether slave or free.* Ephesians 6:8

I magine working for a supervisor who sees every good deed
that you do for the company. No more hidden sacrifice or invisible acts of service no one notices, but instead, every good deed done
by you is documented for repayment. In fact, that supervisor personally credits your good deeds to your account and then takes on the
responsibility for paying the debt themselves to make sure you are
rewarded. *This* is the promise God makes to you. It's astonishing
but consistent with the reoccurring themes throughout Scripture.
"Give, and it will be given to you" (Luke 6:38); "He who waters will
himself be watered" (Proverbs 11:25); "One who is gracious to the
poor lends to the LORD And He will repay him for his good deed"
(Proverbs 19:17); "To the extent that you did it for one of the least of
these brothers or sisters of Mine, you did it for Me." (Matthew 25:40)

Your heavenly Father is the most generous Dad in the universe. The Law of Giving says that when you add value to another,
it triggers an invisible return to you. When serving others, serve as
you would to the Lord because it is He who returns the same and
more to you.

Whatever need you have in your life, find someone to give that
very thing to. If you have nothing tangible to give, give of your time
and talent or whatever God prompts you to give. As you are meeting
someone else's need, watch how God shows up to meet yours. You

will not always reap where you sow, so allow God to reward you in the way He feels best and thank Him for it.

The story of the widow's mite reminds us that God gives weight to the meaning and sacrifice of a gift over the measure or amount. No matter how small, if you sow in sacrifice to God in how you give and serve, He will find a way to return to you the good you have done for another.

REFLECT TO CONNECT

1. What do you have in your possession that you value that could be used to sow into someone's life?
2. Who is God calling you to approach today and perform an act of service for?
3. Do you have a clear-cut picture of what it is you are seeking from God in your life today?

Serving others in God's economy triggers a guaranteed return where God takes on the debt of your service, and He always repays.

THE ANKLE WEIGHTS OF LIFE
WEEK 20 | FRIDAY

Therefore, since we also have so great a cloud of witnesses surrounding us, let's rid ourselves of every obstacle and the sin which so easily entangles us, and let's run with endurance the race that is set before us, looking only at Jesus, the originator and perfecter of the faith.
Hebrews 12:1-2

W hat you "set your eyes on" is what you move toward. The story is told of a cargo plane that could not reach its designed altitude. After investigating, the pilot realized the plane was overloaded. After emptying some of its cargo, it was then able to reach its designed altitude and fulfill its mission. In the same way, the Holy Spirit reminds us that there are weights in life that can slow us down and wear us out, even if we are unaware of them. Left unchecked, weights can stop a person from fulfilling their purpose or a company from reaching its goal. What weights have been hindering you as you run your race?

Ankle weights are great for strengthening during conditioning but hindering when it's time to run the race. Leaders must regularly take inventory to assess whether or not they've taken on unnecessary cargo while passing through the seasons of life.

Weights that Slow You Down	Solutions that Speed You Up
• Sin	• Sanctification
• Conflict	• Resolution
• Unforgiveness	• Forgiveness
• Bitterness	• Gratefulness
• Pride	• Humility
• Self-Hatred (listening to the enemy)	• Valuing Yourself (listening to God)
• Reliving Regret from the Past	• Reconciling the Past to Focus on the Future
• Fear (too much focus on self)	• Confidence in God (thinking God's perspective)

God desires to help set you free from the pains that weigh you down. Ask Him for His help today and listen for direction; you will always play a part in your miracle, which is conditional on obedience.

REFLECT TO CONNECT

1. What are the "weights" in your life that bring a "heaviness" to you?
2. What advice would you give to someone who has weights in their life they need to lay down?
3. Is there an expert, mentor, or counselor you can reach out to for insight or perspective to help you break through?

What you "set your eyes on" is what you move toward.

THE CITY OF CALLING

WEEK 21 | MONDAY

Arise, go to Zarephath, which belongs to Sidon, and stay there; behold,
I have commanded a widow there to provide food for you. 1 Kings 17:9

Provision comes through a person or place—that is how God provides. God could have supernaturally fed Elijah where he was, but He commanded ravens to feed him day and night only after Elijah had gone to the PLACE God told him to go. Providing for Elijah again, God commanded a woman at Zarephath to feed Elijah, but he had to travel to a PLACE OF PROVISION and find a specific person. In the same way, there are seasons in our life where we, too, have a "city of calling," a place where we will find provision and people God has assigned to us and whom we have been assigned to. It is the place where God has asked you to go or to remain. There are provision, prosperity, and relationships in the PLACE God has told you to go.

FOUR INSIGHTS ABOUT THE PLACE OF PROVISION:

1. There is a timing element: Go "when" God tells you to go.
2. There are places you must go to be in obedience: Where has God called you to be or go?
3. There is favor in the place God has called you to. God can speak to people on your behalf before you even arrive. Where and with whom do you have favor? This is a clue to your provision.
4. Obedience precedes provision. Provision is waiting for you where God tells you to go (geography), in what God calls you to do (assignment), and with whom God calls you to serve (people).

REFLECT TO CONNECT

1. What was the last instruction God gave to you with regard to people and places?
2. Know that your calling is geographical. Where is the PLACE God wants you?
3. Is there a place or person you feel a gravitational pull to?

Provision is waiting for you where God tells you to go (geography), in what God calls you to do (assignment), and with whom God calls you to serve (people).

IS THAT YOU, LORD?
WEEK 21 | TUESDAY

Then the LORD came and stood, and called as at other times: "Samuel! Samuel!" 1 Samuel 3:10

Do you remember the first time you had an encounter with God? Would it surprise you to know that one of the greatest prophets in the Bible could not discern the voice of God at first? He had to learn it, and so do you. Prior to relationship and revelation, Samuel could not hear God. It is the same way with us. Do you remember the day you first met the Lord? Maybe it was at church, or with a friend. Or maybe you were alone reading or listening to a message. One thing is for certain: on that day when you chose to believe, there was no doubt about Whom you had met and what you felt and heard. The atmosphere on the inside was different; you had new sight and a new you. You knew you were changed.

How can you tell when God is speaking to you? There are many different ways, but oftentimes, like the day you first heard Him, you just know. When it's not God, you also know. You may feel yourself thinking through or rationalizing the matter, but it doesn't carry conviction. And this is a clue. When God speaks through our spirit, we receive and know. When it is only our own voice, we can often feel our mental motor turning in our brain. God's word isn't a product of our own reasoning; it's received. It is deposited in us, not decided within us. Our self-talk, on the other hand, is generated through our own thinking and nothing else.

You are meant to make a living in the lane of your assignment, but you are also meant to make a difference. To be successful, you must distinguish between God's voice and all others. Ask God today to speak to you and then wait for Him over the minutes, days, or weeks to gently drop His words of love, affirmation, and instruction into your heart. He wants you to hear Him more than you want to hear Him.

REFLECT TO CONNECT

1. When did you first hear God speak to you?
2. What was the first thing God asked you to do?
3. What is it you "know in your knower" today about God?

God's word isn't rationalized; it's received.
It is deposited in us, not decided within us.
Our self-talk, on the other hand, requires thinking through.

PICTURE OF A PROMISE

WEEK 21 | WEDNESDAY

"I will surely bless you and I will surely multiply you."
And so, having patiently waited, he obtained the promise.
Hebrews 6:14-16

There are two types of waiting: passive and active. If you are passive in your waiting, you may have a "set it and forget it" attitude. If you have received a sense of full assurance of your answer, you can wait without doubt for a promise to arrive. Active waiting means you are intentionally clinging to hope and staying in faith. Abraham kept his eyes on the stars as a picture of his promise as he waited on God. What picture has God given to you to meditate on while you wait?

The main ingredient in prayer is faith. Its main enemy is doubting that what you prayed for will come to pass. We know that without faith, it is impossible to please God, so how do you stay in faith when the waiting is longer than you expect? Active waiting is a verb—it is active and "in action." Here is how you can get into action when it's time to wait on God:

TRUSTING: Feeding your faith and starving your fears can be a moment-by-moment process at times. It involves "taking every thought captive to the obedience of Christ" (2 Corinthians 10:5) to not allow any thought to contradict your seed of faith. If you find yourself switching from waiting to worrying, that is not God. Once you give your request to God, do not take back what you've placed into His hands. Let "it" go, and let God do His part.

LOOKING: Like watchmen that wait for the morning, we wait for the Son to show us His solution to our request. Don't abandon your post; continue to look to the horizon for your answer. There are times and seasons God has appointed for you to wait on Him. It is in the "waiting time" that He is shaping you and building your spiritual muscles.

BIRTHING: The gestation period for a baby is nine months. Depending on the size of your request, your dream, or your problem, an answer could take shorter or longer. Give God time to work. He does not pop out like a genie in a bottle.

HOPING: Grab it, grip it tightly, and hold onto the hope that has been deposited within you. God has deposited within us an "earthen treasure" that acts as an anchor of the soul. That anchor is the Holy Spirit. Your faith may feel worn down at times while waiting but never let go of hope—your hope in Him inspires God.

SINGING: Paul and Silas sang their way out of prison. David's harp sent Saul's evil spirits fleeing. Songs are like passcodes that can unlock divine assistance. It's amazing the power of a song in the spiritual realm to break through enemy lines. God dispatches heavenly resources to your aid when He hears you singing a love song to Him. Find yourself a song for this season.

REFLECT TO CONNECT

1. Is there something that, through patience, God wants to break in you so He can birth something new?
2. What specific requests have you made of God that you are waiting on Him for?
3. What specific requests has God made of you that He is waiting on you for?

Spiritual "thoughts" are the God-nutrients
that water your heart to feed your faith.

THE DUAL ASSIGNMENT
WEEK 21 | THURSDAY

But seek first His kingdom and His righteousness,
and all these things will be added to you. Matthew 6:33

What is more important, heavenly priorities or earthly priorities? The answer may seem obvious, yet many find themselves wrestling between the secular and the sacred, as if they can be separated. We are commanded to walk *in* the world yet not be *of* the world. Talking out practical steps is often easier than walking them out.

Putting God first in all things is not a permission slip to skirt earthly responsibilities.

A vocational calling in the marketplace is no less sacred to God than a call to vocational ministry. Why do people elevate one and discount the other if God is the head who gives out both marketplace and ministry assignments? Is God less practical than He is spiritual? Of course not. He gives each person an assignment **predetermined** before the foundation of the world.

If you live in a performance-driven environment, you are faced with daily demands, ongoing accountability, and systems that track your progress against expectations. God does not expect you to ignore the practical and only follow the spiritual. God is reasonable and understands the tug of war you face on your time and wants you to integrate Heaven's priorities with earthly living. It's not one or the other, but both. Consider how God may intermingle heavenly and earthly priorities.

ATTITUDE: How you feel and think, not only what you produce.

CONNECTION: The health of our relationships with others and God. Does God care more for your relationship with Him and less for your relationship with others?

COMMUNION: Intimacy with God and those we are responsible for and to.

STEWARDSHIP: Your use of treasure, talent, and time at home and at work.

OPPORTUNITY: On the hunt for finances or saving souls. Are not both important?

RESOLUTION: Fixing problems in your business and God's. The kingdom of Heaven is a government and business that requires your problem-solving participation.

CAREER: Finding the vocational lane you can thrive in and minister in at the same time.

REFLECT TO CONNECT

1. If you had to make you and God a "to-do list," what would that look like?
2. In what ways would God remake your priorities?
3. What do you feel compelled to add to or eliminate from your list of priorities?

If you don't decide your earthly and heavenly priorities,
one will get lost.

A BASE HIT IS ALL IT TAKES

WEEK 21 | FRIDAY

Concerning him we have much to say, and it is hard to explain,
since you have become dull of hearing. For though by this time you
ought to be teachers, you have need again for someone to teach you
the elementary principles of the oracles of God, and you have come
to need milk and not solid food.
Hebrews 5:11-12

Whether they run like rabbits or walk like turtles, God expects His children to make progress in their walks with Him, in their work lives, habits, thought lives, relationships, etc. The author of Hebrews, under the inspiration of the Holy Spirit, comes right to the point in a moment of accountability. He says, in essence, that some should be teachers by now, yet expresses his disappointment that they are not. God, in His patience, takes us through seasons of challenge and change but does not like complacency. Are you making progress or defending a comfort zone? The God we serve is also a God of ROI, Return on Investment. Ask yourself the following progress challenge questions:

LIVING IN THE PAST: Are you still talking about yesterday's victories? If the "good old days" are the only areas of success you have to point to, it may be time to ask God what He would like to accomplish with you and through you today. God can help you create momentum from just one step in the right direction.

GETTING UNSTUCK: Are you still struggling with the same challenges or sins from a year ago? If so, it's time to set aside—once and for all—the encumbrances that are holding you back. You are never more than one person or one idea away from a breakthrough. Visit an online bookstore or watch a YouTube video today and find out how others have persevered and broken through what you are going through. God is on your side.

With every step you take toward transformation, you are breaking through and making progress, even if it is only an inch at a time. God will wait for you if you are slow-moving, but He won't do the walking for you.

God never expects more than we have, but He does expect us to give Him all that we have. A successful strategy might include getting 1% better today than you were yesterday. For the steps toward success that you need to take, you don't need to hit it out of the park with one swing; focus on a base hit and let God bring you home.

REFLECT TO CONNECT

1. Do you have growth goals written out in stages?
2. Whom do you know that models ongoing growth and progress that you can follow?
3. How much time per day is God leading you to commit to growing yourself in order to achieve incremental progress?

If you are stuck in neutral, it's possible
you are defending your comfort zone.

WALK RIGHT IN

WEEK 22 | MONDAY

*Therefore let us draw near with confidence to the throne of grace,
so that we may receive mercy and find grace
to help in time of need.* Hebrews 4:16

I n Old Testament times, there was a protocol where if you entered the presence of the king without being summoned, and the king did not extend his scepter to you, it meant death for you. The author of Hebrews penned that we are children of grace who have an *open invitation* whereby we can enter into God's presence any time we want to. When we seek an audience with God and we enter, we should do so with confidence, even boldness, because we have righteous standing before God because of what Jesus did. Once in His presence, He not only hears us out but promises to help us with our need. Today, He is waiting for you to enter in. Once in God's presence, what will you say? What will you ask? Knowing you have unfettered access, how will you use it? God is not only concerned with heavenly purposes, but also earthly matters that impact your life. Make your request.

REFLECT TO CONNECT

1. Do you believe you have 24/7 access to God, and He will answer your requests?
2. Why do you have confidence before God?
3. Do you believe God answers one person's prayers more than another's?

God awaits your arrival;
It is not you who is waiting on God, but
He who is waiting on you.

HOW TO WALK IN THE SPIRIT
WEEK 22 | TUESDAY

... Be filled with the Spirit, speaking to one another in psalms and hymns
and spiritual songs, singing and making melody with your heart
to the Lord; always giving thanks for all things in the name of our
Lord Jesus Christ to God, even the Father.
Ephesians 5:18-20

The minute I turn on Christian music and begin to sing along in my heart, God enters my car and pulls me into His presence. You are never more than one song away from entering the presence of God. Paul tells us the secret for what attracts God's presence: making melody in our hearts to the Lord. God can't resist a love song sung by His children. The moment you start singing to Him or about Him, He draws near to you, and the moment He enters, everything changes. You can start strengthening yourself by reading, meditating, and singing the words of God. When you say or sing what God has said, you will feel strengthening from God. For where His presence goes, His Spirit blows with the wind of inspiration. When you experience low points or valleys in the middle of your day, steal away for 5 to 10 minutes to strengthen yourself in the Lord with a song.

Here are a few ways in which God may strengthen you as you enter His presence.

1. Solutions to your problems can appear in an instant.
2. You are refreshed and strengthened mentally and spiritually.
3. The atmosphere may feel charged with energy or a peace unmistakable.
4. Your challenge becomes God's challenge as He breathes a word into your heart.
5. You may hear an answer, a Scripture, a whisper, or sense a word of wisdom has been deposited.

A song often brings instant reinforcement. Other times, it will bring peace or a sense that God has your back. Remember to give God time to work behind the scenes to line things up, and as you wait, stay in faith.

REFLECT TO CONNECT

1. Whom do you know that lives a life of "walking in the Spirit"?
2. Have you ever put your 10 favorite worship songs on a playlist and sung them under your breath as you walked through your day?
3. What is God's favorite song that you sing to Him? (Ask Him.)

Where God's presence goes,
His Spirit blows with the wind of inspiration.

THE SHARPENING STONE
OF SUCCESS

WEEK 22 | WEDNESDAY

For it was fitting for Him, for whom are all things, and through whom
are all things, in bringing many sons to glory, to perfect the author of
their salvation through sufferings. Hebrews 2:10

I t's not popular, and it doesn't preach well, yet Scripture speaks
of sacrifice and suffering as part of the heavenly steps toward success. "Suffering according to God's will" is a mystery, but it is one of
God's ways, a sort of sharpening stone to remake His children into
His likeness. Jesus learned obedience through suffering. Job 13:15 says,
"Though He slay me, I will hope in Him." Then Jesus spoke of the
greatest apostle of all time when He said to Ananias about Paul, "I will
show him how much he must suffer for My name's sake." (Acts 9:16)

If success were easy and sacrifice enjoyable, everyone would have
it. Many want the fruits of success but are unwilling to pay the price,
and many seek the hand of God but neglect the heart of God. But
success comes with a price. The fruit of success always includes a
degree of sacrifice. God will not cease in growing you unless you
become unwilling to keep journeying with Him. If God is willing
to grow you, but the price is to sacrifice or suffer for a season, are
you willing to submit to His way? Here are some guiding questions
along the road toward growth to consider:

- What sacrifices is God asking me to make in the arena I am
  called to?
- Whom should I be submitted to in this season to level up in life?
- For the suffering and injustices I face, how can I suffer according
  to the will of God?

- When have I suffered because of my mouth, attitude, or actions?
- Am I willing to stretch and change in the way my spouse, supervisor, or friends have intimated to me?

REFLECT TO CONNECT

1. Do I embrace the biblical truth that suffering often surrounds a sanctifying work?
2. Have I identified the "price I must pay" to do what God has called me to do?
3. Am I a "Type A" personality that pushes God and His timeline or a "Type S" in the kingdom that submits to His way of service and sacrifice?

The journey toward growth ceases when you stop climbing.

———————————◆———————————

THE CHRISTIAN DRIFT
WEEK 22 | THURSDAY

For this reason we must pay much closer attention to what
we have heard, so that we do not drift away from it.
Hebrews 2:1

"The Christian Drift" sounds like a folk song or a new dance, but the Holy Spirit felt it important enough to include the word "drift" in Scripture and point to the inevitability of a spiritual drift away from God we are prone to experience. This is true for you, the angels, and anyone who has free will. There are times when your mind is right, but your feelings are wrong and times when your heart should be trusted, and your thoughts ignored. But how can you tell which to follow? Like a car at highway speed with two hands firmly holding the wheel, so must we intentionally steer ourselves into the will of God. God's will is not automatic in your life—you will play a role in bringing it to pass. There is no cruise control in the kingdom of Heaven.

It's not enough to hear or possess knowledge to be successful; we must hear and heed what we have learned whether we are working on our walk with God or our daily work in the marketplace. You can avoid drifting off course by:

RECOGNITION: Mature saints recognize that the drift is natural and are aware when it happens.

RESPONSIBILITY: Mature saints take ownership of the fact that God has given them control to steer and submit their walk and work to the will and works of God.

RETURNING: Mature saints return daily to the point of entry for all renewal, the presence of God to wash and renew their minds in the Word. Developing a daily cadence of letting the Word read you as you read it ensures we are made aware of adjustments we need to make.

REFLECT TO CONNECT

1. What areas of weakness are you vulnerable to drift in?
2. Do you have a daily, scheduled time for the washing and renewing of your mind in the Word?
3. When you sense a "drift," is your tendency to keep going or stop moving and ask God for help?

All saints drift, but those who catch themselves
and course correct, happy are they.

SUPPORT THE BOSS

WEEK 22 | FRIDAY

Remind them to be subject to rulers, to authorities,
to be obedient, to be ready for every good deed. Titus 3:1

It's easy to be submissive to those above us when it doesn't come with a cost. It's easy to come into agreement with those we agree with. The challenge is to bring your heart and actions into conformity with those in authority over us when we do not agree with a decision or direction of leadership. It is one thing to know the "right" thing to do but quite another to make oneself do it with a good attitude.

Everyone reports to someone. This is true in Heaven and on Earth. For every decision a person is saddled with by a supervisor that they don't agree with, the decision to follow vs. fight allows one to remain in relationship and harmony with those in authority. On the other hand, the decision to fight authority puts a spotlight on one's attitude and alters the course of favor over time. If you are at odds and struggling to support one who is in authority over you, follow the "Rule of Three":

1. Look for one thing you can agree on, then give 100% of your support to the 1% and let God build the rest.
2. Look through the unbiased eyes of God and try to see and support what He sees in the authority you are struggling to buy into.

3. If you cannot bring yourself to get along, decide to go along and reserve judgment until God opens your eyes to see another perspective.

Leaders adapt to everyone so they can get along with everyone. Paul was a Roman to the Romans and a Greek to the Greeks; he learned to adapt to people and environments everywhere.

REFLECT TO CONNECT

1. What initiative, goal, or way of thinking are you struggling to come into agreement with in this season?
2. Looking through the eyes of Christ, what is the biblical perspective on the situation at hand?
3. Who in your world models submitting to authority the best?

Learn to "go along" to "get along,"
and your heart will eventually follow.

DOING BUSINESS GOD'S WAY

WEEK 23 | MONDAY

*Hear this, you who trample the needy, to do away with the humble of
the land, saying, "When will the new moon be over,
So that we may sell grain, And the sabbath, that we may open the wheat
market, To make the bushel smaller and the shekel bigger,
And to cheat with dishonest scales" ... The Lord has sworn by the pride
of Jacob, "Indeed, I will never forget any of their deeds." Amos 8:4-5, 7*

As God is going through the list of deeds that anger Him,
cheating a neighbor, dishonest gain, and doing business in
a way that takes advantage of others are among them. When businesspeople use dishonest gain as a strategy for profit, God promises
future consequences.

God is a businessman who honors honest gain; He, too, wants a
return on investment for His distribution of talents to His children.

People are money conscious and money motivated. There is
nothing wrong with desiring to make a profit or improve your
standard of living. Doing business God's way involves doing things
the right way and for the right reasons. The litmus test for integrity
in the marketplaces removes the gray areas by answering three
questions:

1. What would God say about the way I am structuring the
   transaction? Am I taking care of or taking advantage of the
   other party?
2. What does my conscience say? Who is helped or hurt by my
   plans, processes, or profit motives?
3. What would others say? Never do anything you would not
   want to read about online.

1. Are there any deals or negotiations in your memory that God is speaking to you about?
2. Are there any changes you need to make in your plans or processes to ensure you are honoring God and His ways in how you do business?
3. Who comes to mind when you think of people who represent honest or dishonest business practices?

Transactions are tracked in a ledger on Earth
and in Heaven, so act accordingly.

ANGER REDIRECTED

WEEK 23 | TUESDAY

I hate, I reject your festivals,
Nor do I delight in your solemn assemblies. Amos 5:21

I t doesn't preach well. Nobody likes to talk about it, yet it is true. God, like any parent, gets angry at times with His children. In the case of religion, God hates and rejects religion for religion's sake when the heart toward Him is not right. Yet God channels His hate, frustration, and disappointment in a productive way to bring His children back. In this case, we can see that negative emotions carry the power to be destructive *or* constructive. They can provide a powerful energy when channeled to create positive results.

Leaders face frustrations like anyone else; however, they learn to control their emotions and channel them into productive uses throughout their day. You will encounter anger, disappointment, frustration, rejection, betrayal, and many other negative emotions. However, how you redirect these powerful energies will determine if they produce a productive or destructive force. Jesus speaks of great rewards for those who overcome. Are you in control of your emotions, or are they in control of you? If you had to make a list of the top two frustrations that negatively impact you in the work environment, what would they be? How would God advise you to handle them?

1. _____

2. _____

REFLECT TO CONNECT

1. How did you respond the last time you were rejected, angered, or betrayed?
2. Do you have a "redirect" plan for settling yourself down when overcome with powerful emotions?
3. What is God speaking to you now about redirecting negative emotions?

Things work out the best for those who make the best of the way things work out.

EMPOWERED TO STOP

WEEK 23 | WEDNESDAY

Furthermore, I withheld the rain from you while there were still three months until harvest. Then I would send rain on one city And on another city I would not send rain; One part would be rained on, While the part not rained on would dry up. "So two or three cities would stagger to another city to drink water, But would not be satisfied; Yet you have not returned to Me," declares the Lord. Amos 4:7-8

Four times in Amos 4, the Lord says, "You have not returned to me." Have you ever known there was something you needed to do but continued to put off? It was better to take the easy road than the right road. God is long-suffering, wishing all to come to repentance; however, He does have a limit and, at some point, declares that time is up. The consequences of delayed obedience can lead to a shot over the bow from the Lord or, if ignored long enough, can lead to a "time is up" scenario where God declares an end to one season and the beginning of the next. God often holds back the arm of consequence from the choices we make to give us time to change our ways.

Israel didn't become disobedient as a nation all at once; it happened one decision at a time. It is often the many micro-decisions that lead to a big event in our life. Successful people are diligent in building habits that keep them doing what *is* right vs. doing what *feels* right. Success habits are built one decision at a time. However, steps to failure are also made one decision at a time. Decisions compound over time, creating our future. What direction are your habits and micro-decisions taking you today?

Empower yourself by separating from yourself! Conscience is the primary mechanism by which God speaks to us. There are hundreds of micro-decisions a person makes each day. One practice that will allow you to empower yourself when decision making is to view yourself as one up in the stands observing the people below on the stage making decisions. What advice would you give to them? What choice would you make if you were in their shoes seeing from a different perspective? This practice of being able to emotionally separate yourself from a situation can provide you the perspective to be able to separate what "feels" right at the moment from what you know to be right. Setting your emotions aside and clinging to God's tap on your conscience will keep you on course when tempted.

REFLECT TO CONNECT

1. What decisions have you made that have brought you to where you are today?
2. Are there things you blame God or others for that are the result of your own doing?
3. If you had to reverse engineer one of the most important decisions you've ever made, what was the thinking process or steps that led you to decide what you did?

Feeling right comes from doing right.

———————————◆◆◆———————————

FINISH YOUR RACE

WEEK 23 | THURSDAY

I have fought the good fight, I have finished the course,
I have kept the faith. 2 Timothy 4:7

S ome believe that if it's God's will, then nothing will stop it. But God also has willed that we be free and has permitted our free will decisions to have an impact on the world around us, for better or for worse. It is not God's will for a drug dealer to deal drugs, but they deal. It is not God's will for car accidents to happen, but they do. It is not God's will for people to be led astray, but many are. It is not God's will that any would perish, but that all would come to a saving knowledge of Christ. Yet many will perish by the choices they make.

Not everyone Paul persuaded to join him in his beliefs and his cause stayed with him. Many abandoned him, and some even shipwrecked their faith. To finish well, it's not enough to start strong; a saint must remain strong. The Apostle Paul, toward the end of his calling, was able to declare that he had finished strongly. In what ways did Paul live out his calling so he could stay the course and finish well?

Purpose: Paul knew not just what he was doing but why he was doing it. What is your "why"?

Persuasion: Paul was fully persuaded, convicted, and convinced of the worthiness of his pursuit. What are you convinced of?

Passion: Paul was driven daily by the motivation of the One who called him. What relationships drive you each day to do what you do?

Perseverance: Paul was not sidetracked by struggle, sacrifice, or seemingly unimportant distractions—his eyes stayed fixed on the finish line. Are you focused on daily circumstances or final outcomes?

"When there is hope in the future, there is power in the present."
John Maxwell

REFLECT TO CONNECT

1. How do you define your purpose in this present season?
2. How does your vocational calling complement your heavenly calling?

3. What are you fully persuaded of with regard to your assignment?

Your "WHY" is decided by God but discovered by you.
When you know your "WHY," you'll know your "WAY."

DIVINE INTELLIGENCE
IN THE SCRIPTURES
WEEK 23 | FRIDAY

Always learning but never able to come to a
knowledge of the truth.
2 Timothy 3:7

Have you ever heard the phrase "use it or lose it" before? Like a muscle, knowledge atrophies if not put into action. If it is acted upon, it can increase and strengthen. If learning is not acted upon, it may accumulate but not benefit anyone. It is possible to create the habit of learning but not experience the *benefits* of it.

A sponge can reach its limit as to how much liquid it can hold. It must be wrung out if it is to take on new liquid. In the same way, saints studying Scripture can wring out their sponges by putting into action what they learn. Once wrung out, the sponge is ready again to take on more.

Consider how a leader guarantees transformation by daily downloading intelligence provided in Scripture from the inspirational mentors in the Bible by following the C.I.A. process.

C onnecting: What **connection** are you experiencing as you read? Some verses will resonate with you, and others will not. As you read, be aware of areas of Scripture that seem to "jump off the page" and grab your attention. Once you identify an area of connection with God, stop reading and start reflecting. Once you discover something God is illuminating to you, STOP and remain in that area.

I nsight: What **insight** did you receive from what connected with you? If God is illuminating a verse to you from your daily reading, it is because He wants to have a conversation with you about it.

A ction: What **action** can you implement as a result of what God spoke to you about today? Transformation is a calendar event. What gets scheduled gets done. By incorporating what God is telling you to do into your daily routine, you are guaranteed change in your life.

REFLECT TO CONNECT

1. What is the last thing God impressed upon you that you have yet to put into action?
2. Who in your life is a model of being a "doer" and not merely a hearer of the Word?
3. What would be the outcome if you act upon what you have recently learned?

Illumination is the internal stirring God uses
to let you know it is Him inspiring you.

THE HOUND OF HEAVEN

WEEK 24 | MONDAY

But Jonah rose up to flee to Tarshish from the presence of the Lord.
So he went down to Joppa, found a ship which was going to Tarshish,
paid the fare and went down into it to go with them to Tarshish
from the presence of the LORD. Jonah 1:3

If you've ever gone the other way on something you knew you were supposed to do, you know why Jonah did what he did. Nonetheless, Jonah was without excuse. He knew the right and did not do it. He knew God wanted to show kindness to Nineveh and forgive them, and he knew he was going to be the vessel of God's goodness to those he considered enemies.

I imagine a mailroom in Heaven. One prayer request comes up, and another goes down. While God is using someone close by to answer your prayer, He wants to use you to be an answer to someone else's prayer. Consider that the next time you resist what God wants to do in your life. God chooses the way in which He will answer your prayer and through whom. Like Jonah, you are never more than one decision away from getting right with God.

A leader's day is filled with fast-paced decision-making. God is faithful to send his Holy Spirit, the "Hound of Heaven," and He will not let you get off track without pinging you in your conscience to bring you back. If you are getting a ping from God in your heart, do as Jonah did and repent (change direction) but do it earlier before a big fish of consequence comes to swallow you up (pun intended). God will use your turnaround to do a great work in someone's life.

GET ON THE TURNAROUND TRACK

1. **HEAR:** Do not resist the conscience-correcting work of the Holy Spirit.
2. **HEAL:** Remorseful repentance of your choice and acceptance of God's voice will heal your conscience.
3. **HEED:** Make the decision to follow the direction or nudge the Holy Spirit is giving you.
4. **HARKEN:** Peter in Acts pointed out that David was a man after God's own heart because he did what God asked of him. David wasn't perfect, but he was correctable, and that made him near and dear to God's heart. You, too, become near and dear to God's heart when He knows He can count on you to course correct when He calls.

REFLECT TO CONNECT

1. What was your experience the last time you resisted God?
2. Have you felt a nudging from the Hound of Heaven?
3. Whom do you know that is easily correctable?

"There's a little bit of Jonah in all of us."
Wayne Cordeiro, Founding Pastor, New Hope Oahu

———————————◆———————————

SCREEN TIME IN THE SPIRIT

He fixed his gaze steadily on him until he was ashamed, and the man of God wept. Hazael said, "Why does my lord weep?" Then he answered, "Because I know the evil that you will do to the sons of Israel: their strongholds you will set on fire, and their young men you will kill with the sword, and their little ones you will dash in pieces, and their women with child you will rip up." Then Hazael said, "But what is your servant, who is but a dog, that he should do this great thing?" And Elisha answered, "The LORD has shown me that you will be king over Aram."
2 Kings 8:11-13

Did you know that your spirit is connected to God's Spirit, which allows you to receive directly from God? God gave Elisha a vision in the middle of a conversation he was having with Hazael. Have you ever lost yourself in thought and found yourself watching what is like a play enacted on the "screen" of your mind? Divine inspiration can come during meditation, while thinking on a subject, during mental preparation, while reading Scripture, and even in the middle of a conversation. Jesus spoke of a process of seeing before doing when He said that He could only do what He saw the Father doing.

You have the power to trigger vision in your life. One characteristic of intuition is the ability to see or sense something before it happens. The process of mental preparation allows one to exercise their imagination to "see it before they do it," "hear it before they say it," or "experience it before it happens." Successful saints practice the daily habit of taking their plans into their prayer closets to submit them to the Lord. While in His presence, thinking through, talking through, and working through one's plans and conversations for the day gives God an opportunity to weigh in and share

His perspective with you, which is often accompanied by an idea, insight, or vision.

Whether selling, managing, coaching, parenting, teaching, or working in a service or support role, mentally pre-planning events and conversations in an attitude of prayer will ensure you bring God into your day. Planning ahead with God also allows one to foresee potential opportunities or pitfalls in the future before they occur.

Wayne Cordeiro, Founding Pastor of New Hope Oahu, once said, "Prayer is thinking deeply in the presence of God." Next time you are thinking deeply in God's presence and submitting your plans to Him, be aware of the theatrical scene or conversation God may enact on the screen of your mind. It is through vision that He makes His secret plans for you known.

REFLECT TO CONNECT

1. When was the last time you experienced a vision being enacted on the screen of your mind? It might have even felt like a daydream.
2. What is your process for submitting your plans and conversations to the Lord?
3. Whom do you know that has a gift for always being prepared, and what is their secret?

Roleplaying during "screen time with God" is one way to submit your plans to see what He sees.

TAKE YOUR STAND
ON YOUR KNEES

WEEK 24 | WEDNESDAY

You need not fight in this battle; station yourselves,
stand and see the salvation of the LORD on your behalf,
O Judah and Jerusalem. Do not fear or be dismayed; tomorrow go out
to face them, for the LORD is with you. 2 Chronicles 20:17

Surrender to God when surrounded by circumstance. A great multitude was coming against Jehoshaphat, King of Judah. Upon hearing what he and his nation were up against, the king knew he had no chance, and he experienced great fear. Outnumbered, afraid, and doomed for destruction, Jehoshaphat sought the Lord and declared a national fast. When the chips are stacked against you, taking a knee is how a saint stands before God. Bowing before God will allow you to stand before men.

When you kneel down, God stands up on your behalf. There is not a person alive who doesn't find themselves over their head from time to time. If you are unsure of what to do with a supervisor, customer, or a child, remember that God knows the heart of everyone. He knows not only your plans but theirs. When your back is against the wall, God knows the way to victory. Hillsong music once recorded a song called "Touch the Sky" with a lyric that read, "My hands touch the sky when my knees hit the ground." The best place to receive the strategy of God for your circumstance is to visit the war room of prayer and supplication and let God fight for you.

1. When feeling afraid or intimidated, is your first response to bow your head or buck up?
2. What was the last victory that you experienced with the Lord?
3. Who is an example in your life of a warring person of prayer that seeks God when trouble comes?

When the chips are stacked against you,
taking a knee is how a saint stands before God.
Bowing before God allows you to stand before men.

TEAM FIRST

WEEK 24 | THURSDAY

I thank Christ Jesus our Lord, who has strengthened me,
because He considered me faithful, putting me into service.
1 Timothy 1:12

It's easy to forget that we are part of something much greater than ourselves. God assigns each one a personal and corporal call. One is specifically relevant to one's walk, while the other is in service to the body of Christ. The Great Commission has an assignment for everyone right where they are, regardless of their station in life. The Apostle Paul taught in Acts 17:26 that God has set the dates and places that we live. If you have been called in this place for this time, then whom are you called to serve? Timothy served Paul, Elisha served Elijah, David served Saul, and Joshua served Moses. God uses service to others to qualify us for roles of leadership both in this life and the life to come. Service to another requires sacrifice of self, putting an individual's or a team's interest above our own. Here are a few successful behaviors of a team-oriented saint. Team players:

- Put the team needs above individual needs.
- Defer to the team direction vs. personal direction.
- Are committed to the best idea vs. their idea.
- Embrace the idea that "all of us know more than one of us."
- Work for a win-win. When the team wins, everyone wins.

REFLECT TO CONNECT

1. What position does God have you playing on your current team?
2. In those you are called to serve in this season, how would you rate yourself as a team player on a scale of 1-10?
3. What could you do today to increase your level of contribution toward the team?

Jesus used a team of 12; who are your 12 picks
for the team to get you through life?

———————◆◆———————

MUSIC THAT ATTRACTS MIRACLES

WEEK 24 | FRIDAY

Elisha said… "But now bring me a minstrel." And it came about,
when the minstrel played, that the hand of the LORD came upon him.
He said, "Thus says the LORD, 'Make this valley full of trenches.'

For thus says the LORD, 'You shall not see wind nor shall you see rain;
yet that valley shall be filled with water, so that you shall drink,
both you and your cattle and your beasts.'"
2 Kings 3:14-17

Wherever there is music unto the Lord, there is the potential for a miracle. Music in celebration of the greatness of God ushers in His presence. Even the Psalmist testifies to the protocol for entering His presence when he said, "Enter His gates with thanksgiving *And* His courts with praise." (Psalm 100:4)

Elisha was reluctant to perform a miracle, yet he knew music brought him into the presence of God. Are you needing a miracle in your life? If so, draw near to God, and He will draw near to you. A song is a simple way to unlock the door to His presence in your life. Here are a few reminders the Holy Spirit penned to show us that we are only a song away from the Savior:

1. Be filled with the Spirit by singing to yourself in songs, hymns, and spiritual songs. (Ephesians 5:19)
2. God inhabits the praises of His people (Psalm 22:3), so praise Him whether under your breath, in your heart, or from the top of your lungs.
3. Worship is a weapon that makes the enemy flee. David played the harp, and the evil spirit left Saul.
4. "Where the Spirit of the Lord is, there is liberty." (2 Corinthians 3:17)
5. Sing your way to freedom as Paul and Silas did. When they sang, the walls in the prison fell.

Whether you prefer to sing a hymn, a song you learned in church, or a song from the radio, raising your spirit to God in celebration gets Heaven's attention. If you can't think of a song to sing, ask God to give you a song just for you. See what words He brings to your mind, then hum them and watch Him draw close to you.

REFLECT TO CONNECT

1. When was the last time you entered into His presence with a song as the entry point?
2. Did you know that God hears the heart, not only the voice, when you sing?
3. Have you ever considered doing a daily prayer walk whereby you pray, sing, and meditate as you walk? God waits for you on the road.

Like bees to honey, so is God to saints who sing to Him.
Singing to God joins you with the heavenly choir who sings
His praises without ceasing day and night.

BECOMING A SUCCESS SCIENTIST

WEEK 25 | MONDAY

Now Jehoshaphat the son of Asa became king over Judah in the fourth
year of Ahab king of Israel. Jehoshaphat was thirty-five years old when
he became king, and he reigned twenty-five years in Jerusalem.
And his mother's name was Azubah the daughter of Shilhi.
He walked in all the way of Asa his father; he did not turn aside from it,
doing right in the sight of the LORD. 1 Kings 22:41-43

Mentors and mistakes are the most memorable teachers. Jehoshaphat had a path of success to follow: his father's. Example is the best teacher, and the best teachers have been mentors throughout time. It is said that we "learn from mentors or mistakes." For this reason, God has given thousands of examples of what success and failure look like in the context of relationship with Himself and others in the Bible. He did this so we would have an example to model and mimic.

Success leaves clues; so does failure. Scripture is loaded with both. Smart people know how to take on the mindset of a "Success Scientist." Success Scientists learn from other people's experiences, whether they be good or bad. They are selective about whom they choose to learn from as well as whom they model their life and behavior after. While they are particular about whom they follow and learn from, they are also aware that others are observing them, being influenced by them, and will model their examples. Everybody influences somebody.

Study success and failure. People model, mimic, and reproduce that which they see. Whether in the work environment, the classroom, the sports arena, or the neighborhood, someone is always watching. Consider the ways in which you may be impacting the environment around you.

Home Environment: If you treat others with respect, you will reproduce respect.

Work Culture: If you act with integrity, people will observe your standard.

Parenting: If you are kind to strangers, your children will learn to be kind.

Church: If you have intimacy with God, others will believe they can, too.

Values: If you put doing "right" above doing what "feels right," God will be honored.

"Your actions speak so loudly I can't hear your words!" said the child. Always remember that as you learned your ways from those who went before you, there are those who are finding their way by observing your ways.

REFLECT TO CONNECT

1. Whom do you look up to that you desire to be like?
2. Who are the heroes of your kids, friends, or spouse?
3. Are there habits in your life that are positive or negative examples?

The secret to mastery is to become a student.

———————————◆◆◆———————————

MAJESTIC MELODY

Let the word of Christ richly dwell within you, with all wisdom teaching and admonishing one another with psalms and hymns and spiritual songs, singing with thankfulness in your hearts to God. Whatever you do in word or deed, do all in the name of the Lord Jesus, giving thanks through Him to God the Father. Colossians 3:16-17

Making melody in your heart to God ushers in His presence. To "dwell" on the word of Christ means to think consistently on a passage of Scripture or rehearse a song to God or about God in your heart. When you dwell on what God said or begin to sing to Him, it triggers His promise that if you draw near to Him, He will draw near to you. Dwelling on His Word means to remember what He said.

As you dwell on God, you will begin to experience:

- The mood change within you. He's drawing near to you to be with you.
- Inner peace wash over you. God has entered the room and is letting you know He has arrived.
- A mental picture, memory, or sort of "daydreaming" experience whereby you are watching yourself perform something in the past or future. This is how God shows you things in the present.
- An inward prompting or train of thought that takes you from one thought to the next. He is leading you.

To "dwell" on God is how a saint remains filled with the Spirit. The Apostle Paul's prescription to the Colossians is to be FILLED with God in the same way he learned to be with the Lord continually, regardless of the circumstance he was in. Nobody can rob you of your inner life without your permission—the Apostle Paul proved this.

Redeem the seconds! We spend much of our day just waiting, in lines, for people, or for other reasons. "In-between times" can be redeemed into TIME SPENT WITH GOD moments. If you are feeling empty, unsure, or could use a season of strengthening from God, refill with song, word, and thankfulness in Christ by singing in your heart or meditating on the words of Christ. As you do, you will feel God draw near and His divine presence embrace you.

REFLECT TO CONNECT

1. How do you make the most of your "in-between times" during your days?
2. How does God recharge and restore you while in His presence?
3. What other practices do you employ to reengage God's presence in your life?

Nobody can rob you of your inner life without your permission—the Apostle Paul proved this.

———————————◆———————————

THE JESUS JOURNEY IN THE MARKETPLACE

WEEK 25 | WEDNESDAY

See to it that no one takes you captive through philosophy and empty deception, according to the tradition of men, according to the elementary principles of the world, rather than according to Christ. For in Him all the fullness of Deity dwells in bodily form, and in Him you have been made complete. Colossians 2:8-10

The new shiny penny is exciting, but could be a New Age entrapment. You will encounter many belief systems in the marketplace. The one thing that distinguishes Christianity from other religions is that we follow a Person, not a philosophy. We serve a living God, not a set of rules or traditions. With Christ, there is FREE forgiveness for your sins when you repent, a GIFTED inheritance as a child of God, and ACCESS to a personal relationship with God. In every other religion or philosophy, the debt of sin never entirely goes away, the conscience isn't cleansed, and there is no personal relationship with God. This is how you can distinguish philosophies and religion from Christianity, the genuine Jesus from the temporary counterfeit feeling many marketplace philosophies provide.

The threat in the marketplace to your relationship with God is mixing in other philosophies. Here is a checkup you can give yourself to see if you need a self-correcting tune-up.

Y/N   Can you distinguish between marketplace philosophies and kingdom culture?

Y/N   Do you struggle from time to time having to say "no" to worldly opportunities that conflict with your faith?

Y/N   Do you have a reputation for being a Christ follower, or do you blend into the marketplace?

Y/N   Do you filter big decisions through God and what His Word says?

Y/N   Do you sense Jesus on the journey with you as you walk out your calling?

If you can answer "yes" to all of these all the time, congratulations! You are a perfect person. All kidding aside, it is unlikely you will always be successful, but the fact that you keep climbing and choosing to self-correct when Jesus prompts you to is what pleases God.

REFLECT TO CONNECT

1. What one thing could you do today to make yourself more like Christ?
2. How would you describe the trajectory of your life right now?
3. Are there worldly philosophies that have mixed in with your faith you need to root out?

Adapt to others without adopting their views;
this is how you can become "all things to all people"
so that you can win some.

ACCEPTING THE ASSIGNMENT

WEEK 25 | THURSDAY

So he returned from following him, and took the pair of oxen and
sacrificed them and boiled their flesh with the implements of the oxen,
and gave it to the people and they ate. Then he arose and followed
Elijah and ministered to him. 1 Kings 19:21

No going back! After Elisha experienced Elijah's mantle falling on him, he would never be the same. As the final act of his former life, he cooked his oxen using the farming tools he used to make his living with and bid it farewell. Elisha wasn't just saying goodbye to his people; he was closing the door on his whole former way of life by burning the tools he used to make a living. Elisha made the decision to follow God and follow the mentor God had given him by closing the door on his past. When God taps you on the shoulder, it's time to let go and let God lead.

Successful businesspeople often practice the art of "hedging their bet" as a way of giving themselves options in case plan A doesn't work out. This is a good strategy and sound advice for preparing in advance for all eventualities. However, hedging in business must not be transferred to the call and commitment to God. When God gives you an assignment, you must be in or out. Consider what Elisha did when the presence of God showed up in his life, and he was invited to follow the mentor God assigned to him.

FIVE WAYS ELISHA RESPONDED TO THE CALL OF GOD

1. Elisha received the call.
2. Elisha made the decision to follow.
3. Elisha celebrated the new beginning with friends and feast.
4. Elisha closed the door on his old life so there was no going back.
5. Elisha fully committed himself to serving God by serving the man, prophet, and mentor that God provided in Elijah.

God often "calls" a person through a mentor. Whom has God put on your path that has reached out to you? The way to serve God is to serve those He sends to you. God-given mentors are not always people you will like. They can be the sandpaper God uses to remove your rough edges and the instrument God uses to chisel His character into you.

REFLECT TO CONNECT

1. In your past, have you made a "no-going-back" decision?
2. Can you give an example of when you had to close a door permanently in your life?
3. What sacrifices have you had to make for the "sake of the call"?

Serving God starts by serving those
God sends to you.

RECHARGE ON THE RUN
WEEK 25 | FRIDAY

*The angel of the LORD came again a second time and touched him and
said, "Arise, eat, because the journey is too great for you."* 1 Kings 19:7

Have you thrown your heart over the line for God? Elijah did, and all those who engage in the "call of God" on their life must. After Jezebel threatened Elijah, he was on the run, tired and ready to quit on God. God's response to Elijah is interesting... He sent an angel to feed him twice. Do you find it interesting that God repairs and restores physically before attempting to communicate with us spiritually? Next time you are feeling fragile, emotionally drained, or spent, consider pulling back, taking a breath, and recharging before making any major decisions.

When you are feeling your best, you make your best decisions. But the opposite is also true. Leaders pour out emotional and physical energy all day long. With a full tank, you feel charged, unstoppable, and ready to embrace whatever challenges arise. With an empty tank, you become vulnerable to attack, open to bad attitudes, and may even want to avoid work. Consider a daily routine for recharging on the run to avoid low energy which leads to poor performance.

MAINTAINING STRENGTH AND BALANCE

A.M. FILLING: Fuel up physically with breakfast and exercise following your devotions. Consider multitasking your morning ritual to include prayer walks, exercise while listening to the Bible audibly, or enjoying Christian music in the cadence of your routine.

MIDDAY REFUELING: Midday choices will dictate your afternoon. Be intentional with what you choose to put in your body and mind during the lunch hour. Although He is always with you, a midday check-in with God can give you a bounce in your step to take you through the afternoon.

P.M. DOWNTIME: The first decision of the day always starts with how you finish the day before. The decision of what you fill your mind with will dictate what it meditates on while you sleep. In order to remember what God has done and is doing through you, journaling or quiet time in the evening will produce more refueling than screen / TV time.

REFLECT TO CONNECT

1. Do you notice the shift in performance and attitude when your energy stores are low?
2. Have you ever made a bad decision or said something you regretted as a result of being spent emotionally, physically, or spiritually?
3. What routine can you initiate that will empower you to refill your energy stores throughout the day?

God doesn't begrudge a person for taking a rest,
but if you run yourself ragged in a way that affects
your moral judgment, He will hold you accountable.

NO SUCH THING AS BLIND FAITH

WEEK 26 | MONDAY

At the time of the offering of the evening sacrifice, Elijah the prophet
came near and said, "O LORD, the God of Abraham, Isaac and Israel,
today let it be known that You are God in Israel and that I am Your
servant and I have done all these things at Your word."
1 Kings 18:36

In one of the biggest showdowns in the Bible between God and evil, Elijah challenges over 450 prophets to public demonstration to once and for all prove whose God is real and whose is false. Elijah wasn't content to just win the victory; he taunted the enemies of God. Where did he get that confidence from? Elijah had full assurance that God would do what He said He would do because he had heard a sure word from God.

God never misses an appointment He has scheduled. A leap of faith is a step toward something when you "know in part" but don't have the full picture. Walking in faith always begins with a sense of a step you believe God is leading you to take. To trust God means to move toward what you believe He has asked you to do when you don't have all the information. However, you have enough information and a sense of hope in your heart that He is leading you. That hope planted by Him is the substance He asks you to cling to as you "walk by faith, not by sight." (2 Corinthians 5:7) Consider the difference between taking a step of faith vs. walking in blind faith.

BLIND FAITH
- No word from God
- No confirmations
- No evidence of leading

STEP OF FAITH
- Received a message from God
- Received 2-3 confirmations
- Received an inward pull from God

- Nothing to trust but self
- Requires hope in outward circumstances

- Requires trusting God
- Clings to inward evidence of hope in God

REFLECT TO CONNECT

1. Do you believe Elijah had full confidence in God when he challenged the false prophets to a showdown, or did he wonder if God would have his back?
2. What do you feel God is leading you to do that requires you to trust Him more?
3. If you feel God has ever let you down, what would be His perspective on the situation?

Walking by faith requires the evidence of hope and an assurance you are clinging to in your spirit.

THE PLACE OF PROVISION

WEEK 26 | TUESDAY

The word of the LORD came to him, saying... 1 Kings 17:2

One of the greatest prophets in the Bible enters God's storyline of humanity in 1 Kings 17, and his name is Elijah. In one chapter, Elijah is commanded to do two things, does both, and God provides for him at the end of each act of obedience. God commanded Elijah to go to a brook and then to a widow in Zarephath, and the Scriptures in both cases say, "I have commanded a widow" or "I have commanded a raven to feed you there." Provision for what you are needing is always found in the place of obedience. What instruction is God giving you today?

Mature saints feed off the Word and whisper of the Spirit daily. Like daily bread, they are eager to receive direction from God on where to go, whom to call, what to say, and how to think as Jesus would think about a situation. God doesn't give minute-to-minute directions, but He does like to be included when deliberating on the details of a situation. Saints seeking provision can rely on God as Elijah did. God may not always answer on your timeline, yet when He speaks and you obey, He will be waiting for you in the place of obedience, and there is always provision where God is. Where is God guiding you today that He may provide?

REFLECT TO CONNECT

1. What is the last instruction God gave to you?
2. Whom has God told you to talk to that you have not? Delayed obedience is the same as disobedience.
3. Where has God told you to go that you have not gone? God's presence is waiting for you in the PLACE of obedience.

When you come to God with a need,
He will give you an instruction to follow.

———————◆———————

SUPPORT FROM GOD

WEEK 26 | WEDNESDAY

For the eyes of the LORD move to and fro throughout the earth that
He may strongly support those whose heart is completely His.
2 Chronicles 16:9

The Holy Spirit wants you to know the secret to getting God's support in your endeavors. It may sound counterintuitive, but the secret to getting God on your side is to get on the side of the situation that God is on. A fully devoted heart is so precious to God that He has dispatched His Spirit to seek out those who are "ALL IN."

There is nothing more powerful for a saint than to have the confidence that God is on their side. How would it feel to go into every meeting, every challenge, and every new relationship knowing that God is your "wingman," willing and working the situation to His purposes and your benefit? King David had that level of faith. The Apostle Paul knew nothing could separate him from the love of God (Romans 8:39) and acted in boldness, understanding Romans 8:31: "If God is for us, who is against us?" If the acid test of being "completely His" is the entry point of divine assistance, is there anything you are holding back from God that, when given to Him, would make you completely His?

REFLECT TO CONNECT

1. In what way do you define being "ALL IN" for God?
2. If God were to rate your "ALL IN" commitment level on a scale of 1-10, where do you feel you would rate?
3. If you went "ALL IN" with God, what would you be capable of?

If you went "ALL IN" with God,
what would you be capable of?

PAUL'S SECRET SOURCE

WEEK 26 | THURSDAY

I have learned to be content in whatever circumstances I am.
I know how to get along with humble means, and I also know how to
live in prosperity; in any and every circumstance I have learned the
secret of being filled and going hungry, both of having abundance and
suffering need. I can do all things through Him who strengthens me.
Philippians 4:11-13

Paul uses the word "secret" when describing how he has been able to bear the difficult circumstances in his life. When the weight of responsibility is crushing, Paul's secret was to lean on the Lord. As the supplier of his strength, Paul learned to become dependent on God for all things.

Faith is voice-activated. Faith can rise up in silence, but when spoken out loud, it takes on new life. When you say the words of the Bible out loud, the same power that dwelt in Christ is activated in you. Proclamation of God's Word always produces an uncommon faith and energy. You will face days when you feel punched, pushed, and plowed over. When you do, remember the battle cry of those who have gone before you in the words of Philippians 4:13, "I can do all things through Christ who strengthens me," and you will be given strength in the same hour to persevere through your trial. With God as your source, you cannot lose. If God is for you, who can stand against you? Let this be your confidence in Christ Jesus, that He who resides within you will supply ample strength to you in the moment you need it.

REFLECT TO CONNECT

1. When you are hurting, whom is your first call to?
2. What secret place could you adopt during your day to pray in private and receive strength?
3. What is your favorite Scripture—start by saying it out loud until you feel Christ rise within you.

The secret to feeling strong is to stay plugged into the Source, The Spirit of God.

STRESS-ELIMINATING STRATEGY
WEEK 26 | FRIDAY

The Lord is near. Be anxious for nothing, but in everything by prayer and supplication with thanksgiving let your requests be made known to God. And the peace of God, which surpasses all comprehension, will guard your hearts and your minds in Christ Jesus.
Philippians 4:5-7

I s peace a feeling to pursue? Peace is a Person, and Paul reminds us that the Prince of Peace is near to us. He gives us the recipe for drawing the Prince of Peace close. Scripture constantly reminds us that we are never more than one step away from God. If we draw near to Him, He will draw near to us.

Scripture isn't just words; it is a living and active strategy manual that creates victory for the saints. It's not uncommon for a businessperson to have their cage rattled in the marketplace or at home. Anxiety is a normal byproduct of stress. But thanks be to God that the saint gets to choose a quick cure. To worry is to meditate on the problem and compound the pain. To turn our attention to Jesus, the Prince of Peace, is to receive relief. There is a process God wants to create in you in order to guide you in what you are going through. In the middle of crisis, Paul encourages a battle-worn saint to:

1. Not to be anxious.
2. Recognize that Jesus is close by.
3. Put your request for help before God but come with a thankful heart.
4. Peace will guard your heart. When we are peaceful, it is easier to hear a word of wisdom from above in response to our request. When our hearts are troubled or minds going a million miles an hour, even Heaven has a hard time getting our attention because the anxiety clogs the ears of our heart.

Trouble visits everyone; let the Prince of Peace guide you through the storm.

REFLECT TO CONNECT

1. Is there anything you are struggling with that you need to bring to the foot of the cross?
2. What causes you anxiety throughout your day?
3. Who in your world handles stress and anxiety well—how do they do it?

Anxiety is the byproduct of focusing on the problem;
peace is what you get when you focus on the Prince of Peace.

PEACEFUL FEELINGS ON DEMAND

WEEK 27 | MONDAY

Finally, brethren, whatever is true, whatever is honorable,
whatever is right, whatever is pure, whatever is lovely, whatever is of
good repute, if there is any excellence and if anything worthy of praise,
dwell on these things. The things you have learned and received and
heard and seen in me, practice these things, and the God of peace
will be with you. Philippians 4:8-9

Your mindset will determine whom you attract. The Apostle Paul is giving two instructions. One instruction is giving us eight examples of what to occupy our minds with, and the other is to "follow him" and his example. In other writings by Paul, he describes how to "put on the "mind of Christ" and walk in the Spirit. In concert with Paul's walk, we, too, can feel the way Paul feels and walk in the Spirit by focusing our minds on what Paul is focused on.

High-functioning people are able to create mental tracks for their thoughts to run on. By focusing their thoughts, they are able to self-direct their feelings in order to create performance on demand. Feelings are the fruits of focused thought.

Your focus will decide your feelings. William James, the American psychologist, once said, "The greatest discovery of my generation is that we can change our feelings by changing our thoughts." God created in you an amazing ability to mentally compartmentalize. Those in business must develop this skill in order to be able to function. It allows them to set aside negative emotions that may be triggered by events during their day in order to continue to perform at a high level. If you want to change the way you are feeling, think on these eight things as Paul did, and you will feel as Paul felt. These eight are also a clue to what creates an environment conducive for the Holy Spirit to work in. (Hint, hint.)

EIGHT MENTAL STRATEGIES FOR CREATING INNER PEACE

1. What is true in your life?   _____
2. What is honorable in your life?   _____
3. What is going right in your life?   _____
4. What is pure in your life?   _____
5. What is lovely in your life?   _____
6. What has a good reputation in your life?   _____
7. What is excellent in your life?   _____
8. What is worthy of praise in your life?   _____

REFLECT TO CONNECT

1. How do you change your feelings at will?
2. What examples of compartmentalization can you practice on a daily basis?
3. Why does thinking on Paul's eight things usher in the presence of God?

Feelings are the fruits of a focused thought life.
Change your mind to change your emotions.

———————◆———————

THE UPWARD CALL

WEEK 27 | TUESDAY

Not that I have already obtained it or have already become perfect,
but I press on so that I may lay hold of that for which also I was laid
hold of by Christ Jesus. Brethren, I do not regard myself as having

laid hold of it yet; but one thing I do: forgetting what lies behind and reaching forward to what lies ahead, I press on toward the goal for the prize of the upward call of God in Christ Jesus. Philippians 3:12-14

W hat is your "upward call"? Paul's upward call was that of an apostle. Your upward call could be that of a leader, a carpenter, a craftsman, teacher, or so on. Whatever your vocational assignment, that is your "upward call," which is also the highest and best use for your talents. In order to be successful in his pursuit, Paul outlines a few strategies for goals associated with his upward call:

FOUR STRATEGIES FOR FINE-TUNING
YOUR UPWARD CALL

ACKNOWLEDGMENT: Paul admits he has not achieved his goal yet. Successful people always start with defining present reality so they can work to close the gap between where they are and where they want to be.

LET GO TO LEVEL UP: Paul says in Philippians 3:13 that he is *willing* to let go of the past, "forgetting what lies behind," knowing it will slow him down in the future. Not letting go of the past is like running a race with ankle weights. Those in the marketplace have regular wins and losses in business and have to manage a "well of emotions." If negativity isn't filtered daily, it will build up like toxins in your system and poison your spiritual well. You can flush your toxins daily by focusing on what God has put in your control and leaving the "uncontrollable" to God.

REACHING: Paul's eyes are FIXED ahead, as he says in Philippians 3:14, "I press on toward the goal." We naturally move toward that which holds our attention. To be FIXED forward means to have unbroken focus and not be moved by outward circumstances because the inward focus has been FIXED. Achievers don't have a rearview mirror.

PRIORITIZATION: Paul points out an "upward call," signifying that there are other important callings he could be sidetracked by, but he remains steadfast on the "upward call," which is God's highest call for his life. For you to be successful, at some point, you will have to let go of GOOD pursuits so you can focus on the BEST pursuits God has designed you for. This is the highest upward call upon your life.

REFLECT TO CONNECT

1. How would you describe God's "upward call" in your life?
2. What goals are you FIXED on, and which are you flexible on?
3. What is holding you back that you need to let go of?

When God directs your goals,
He sets a roadmap in place to achieve them.

———————◆———————

GOD'S PATIENCE METER
WEEK 27 | WEDNESDAY

When the Lord saw that they humbled themselves,
the word of the LORD came to Shemaiah, saying,
"They have humbled themselves so I will not destroy them,
but I will grant them some measure of deliverance, and
My wrath shall not be poured out on Jerusalem by means of Shishak.
But they will become his slaves so that they may learn the difference
between My service and the service of the kingdoms of the countries."
2 Chronicles 12:7-8

Y our behavior is a picture of whom you are obeying—pick your master wisely. There is a beginning and end to all things, including the patience of God. Everyone knows God's patience has its limits, but nobody believes it. If we did, we would live differently. There came a moment in 1 Kings 14:9 when God told Jeroboam that He had had enough and would remove him from the throne for his evil works and because he had led Israel astray. Then in 2 Chronicles 12:7-9, God loses His patience with Rehoboam. Because Rehoboam humbles himself, God allows him to live but gives Judah over to slavery. In an interesting judgment, God may at times give us over to new taskmasters *so as to* demonstrate how we are better off serving Him over worldly masters. Where do you put your trust?

People work in professions where there are beginnings and ends every day, along with positive or negative consequences for our actions and choices we make. If this is true in earthly matters, why do people not think it is true in spiritual matters? As you consider God's patience and the patience of those around you, do you sense an "ending" or event on the horizon? Is there an adjustment you need to make today to change the trajectory of your behavior? Rehoboam made an adjustment, and God took notice; you can do the same, too.

REFLECT TO CONNECT

1. Is there any area of self-correction you have been putting off in your life?
2. Who needs to hear the "time is up" message in your circle of influence?
3. Why do we resist the signs to upcoming consequences?

Everyone knows God's patience has its limits,
but nobody believes it.

SEEKING BALANCE
AND SELF-CARE

WEEK 27 | THURSDAY

Do nothing from selfishness or empty conceit, but with humility
of mind regard one another as more important than yourselves;
do not merely look out for your own personal interests,
but also for the interests of others. Philippians 2:3-4

P aul's instruction to put on a mindset of humility and to have an "others-first" mindset is in response and contrast to those who were being driven by self-interest (Philippians 2:20-21). Everyone at some point fails to practice the Golden Rule. But don't think that it's okay to only focus on others and neglect yourself. After all, we are to love our neighbors *as ourselves*. If, by God's grace, we don't love ourselves, how can we ever love others?

If you only serve others while sacrificing yourself, you are out of balance and heading for burnout. It is not wrong to focus on yourself from time to time. In fact, it is even necessary. If you don't build yourself up, it will be difficult for you to build others up. If you don't attain a degree of success, how can you teach others to become successful? If you don't earn more than enough to meet your needs, how can you become generous on all occasions? Taking care of self and others is a kingdom virtue.

Achieving balance is never permanent. How does a saint strike a balance in serving oneself and serving others? Consider checking your motives on a regular basis as a way of getting to the heart of the matter. Here are a few questions you can consider with God listening in. But remember, balance fluctuates and requires recalibration constantly as stress, crises, and unplanned events enter our lives. Sometimes you will attain balance, and sometimes you won't. The important thing is to recognize when you are out of balance and to set your aim to rebalance when necessary.

REFLECT TO CONNECT

1. When was the last time you were confronted with the choice to sacrifice for another?
2. What example of balanced and out-of-balance seasons have you experienced?
3. In what ways are you taking care of yourself so you can be strong to serve others?

Seek balance and settle for progress,
for balance is a practice, not a "set-it-and-forget-it"
state of being.

———————————◆————————————

BIG DECISIONS REQUIRE EXPERTS, NOT FRIENDS
WEEK 27 | FRIDAY

But he forsook the counsel of the elders which they had given him, and consulted with the young men who grew up with him and served him.
1 Kings 12:8

G rowth and wisdom often come outside of one's peer group. In one weighty decision, Judah split from Israel, and one nation became two. Rehoboam, who was Solomon's son, became king over Judah, while Jeroboam, who worked for Solomon running the labor camps, became king over the rest of Israel. Rehoboam, in one unwise decision, incited one nation to break into two by pushing it over a tipping point. Why? Because Rehoboam misjudged the environment and followed the youth he grew up with vs. the wise counselors who had experience in counseling the king. Although verses 8 and 15 show that these events were from the Lord, we've shown them as an example of what not to do in order to make wise decisions.

When I decided to become an author, I sought out advice and made friends with publishers and other authors. When I desired to take up racing as a hobby, I sought out the counsel of drivers and teachers of drivers. When I have big decisions to make, I seek out experts before considering a friend's advice who has no experience in the area.

Everyone gets over their head at some point in their career like Rehoboam did. When you find yourself in the deep end of the pool, you will need an idea, a brainstorm, counsel on a decision, or an insight into a situation. Consider the process of wise decision-making:

INVESTIGATE: Evaluate all the facts from multiple perspectives.

SEEK P.O.V. Seek counsel from different points of view.

EXPERT INPUT: Who within reach has made this sort of decision before? Seek them out and gain their input. Someone, somewhere, has been through what you are going through.

ASK GOD: "If any of you lacks wisdom, let him ask of God, who gives to all generously and without reproach, and it will be given to him." (James 1:5) God, who sees the future, will always guide your steps if you ask Him.

DISCERN: After you have considered the facts, the input, the opinions, and the options, lay them all out before God and let Him guide you.

REFLECT TO CONNECT

1. Whom in your inner circle do you usually turn to for advice?
2. Do you tend to seek out the advice of a friend or experts in the area of decision you need to make?
3. What was the last piece of advice God gave you when you sought Him out?

Spending time with the wise makes one wise,
and the opposite is true.

PROGRESS MANDATORY, PLATEAUING COMMON

WEEK 28 | MONDAY

For I am confident of this very thing, that He who began a good work
in you will perfect it until the day of Christ Jesus.
Philippians 1:6

G od is a finisher. God is a fixer. God is a carpenter. As the architect in the soul of man, He transforms our character into His likeness while maintaining our uniqueness. As the old nature dies, a new nature emerges. God invests time to fashion you into the image of His Son. His ultimate goal is to imprint the image of Christ onto the tablet of your heart, so your desires, purposes, and pursuits are of the highest call. For that to be possible, God invites you to participate in the transformative work of becoming a new creation. With a willing spirit, nothing is impossible for God to accomplish through you.

God never bullies. He asks for cooperation and commitment, yet He won't force His way with you; you get to opt-in or opt-out. Many sinners and saints say "no" to God every day, albeit unintentionally. Consider some of the ways His master craftsman, the Holy Spirit, engages you in the process of divine transformation.

Transformative Act	Required Cooperative Action
• Obedience	• Willingness to put God's desires ahead of your own.
• Mental Recalibration	• Willingness to turn away from thoughts contrary to Christ.
• Conscience	• Willingness to confess and repent without delay when convicted.

- Correction
  - Willingness to adjust behavior and words to Christlikeness.
- Identity
  - Willingness to let God define your value in Christ.

Without change, transformation is impossible. What got you to your current level of success will not be enough to keep you there. You were not meant to plateau, but to progress. The willingness to progress is necessary for growth—what are you willing to do in order to move forward in your life? Growing up requires stepping up and stretching forward. Like a rubber band, stepping out of your comfort zone and embracing the "heavenly stretch" is what will help you to take a quantum leap in the kingdom of God and in the kingdom of men.

REFLECT TO CONNECT

1. Who is most Christlike to you?
2. What is God asking you to give up so He can help you step up?
3. Why is sanctification important in readying you for the day we will meet Christ?

God never bullies. He asks for cooperation and commitment,
yet He won't force His way with you;
you get to opt-in or opt-out.

THE LORD WILL PROVIDE

WEEK 28 | TUESDAY

*He said, "Do not stretch out your hand against the lad, and do nothing
to him; for now I know that you fear God, since you have not withheld
your son, your only son, from Me." Then Abraham raised his eyes and
looked, and behold, behind him a ram caught in the thicket by his horns;
and Abraham went and took the ram and offered him up for a burnt
offering in the place of his son. Abraham called the name of that place
The LORD Will Provide, as it is said to this day, "In the mount of the
Lord it will be provided." Genesis 22:12-14*

There is a place called "The Lord Will Provide." In every season of life, God sets the time, place, and manner in which we will be tested. God gives tests as a way of proving that we have persevered through the present season and are ready for the next. When you face a test, God is building a testimony. Abraham was about to face the ultimate test, the willingness to give up what mattered so much to him to show God that He still mattered most. A few thousand years later, God would pass the same test on a hill called Calvary when He would sacrifice His son for the sins of the world.

When you are doing what God asked you to do and doing it the way God asked you to do it, God provides. For leaders, He provides in many ways. Consider the ways in which you can rely on God to supply your need as you fulfill your vocational calling in the marketplace.

- God can give you insight into a situation you are facing.
- God can guide you on whose advice to seek when you are facing an uncertain situation.
- God can give you strategy for the battle ahead or the business you are going to start.
- God can show you where to sow your seeds so you reap the largest possible harvest.

- God can open your eyes to see what He's already provided, like He did with Abraham.
- God can reveal a creative idea to you that becomes a key that opens the door to success.

REFLECT TO CONNECT

1. With God as your provider, what are you trusting Him to provide?
2. Is there an instruction God is waiting for you to fulfill before He can do His part?
3. Which parts of your leadership have you turned over to God, and which parts are you relying on your own power?

Through obedience, God will bring you to the place called "The Lord Will Provide."

THE PLANTER'S PROMISE
WEEK 28 | WEDNESDAY

Cast your bread on the surface of the waters, for you will find it after many days. Divide your portion to seven, or even to eight, for you do not know what misfortune may occur on the earth. Ecclesiastes 11:1-2

The law of sowing and reaping can be seen in every walk of life. Jesus spoke of some seeds producing little and some producing more, but He instructed us to keep planting because we do not know which will return and in what quantity. The ability to persevere, not give up, and maintain hope when you see little results for your labor is a hallmark of a persevering saint. However, those who work as "unto the Lord" have learned through experience that seeds planted using the Word of God will not return void. They produce a reward in this life and the life to come, even if we can't always see which seeds God is causing to grow. Seeds are underground and out of sight. That is why planting requires faith. Much of what God is growing in your life is invisible to you, happening behind the scenes in the spiritual realm.

In the profession of sales, prospecting (customer acquisition) is the hardest part. It's not uncommon for a seller to knock on 10 doors in order to get one appointment. That means 90% of seed planting or "the casting of bread upon the waters of the marketplace" can go without an obvious return. Only 10% of your efforts may be successful, but you don't know which 10%. That's a lot of rejection one must process and reframe. What is the hard planting you must do in your profession where the return is slow?

It requires faith to plant and leave the return on investment to God. Thanks be to God that the One who waters our efforts and the One who moves the hearts of people is also sowing alongside us to accomplish His purposes in our lives. As you sow your seed in the marketplace, remember...

1. **God is your co-laborer in the heavy lifting.** One person plants, another waters, but God gives the increase. It's not only your efforts that create the harvest in your life but His blessings.

2. **Trust God to deliver the ROI.** The planting is your responsibility; the return is God's. When you feel discouraged and want to give up, remember that God counts each seed, sacrifice, and step you make in keeping faithful to do what He has called you to do.

3. **God is the Master Planter.** As you would ask God to help you in your household matters, ask His assistance in your business matters. God always knows which ground will yield the highest return.
4. **Don't take rejection or failure personally.** Be patient with yourself and remember to "take a breath" when you are rejected. Learn to turn rejection into redirection.
5. **Keep planting in good and soft economies.** Do what Solomon did and STAY THE COURSE. Consistent work habits produce a compounding ROI over time.
6. **JUST DO IT.** Don't spend another minute procrastinating or talking yourself out of doing what you know must be done. Embrace the heavy lifting that is your cross to carry and watch God use your seeds of sacrifice to birth more of Christ in you.

REFLECT TO CONNECT

1. What is the heavy lifting in your profession?
2. Have you thought about teaming up with someone to help with the heavy lifting?
3. Have you ever asked God to show you the best ground to plant in?

Planting with eternal purpose creates an eternal return from the Lord of Harvest.

BOOMERANG OF BLESSING

WEEK 28 | THURSDAY

With good will render service, as to the Lord, and not to men,
knowing that whatever good thing each one does, this he will receive
back from the Lord, whether slave or free. Ephesians 6:7-8

God's boomerang of blessing. Imagine God taking on the debt and promising to return to us a reward for our good works. In a startling statement, the Holy Spirit instructed Paul to teach us in Ephesians 6:8 that whatever good we do, God will do back for us. God wanted us to know that there was a promise that followed serving with good intentions from the heart. That promise was that God would return the "good" to us when we did good to others. Imagine: God has put you in control of the bounty of blessing you would like Him to bring into your life.

God is a dealmaker who always gives more than He gets. And like a good Father, He will always stack the deck in your favor. He loves to hide blessings for you to stumble into. The Bible has hundreds of promises of God just waiting to be activated in your life. The word "IF" appears over 300 times in Scripture, promising a specific result based on you taking a specific action. This is God's "setup" for your success.

Which promise of God do you need to activate today? Some blessings are free, while others require you to reach for them. What are you waiting on God for today? Is there an action He is waiting on you to take? Whatever need, challenge, or situation you may be facing, there is a promise you can activate to create a God response. God is hoping you will discover the step He is waiting for you to take or realize the opportunity He has planted right in front of you. What breadcrumbs has God left around you so that you may find Him in the middle of your situation? Many blessings are time-based and can be missed if you wait too long. With every step of obedience comes a reward. The promise in the boomerang of blessing guarantees that as you do good to others, God gets into gear to do good for you.

REFLECT TO CONNECT

1. Can you recollect a time when God returned a "good outcome" to you for a "good thing" you did for someone else?
2. Do you believe that you reap where you sow or that God allows you to reap in the place you need it the most regardless of where you sow?
3. Whom in your path can you do a "good thing" for today and serve as "unto the Lord"?

God promises to bring a boomerang of blessing into our life
as often as we do good for and to others.

THE 60-SECOND RULE

WEEK 28 | FRIDAY

Let no unwholesome word proceed from your mouth, but only such a
word as is good for edification according to the need of the moment,
so that it will give grace to those who hear. Ephesians 4:29

Your words create the atmosphere around you and feelings in others. Paul, in the 4th chapter of Ephesians, is teaching on the subject of "putting on Christ"—the new self. Specifically, Paul is asking us to ask ourselves, "What word of encouragement can I speak to the person in front of me right now that will build them up and enlarge them?"

Practice the 60-Second Rule. The 60-Second Rule says, "Say something nice about someone to them in the first 60 seconds you enter their presence." Leaders are in the profession of words. Reading what to say and when to say it based on the need of the moment often determines whether a relationship advances or stalls. Paul was a master of persuasion because his focus was always to address the need of the person right in front of him. In so doing, he always sought to edify and build up the one he was with. Whether communicating in writing or verbally, can you build up someone in a voicemail, text, email, or handwritten note?

Your words attract people to you or repel them from you. Master communicators always make it a point to edify their audience whether they are with one or many. Making others feel good in your presence will create a magnetic pull between you and them. In my best-selling book *PERSUADE*, there are dozens of strategies on how to edify others in "The Law of Connection." Here are a few ways in which you can edify others:

- Initiate a random act of kindness toward them.
- Praise them in public before an audience of their peers.
- Ask about their needs before you talk about your needs.
- Speak to them more about their strengths than weaknesses.
- Find something you admire about them and tell them about it.
- Catch them doing something right and show them appreciation.

REFLECT TO CONNECT

1. Have you ever left a conversation wishing you had not said what you just said?

2. As you emulate Christ today, in what way can you edify another to build them up?
3. Who do you sense should be #1 on your list of people to edify today?

Those who make a habit of making others feel good while in their presence become people magnets who attract larger degrees of influence.

SEASONS OF BARRENNESS

There is an evil which I have seen under the sun and it is prevalent among men—a man to whom God has given riches and wealth and honor so that his soul lacks nothing of all that he desires; yet God has not empowered him to eat from them, for a foreigner enjoys them. This is vanity and a severe affliction. Ecclesiastes 6:1-2

It seems strange that God would grant a person all they desire, yet their soul remains unsatisfied. Have you ever wanted something so badly, and when you received it, it did not satisfy? It is often the process, pursuit, or struggle in obtaining something that God uses to shape His character into us. Feeling "barrenness" is the trigger to draw us back to our source and seek a fresh infilling of the Holy Spirit.

You are God's "workmanship" created in Christ Jesus to do good works which He prepared in advance for you to do. (Ephesians 2:10) But it is possible to be so focused on the work that one forgets to enjoy the fruit of their labor. If God has blessed the work of your hands and has filled your barns, yet there is leanness in your heart, consider asking Him the following questions:

- What is missing in my life?
- Why do I feel the way that I do?
- Is the leanness in my heart Your way of getting my attention?
- Is there a balance You are trying to create in my life that I am resistant to?

The answer to a prayer is often in the question you ask God. What question is bubbling up in your spirit to pose that would address or pinpoint what you are feeling? It's more important to discover the right question than to seek an answer. When you figure out what to ask, the answers take care of themselves.

1. Do you know people who have everything but are not satisfied?
2. How will God use a season of barrenness to grow a saint?
3. What do you believe God is trying to shape you into?

Leanness in a soul can be a sign that a change
of assignment is around the corner.

THE INSTRUCTABLE PERSON

WEEK 29 | TUESDAY

A poor yet wise lad is better than an old and
foolish king who no longer knows how to receive instruction.
Ecclesiastes 4:13

Solomon makes an astonishing statement about being "teachable." The statement that it is better to be poor and wise than king and dumb is hard to understand. However, what the young lad possesses is a teachable spirit that makes him "wise." If you are closed-minded, your lid for learning won't let anything in. Many leave school and place a lid on their potential with the attitude that they're done with learning. Yet God's view on learning is that it never ends for us, for there is always more He has to give us. What is the last thing you learned from God or from another?

"It's what you learn after you know it all that counts."
John Wooden

A wise person learns from other people's mistakes, but the wisest learn from their successes. Age does not create maturity; continual learning does. WHY? Because environments are always shifting, and to remain relevant, you must adapt.

There is always something you don't know. If you maintain a teachable spirit, you will always be able to reach for and read new information necessary to succeed in an ever-changing environment. Teachable people are:

1. OBJECTIVE: You are open to new ideas that are not your own.
2. AWARE: You recognize that there is always something you don't know.
3. HUMBLE: Your way is one of many ways, not the only way.
4. CREATIVE: Your first idea is not your best idea but gets better with others' input.
5. CORRECTABLE: You are not afraid to admit when you've made a mistake.

REFLECT TO CONNECT

1. Ask someone close to you if they perceive you to be teachable—what did they say?
2. Do you have a growth plan where you are pursuing new knowledge?
3. Are you only teachable when you are being corrected, or do you intentionally pursue ideas that are not your own?

Age does not create maturity in business; continual learning does. WHY? Because environments are always shifting, and to remain relevant, you must adapt.

IDEATING WITH GOD

WEEK 29 | WEDNESDAY

Is there anything of which one might say, "See this, it is new"?
Already it has existed for ages Which were before us. Ecclesiastes 1:10

I t's not new, just new to you. Henry Ford once said, "I invented nothing new. I simply assembled the discoveries of other men behind whom were centuries of work." This is an astounding statement by the man credited with inventing the assembly line in American manufacturing. Solomon and Henry Ford both were known for doing in their generation something that had never been done before. Solomon built a temple and a palace, and Henry Ford built cars; both ideas came from a place of inspiration.

God has thousands of ideas to help you in your life; can you hear them? A leader's antenna is always up to receive wisdom from on high of how God would inspire them to assemble or reassemble a series of ideas that could benefit them and those they serve. Whether riding in the car, sitting quietly in a devo session, or kneeling in prayer, the successful saint develops an intuitive antenna that listens for the "whisper of an idea" God may blow their way. It is in these "whispers from God" that you will hear a fresh idea and a new way to reinvent.

REFLECT TO CONNECT

1. What is God whispering to you today?
2. Can you distinguish the difference between intuition (a knowing from God) and intellect (a thinking of thoughts)?
3. What is the last idea you received intuitively?

God gives instructions that will feel like an idea when
He wants to birth something new in your life.

CONTROLLABLE VS. UNCONTROLLABLE

WEEK 29 | THURSDAY

What advantage does man have in all his work
Which he does under the sun? Ecclesiastes 1:3

G od will one day ask for an account of what we did with "that which was in our power" to control. Solomon spends the entire first chapter of Ecclesiastes waxing eloquently about the movements of the earth, the sun, and the sea. His conclusion is essentially that "what will be will be," and none of these elements can be changed. This may be true for the "uncontrollable" in our lives, yet there remains a responsibility to influence factors that are in our control. Consider the abilities God gives to you so you can influence outcomes in your life:

Social: You do have the ability to decide which friends to associate with and whom to avoid.
Emotional: You do have the ability to work yourself up or settle yourself down.
Financial: You do have the ability to steward your resources, to say "yes" to necessities and "no" to wants.
Spiritual: You have the ability to choose when and how often you will pursue God.

Vocational: You have the ability to choose your career, work life, and path.

Purpose: You have the ability to discover and follow God's purposes in your life.

Getting out of control vs. having perspective. Perspective is easily lost when experiencing stress, excitement, anger, or emotional ups and downs that accompany day-to-day life. Getting re-grounded in God means remembering what you must leave up to God and what you must take the reins on. Staying grounded starts with getting God's perspective on your situation. He will give you peace, a path for moving forward, and let you know when to take control or relinquish control to Him. The next time you are feeling "out of control," consider outlining on paper what the "controllable" and "uncontrollable" things are in your life. As your pen hits the paper, listen for God's insight and be quick to relinquish those things which only God can control.

REFLECT TO CONNECT

1. What are the "alarm bells" that go off for you when you realize you've lost perspective?
2. What strategies do you employ to help you to reset and get re-grounded?
3. What advice have you given to friends in the past to help them reset or consider another perspective?

When facing an "uncontrollable" in your life,
giving it to God ushers in divine perspective and assistance.

DEFEND THE DEFENSELESS

WEEK 29 | FRIDAY

The righteous is concerned for the rights of the poor,
The wicked does not understand such concern. Proverbs 29:7

Whom has God given you a passion to protect? Those who love God care for what He cares for. God looks out for the little guys because they are the least likely able to defend themselves. In the same way God looks out for us, He asks us to look out for those He puts us in a position to protect. I am called to protect the supervisor God has me assigned to in this season, victims with whom I may relate to their pain, and so forth.

Whom has God asked you to look out for? If you are feeling a burden to protect, look out for, or serve a person or group of people, it is likely God's heart is imprinting on yours. If you are constantly thinking about or concerned with someone or a group of people, it may be God sharing His burden with you. When you feel compassion toward someone, it is often God's compassion coming through. In this way, He will allow you to feel what He feels so you will consider allowing Him to meet the needs of others through you.

Have you developed a trained ear to hear the needs in the marketplace? Successful saints are quick to identify needs, interests, and what people are focused on. They do this by asking questions to uncover pain points and pursuits. As you talk to someone about what they need, it will create a magnetic pull between you and them. A simple, easy way to gain influence with others is to spend most of your talking time asking about them vs. telling them about you. What does this have to do with helping people? Everyone needs something, and when you are serving others in the area of their need, you are acting as the "hands of God" and working the works of Jesus. As God is answering the prayers you prayed this morning; He is using you to answer someone else's prayer.

REFLECT TO CONNECT

1. If you had to make a list of God's top five priorities, what do you think they would be?
2. Whom are you being asked to help today?
3. What is God feeling a burden toward that He has allowed you to share in?

When you care for what God cares about,
He cares for what you care for.

CHANGE THE CHANNEL

WEEK 30 | MONDAY

Like a city that is broken into and without walls
Is a man who has no control over his spirit. Proverbs 25:28

Have you had the experience of catching yourself thinking over and over again about something you can't get out of your head? Like a tape that won't shut off, the internal conversation or scenario won't stop replaying in your mind. Yet, much like a start-and-stop button on a music player, there *is* a shut-off button.

Self-control can be difficult for anyone, especially for someone battling with multiple internal emotional streams all at once. God instilled within us a WILL to direct our mind, emotion, and spirit, and He gives us a heads-up when we've lost control or if there may be enemy infiltration. As a tree is known by its fruit, so is our thought life found out by the emotions it generates within us. Once you seize the talk track in your mind and bring it into subjection to your will, you will have taken control of your city. Here is the strategy God has given you for getting control of a "runaway tape" playing in your head.

What you meditate on is creating your emotions. Consider the following:

1. "By prayer and supplication with thanksgiving let your requests be made known to God. And the peace of God, which surpasses all comprehension, will guard your hearts and minds in Christ Jesus." (Philippians 4:6-7)
2. "Submit therefore to God. Resist the devil and he will flee from you." (James 4:7)
3. "We are taking every thought captive to the obedience of Christ." (2 Corinthians 10:5)

Like a fish caught in a net, we are expected to sift and separate good thoughts from bad thoughts. This can easily be done by journaling your thoughts and sourcing them, which shines a light on the mental tape playing. In the presence of God, His enemies are scattered, and so are yours.

REFLECT TO CONNECT

1. How often do you stop down to scrub your thought life?
2. Do you have a strategy for calming internal chatter and getting yourself into neutral so you can hear God?
3. What habitual thought pattern does God want you to stop?

The enemy's weapon is distraction—to busy you in such a way so you can't concentrate on the work at hand.

RELEASE THE ROPE OF RESCUE
WEEK 30 | TUESDAY

A man of great anger will bear the penalty,
For if you rescue him, you will only have to do it again. Proverbs 19:19

I'm sure we've all heard some iteration of the following quote: "Insanity, by definition, is doing the same things over and over again but expecting a different result." I wonder how long it takes God and His angels to let go and let people "learn the hard way." While a mature saint learns to "let go and let God," I wonder how often God needs to "let go and let us learn"? Letting a friend, coworker, or family member stumble is counterintuitive to our nature to "people please"; however, the above verse from Proverbs promises a "repeat" if we keep rescuing.

Are you a people pleaser? Christians love to serve and save people. But what if serving and saving are working counter to what is in a person's best interest? To repeatedly "break the fall" for someone who consistently jumps off the cliff is to become an enabler to them. Sometimes you need to "let the chips fall where they may" and let gravity have its way.

Next time you catch yourself in an unproductive or unhealthy cycle, choose not to enable but empower. You can do this by breaking the cycle of stepping in to save the day and letting consequence do its work as a tutor. If you don't stop rescuing behavior, you could be interfering with what God is trying to change in a person's life.

REFLECT TO CONNECT

1. Is there someone you continue to rescue that you should not?
2. What is the worst that can happen if you release the rope of rescue?
3. What advice is God giving you now that would help you become an equipper who empowers and not an enabler of bad behavior?

*Pain can be a great tutor if someone
doesn't interrupt the lesson.*

GOOD VS. BAD RELATIONSHIPS

WEEK 30 | WEDNESDAY

He who walks with wise men will be wise,
But the companion of fools will suffer harm. Proverbs 13:20

Environment often dictates who we become. Those whom we spend time around consistently imprint on us and vice versa. Solomon also said in Proverbs 23:7, "For as he thinks within himself, so he is"—he is referring to psychology, not biology. The company we keep contributes a great deal to what we believe, how we think, the decisions we make, and the actions we take. Consider those in your inner circle and ask: which part of their character is rubbing off on you, and which part of you is rubbing off on them?

The Right People in Your Life Will:

- Believe in you.
- Want you to grow past them.

- Want you to grow in your purpose.
- Encourage you to go the extra mile.

- Want you to follow a path of success.
- Set a good example for you to follow.
- Challenge you to be more than you are.
- Encourage you to focus on priorities.

The Wrong People in Your Life Will:

- Foster doubt in you.
- Want you to stay down with them.

- Want you to just get by.
- Want you to take shortcuts with them.

- Make excuses to take the easy road.
- Want you to compromise on principles.
- Want to keep you where you are.
- Distract you from reaching your goals.

Successful saints are selective about whom and what they let in. Proverbs 4:23 expressly instructs us to "watch over your heart with all diligence, For from it flow the spring of life." This means to put a lid with a lock on whom and what you decide to let influence you.

> **"You are the average of the five people**
> **you spend the most time with."**
> **Jim Rohn, Motivational Speaker**

REFLECT TO CONNECT

1. Who is God encouraging you to spend more time with—and less time with?
2. Is there an influence that has entered in that is inhibiting your growth?
3. Do you have someone close to you that is being led off track by an influence around them?

Never let people around you that you don't
want to influence you.

CRACK THE CODE OF DESTINY

WEEK 30 | THURSDAY

The mind of the intelligent seeks knowledge,
But the mouth of fools feeds on folly. Proverbs 15:14

Do you want to be considered intelligent, but maybe you lack a hunger for personal growth? Everybody is hungry for something; you just have to crack your "hunger code" to discover your designed destiny. Find a subject you are interested in and pursue it with all your heart, and you will develop a mind of intelligence in that area. To discover what subject God may be putting in front of you to pursue today, consider the following "Heart Hack" questions to get you interested in the pursuit of knowledge.

1. What challenges are you facing right now? These are an indication of a subject matter God wants you to pursue. Find an expert who wrote on that subject and buy their book today. And as you read the words on the page, listen as God whispers wisdom to you on how to apply what He shares with you.

2. What things are you always thinking of? Google the subject and see if a door of interest opens before you. If the interest remains or builds over time, this could be a clue to something God wants you to pursue. If God is in it, it's for your benefit.

3. Who inspires you? Read a biography on someone that inspires you or of someone who has done what you want to do; this is the first step toward success. God always provides a picture of something or someone that inspires you in the direction He wants you to follow Him.

4. What dreams did you have growing up? Read how someone else achieved a dream you want to live or wish you had. Even if a childhood dream is not your destiny as an adult, God will often start in our past and help connect the dots into our future. As you walk through one door of obedience, another emerges, so just start walking.

Daily growth compounds to birth God's calling in your life. You must "grow up into knowledge" if you want God's best for you in this life. Developing a daily discipline of setting aside a few minutes to read, listen, write, and think on thoughts that expand your knowledge will ensure you are improving your intelligence 1% more each day. After many days of growing daily, the 1% per day compounds into growing up into the calling God has destined you for. As you put into practice what God is prodding you to learn, He breathes on your efforts and multiplies your return.

REFLECT TO CONNECT

1. What areas of interest is God flashing across the screen of your mind?
2. Other than yourself, who will be helped by you learning more in this new area?
3. How might God use a new area of growth in your life to bring you into a new future?

As you put into practice what God is prodding you to learn, He breathes on your efforts and multiplies your return.

———————————◆———————————

THE FOUNTAIN OF FRUSTRATION

WEEK 30 | FRIDAY

A hot-tempered man stirs up strife,
But the slow to anger calms a dispute. Proverbs 15:18

Everybody gets angry from time to time. Anger is energy, and that energy can be used for good or bad. How you direct anger determines whether you use it to satisfy yourself or serve a greater purpose. Consider the choices for how we can use the energy that comes from anger:

Productive Anger	Unproductive Anger
• An opportunity to create.	• A choice to destroy.
• A lesson to be learned.	• A lesson to be taught to another.
• Viewed as a way to strengthen relationships.	• Channeled to destroy a relationship.
• A way to build oneself up if used rightly.	• A way to ruin one's life if used incorrectly.
• An opportunity to correct a wrong.	• A chance to get even.
• An opportunity to teach another.	• A chance to blast another.
• An opportunity to heal within.	• A chance to explode without.
• An opportunity to redirect energy.	• A chance to misuse passion.

We live and die daily on how we use our supply of energy. You can be tossed to and fro emotionally by rejection and injustice, feel disregarded or dismissed in a relationship, or use even the negative, hurtful, and anger-building moments in life to strengthen yourself and others. Frustration and anger, if directed inward, turn into depression and eventually immobilization. However, if the fountain of frustration and anger can be directed in ways that produce better outcomes, nothing becomes impossible for those who follow God in leveraging their emotional resources.

REFLECT TO CONNECT

1. When was the last time you experienced frustration or anger?
2. Consider how you used your last burst of emotional energy; did it help you or hurt your cause?
3. What mental triggers can you put in place that will remind you to redirect the fountain of frustration into a productive outcome?

Like a rock in a slingshot, so is a believer who can harness the energy in anger to serve a greater purpose.

RIDE ON DIVINE TRACKS

WEEK 31 | MONDAY

And we know that God causes all things to work together for good to those who love God, to those who are called according to His purpose.
Romans 8:28

Y ou must choose to stay on the ride. If you've ever gone to a theme park and ridden on a ride that rolls on rails, you know what it means to "go along for the ride." You joined the journey, but you are not driving. Even the water rides at Disney run on underwater tracks that cannot be seen yet are directing the ride. So, who is directing your spiritual journey, you or God?

God will not do for you what He has enabled you to do for yourself. God works alongside us to bring us into His divine and perfect will, but He doesn't control us or make our decisions for us. He leads us, hoping we will cooperate with Him. However, if we get off track or His plan goes off the rails due to others not cooperating, He is able to guide us back onto the divine rails of His will if we follow. God is NOT a fairy godfather who magically controls everything in the world, as many think He is. An employer who has employees on a big factory floor is responsible for setting expectations, then delegating tasks, but is not responsible for every word spoken or action taken by the employees. In the same way, you have your part to play, and God has His.

God's Responsibility	My Responsibility
• Reveal the plan	• Accept His plan
• Direct the plan	• Walk out His plan
• Provide feedback on our walk	• Course correct our walk
• Hold saints accountable	• Accept responsibility
• God does His part	• I do my part
• Rewards obedience	• Be obedient

Believers in business work with marketplace complexity all the time. It's important to embrace our role in following God who leads us in business, not just into eternity. For where He guides you in business, He will provide strategies that bring you into success. God guides, but we must execute what He tells us to do. Hearing and then heeding God's will are not always easy. If God's guidance has become quiet in your business life, it's possible you've gotten off His divine track. Consider going back to the last thing He told you to do and then doing it. As you execute the "last instruction" He gave you, another will emerge. God only stops leading if you stop following.

REFLECT TO CONNECT

1. How many times a day do you turn to God for divine guidance?
2. Who in your life models a cooperative lifestyle with God?
3. What is God directing you to do in your work life?

If you can't hear God's voice, go back and do the last thing
He told you to do. God only stops leading
if you stop following.

THE PROSPERITY DRIFT

WEEK 31 | TUESDAY

So King Solomon became greater than all the kings of the earth in riches
and in wisdom. All the earth was seeking the presence of Solomon, to
hear his wisdom which God had put in his heart. They brought every

man his gift, articles of silver and gold, garments, weapons, spices,
horses, and mules, so much year by year.
1 Kings 10:23-25

Is it easier to remain faithful when you are fighting through painful circumstances or coasting through the vineyards of prosperity in your life? Although we are faithless at times, God remains faithful. Solomon, in his later years, backslid by pursuing self-indulgent purposes. Solomon used the great wealth and wisdom God endowed him with to serve himself. Over time, his appetite became his god. As God answers your prayers and raises you up in position, prestige, and plenty, remember the lessons of Solomon:

1. **KEEP God first!** Solomon abandoned his first love.
2. **SERVE others!** Solomon's focus turned from serving God and His people to serving his appetites. The secret to self-control for saints is to intentionally sacrifice in service to a higher purpose.
3. **PROTECT your environment!** Solomon was seduced away by endless enticements he surrounded himself with. Never let around you what you don't want to grow in you.
4. **STAY single-hearted!** Solomon allowed his affections to be siphoned off into many different directions that included women, wealth, and other worldly pursuits. Don't let anything break your focus on God and Christ in You.

Saints live in environments of emotional highs and lows all day long. Emotions can be a drug, and everyone is easily seduced by something. Consider making a list of what would seduce your heart away from God. You can build a protective barricade around your spiritual walk by identifying your areas of weaknesses.

REFLECT TO CONNECT

1. What are the seducing forces in your life right now?
2. Whom can you confess your struggles to as a way of circum-venting the enemy's strategy and strengthening your resolve to stay on track?
3. Is there someone who is wrestling with worldly temptations you could confront and bring back to God?

Even seasoned saints can be seduced when their area of weakness goes unaddressed—who or what is your Kryptonite?

MASTER YOUR MIND
WEEK 31 | WEDNESDAY

My sheep hear My voice, and I know them,
and they follow Me.
John 10:27

There are four voices within us that we need to be able to distinguish. Knowing their sound, where they are from, and their intent can help you to know which one to follow at any given time and which to ignore all the time.

God's Voice: If you want to know what God's voice sounds like, spend time listening to it *daily* within the pages of the Bible. God's voice might come as a whisper or seem to come from within because He lives within and will never contradict any moral or spiritual principles in the Bible. Remember these hallmarks to God's voice:

1. When God speaks, you are inspired.
2. When God speaks, you know it intuitively because it imprints on you.
3. When God speaks, your confidence level grows—faith comes by hearing.
4. When God speaks, His voice can encourage, instruct, warn, and convict.

Your Voice: Self-talk is the #1 factor that determines how we feel about ourselves. You will never achieve more than the self-image your self-talk has created within you. If you do not like the way you feel, change the way you are talking to yourself. Consider making a list of adjectives of your best qualities and how God sees you and think on these things. Believers often find that God is kinder to them than they are to themselves. Your self-talk can help you or hurt you. If it hurts you, it should be replaced with God's voice by putting His thoughts above yours. You can create a better self-image if you focus on how God sees you vs. how you see yourself.

Others' Voices: People around us and from our past continue to have great influence over us if we let their message play in the background like a music track stuck on repeat. Some of these voices are helpful, and some harmful. Whether from the present or the past, if you are rehearsing conversations in your head that hurt you, stop it by taking every thought captive to the obedience of Christ and submitting it to God's Word. Inspiring voices from the present and the past can be put on "repeat" to energize you; these are healthy memories. Destructive voices and their "rerun tracks" need to be turned off—period.

Enemy's Voice: The enemy's goal is to control your will. If he can dominate you, he will destroy you. Where God wants to empower and release you into His best, the enemy wants to destroy you to hurt God. The enemy's voice masquerades and hides itself behind human thought so as to remain hidden and undetected. If you are ever feeling overcome or pushed into something mentally, this is the enemy bullying you. But submit yourself to God. "Resist the devil and he will flee from you." (James 4:7) Like a counterfeit bill, the devil can be easily spotted if you know what to look for.

It's critical that you can differentiate between the four voices working in your life. Like a traffic cop, some you need to arrest, some you need to let pass, and others you need to talk back to. If you don't talk to yourself, your self will talk back to you.

REFLECT TO CONNECT

1. What is the last thing God has said to you?
2. What is the "talk track" in your head?
3. What is the last thing the enemy said to you to attempt to get you to follow him?

Everyone has multiple voices of influence in their head;
you must distinguish each one so you know who to listen to.

A PLACE TO PRAY AT WORK
WEEK 31 | THURSDAY

Then the Lord appeared to Solomon at night and said to him,
"I have heard your prayer and have chosen this place for Myself as a
house of sacrifice. If I shut up the heavens so that there is no rain,
or if I command the locust to devour the land, or if I send pestilence among
My people, and My people who are called by My name humble
themselves and pray and seek My face and turn from their wicked ways,
then I will hear from heaven, will forgive their sin and will heal their

land. Now My eyes will be open and My ears attentive to the prayer
offered in this place. For now I have chosen and consecrated this house
that My name may be there forever, and My eyes and
My heart will be there perpetually. 2 Chronicles 7:12-16

G od has picked a place to dwell; have you picked a place to pray during your day? God agreed to Solomon's prayer by offering Israel a choice and a place in which He would answer their prayer—in the temple. Today, God doesn't dwell in brick-and-mortar buildings; He dwells in you. Do you recognize when you are near to God?

Believers know how to "turn it on and off" in business based on "who" they are around. When a customer or supervisor walks into the room, they turn on their concern, charm, and a hearing ear, recognizing that dollars and decisions about their future could be decided. God is "always on" and "always in" you, ready to assist you in every conversation and situation. If you consecrate a place in your heart for God as Solomon did in the temple, He will be found by you to guide and direct you. If you have not heard from God in a while, start by seeking Him in prayer, and in no time, you will be restored to sensing His presence. God isn't just concerned with your spiritual health, but also your relational, financial, social, and physical health. He hears every cry and concern, whether spoken or unspoken, and whether you sense He just walked into the room or recognize He has always been there. He wants to hear from you today at work.

REFLECT TO CONNECT

1. What topics is God wanting to discuss with you today?
2. How can you set up reminders to stop and pray throughout your day?

3. Who in your life models a God-consciousness and a daily dialogue that you could follow?

God is always last to leave the conversation;
He desires a dialogue, not a monologue.

———————◆◆———————

THE GREAT ATTENTION-GETTER
WEEK 31 | FRIDAY

"When the heavens are shut up and there is no rain because they have
sinned against You, and they pray toward this place and confess
Your name, and turn from their sin when You afflict them; then hear
in heaven and forgive the sin of Your servants and Your people Israel,
indeed, teach them the good way in which they should walk.
And send rain on Your land which You have given to
Your people for an inheritance." 2 Chronicles 6:26-27

Pain is often the megaphone that causes us to wake up to hearing the voice of God. C.S. Lewis said, "God whispers to us in our pleasure, speaks to us in our conscience, and shouts at us in our pain." Sometimes a harsh word spoken, a blurry line crossed, or a wrong motive can cause the goodness of God to reach out and pull us back over the line so we are saved from creating a negative outcome in our lives. When was the last time God, in His goodness, reached out to correct you or pulled you away from a cliff you were approaching?

Failure is the first step toward success when it brings us back to our faith in God. God raises up successful saints in the marketplace to be rainmakers. Yet in that success, His voice can get drowned out when the rains of success take His place. Failure, pain, missing the mark, or underperformance at work can cause us to look to God for answers or get down and out. God desires that we reach for Him in our pain or self-made mess so He can help us to discover a solution. He will allow events to transpire in our lives as an "attention-getter," then use them to bring us back to relationship... *if* we let Him.

REFLECT TO CONNECT

1. What "attention-getters" has God used in your life before?
2. Is God using anything in your life right now to get your attention?
3. Can you think of a time when God used lackluster results in your life as a way to draw you in so He could speak with you?

Your pain point is a "calendar invite" sent from God so
He can help you out of your mess.

RELATIONSHIPS BUILT TO LAST

WEEK 32 | MONDAY

*"Yet have regard to the prayer of Your servant and to his supplication,
O LORD my God, to listen to the cry and to the prayer which
Your servant prays before You today; that Your eyes may be open
toward this house night and day, toward the place of which
You have said, 'My name shall be there,' to listen to the prayer which
Your servant shall pray toward this place."*
1 Kings 8:28-29

O nce Solomon finished the building of the temple, God filled the place with His glory as a symbol of His arrival, His presence, and His availability. God's promise to hear from on high when we turn to Him is matched by His kind reaction to us when we approach Him with a sincere heart requesting help, forgiveness, or a turnaround. When we draw near to God, He draws near to us. What creates this accessibility? A willingness to be available in a time of need.

Your accessibility shows that you care. People want someone they can count on, not someone they have to hunt down in a time of need. Dependability precedes a reputation for reliability for those laboring in the marketplace. Following God's example, consider making a promise to those you serve to be there when they need you. A promise to be there for someone in their time of need creates a bond of trust, and delivering on a promise is what fortifies the trust. Whether through email, phone, or a text, being ready and willing to help when someone is in need creates repeat business from customers, loyalty from employees, and relationships that are built to last.

REFLECT TO CONNECT

1. Who in your world may be feeling neglected that you have access to?
2. Is there someone you can make yourself more available to at work, at home, or in the church?
3. What advice would you give to someone as to how they can strengthen a relationship?

People gravitate toward people who make themselves accessible in a time of need.

———————◆———————

RESOURCES WITHIN REACH
WEEK 32 | TUESDAY

"Now send me a skilled man to work in gold, silver, brass and iron, and in purple, crimson and violet fabrics, and who knows how to make engravings, to work with the skilled men whom I have in Judah and Jerusalem, whom David my father provided. Send me also cedar, cypress and algum timber from Lebanon, for I know that your servants know how to cut timber of Lebanon; and indeed my servants will work with your servants, to prepare timber in abundance for me, for the house which I am about to build will be great and wonderful. Now behold, I will give to your servants, the woodsmen who cut the timber, 20,000 kors of crushed wheat and 20,000 kors of barley, and 20,000 baths of wine and 20,000 baths of oil." 2 Chronicles 2:7-10

S olomon was known for his wisdom because God provided wisdom for whatever he set his hands to. When God grants wisdom, He provides for each area He guides us into. For your sacred mission, God can do for you what He provided for Solomon and more. In Old Testament times, God didn't grant wisdom to everyone. In New Testament times, God offers His endless wisdom to anyone who wishes to seek it out. When God works a project with you, He will point you to people of provision who are in place to assist you. Here are a few things He provided for Solomon that were already within his reach.

COOPERATION from strangers who were foreigners in the land that agreed to help with the heavy lifting of the work project. Whom might you be able to team up with whereby you can meet their need, and they can meet your need? Be the first to offer help.

TEAMWORK between nations and peoples as they worked side by side and labored together. What commonalities might you have with a people, group, or organization close by that you may not be connected to yet? Reach out today.

PARTNERSHIP with rulers and authorities who were outside of his immediate circle but equipped to help. What authorities has God given you access to?

PROVISION was provided for Huam, King of Tyre, in exchange for the cedars from Lebanon and labor from his workforce. What resource do you have to trade?

God's calling on your life will require others' involvement for you to be successful. God has already given you everything you need. It is within reach, merely awaiting your recognition of it. Ask God today to open your eyes to see the resources and partnerships He's already placed around you.

"Teamwork makes the dream work."
John Maxwell

1. Who is within your reach that could lighten your load by lending a helping hand?
2. Whom do you need to approach to partner with to make you more effective?
3. Are there identifiable barriers or bottlenecks that are slowing you down?

When God calls you to a work, He has provision planned and a team picked out to assist you; do you recognize them?

BATTLE PLAN YOUR DAY

WEEK 32 | WEDNESDAY

Then David numbered the people who were with him and set over them commanders of thousands and commanders of hundreds. David sent the people out, one third under the command of Joab, one third under the command of Abishai the son of Zeruiah, Joab's brother, and one third under the command of Ittai the Gittite. 2 Samuel 18:1-2

Create a repeatable system for what is recurring daily. David was about to carry out a task he had many times before by readying himself for battle, and he had a system that brought him success.

Success in any endeavor requires advance preparation. Here is a simple approach that can help you set up each day for success.

Wars are won one battle at a time, so plan your victories daily.

PRIORITIZE: Delete, delegate, then dive in. Identify what "must" get done today, no matter what. After identifying your top three, prioritize. The most important part of prioritization is elimination of non-essential items so you can focus on what matters most. Anything not mission-critical or that doesn't produce a high ROI from your time and talent should be delegated or deleted from your list of priorities.

ORGANIZE: Take inventory of your resources and determine the scope of work for the day. Time block your day to ensure everything that is priority gets scheduled. What gets scheduled gets done. Be careful not to overcommit yourself—an overflowing cup of to-dos creates unnecessary stress and *ongoing* overflow that can sabotage the next day.

STRATEGIZE: After scheduling your people and projects for the day, it's time to make a plan for each priority. An outline for a meeting will set an agenda and keep you focused. Investing "thinking time" to forecast potential outcomes will not only make you more prepared but help you to anticipate potential problems or roadblocks before they appear. Going into your day with clearly defined outcomes will ensure you walk through your day with purpose, avoiding blind spots and problems.

REFLECT TO CONNECT

1. What issues typically sidetrack your focus during the day?
2. Do you have a success system that you follow?
3. Who is the most organized person you know? What is their success system?

Those who plan ahead get ahead,
and the opposite is also true.

———————————◆———————————

WHO DO PEOPLE SAY
THAT YOU ARE?

Moreover, Husham said, "You know your father and his men, that they are mighty men and they are fierce, like a bear robbed of her cubs in the field. And your father is an expert in warfare, and will not spend the night with the people. Behold, he has now hidden himself in one of the caves or in another place; and it will be when he falls on them at the first attack, that whoever hears it will say, 'There has been a slaughter among the people who follow Absalom.' And even the one who is valiant, whose heart is like the heart of a lion, will completely lose heart; for all Israel knows that your father is a mighty man and those who are with him are valiant men."
2 Samuel 17:8-10

What is your reputation? David and his valiant men got a reputation for being fierce in battle. It started in the days of Goliath, continued while David was on the run from Saul, and continued in victory during David's reign as king. Reputation can be built over years but lost over a single act. The Romans viewed character as the "sum parts" of a person, while the Greeks viewed reputation like a stamp or symbol for what something "looked like." Reputation is who people think you are, but character is who you are.

Reputation has the power to go ahead of you to pave a path of favor and influence. In my best-selling book *PERSUADE*, I cover reputation at length in "The Law of Relationship." When you think about your role in the marketplace, in your work environment, or with family and friends, how would you evaluate your reputation or that of others you know? How do you evaluate others' reputations?

TEN CHARACTERISTICS OF A GOOD REPUTATION

1. Competence: Are they skilled and capable of doing the job? (Can they be trusted with my company, my business, my employees?)
2. Character: What is their total makeup? (How do they behave when things are "otherwise"?)
3. Countability: Can they be counted on? (Do they deliver on what they say they will?)
4. Contribution: What is the value that they add, and how is it measured? (Am I better off with them than without them?)
5. Charisma: Are people drawn to them? (Do people want to spend time with them or avoid them?)
6. Criticism: How do they handle failure? (Do they accept constructive input/feedback?)
7. Correctable: Are they teachable and able to learn from mistakes or repeat the same mistakes over and over?
8. Celebration: How do they handle success and victory? (Does success go to their head, or do they use it as a springboard to go from strength to strength?)
9. Connection: Do they have good people skills? (What is the health of their relationships?)
10. Compassionate: Do they have heartfelt concern for others?

REFLECT TO CONNECT

1. If you were to ask those closest to you, what adjectives would they use to describe your reputation?
2. What one word would you use to describe yourself and why?
3. Your life will likely be summed up in one sentence one day. If you could pick it, what would it be?

Reputation is what others see;
character is what God sees.

MANIPULATORS IN
THE MARKETPLACE
WEEK 32 | FRIDAY

Absalom used to rise early and stand beside the way to the gate; and
when any man had a suit to come to the king for judgment, Absalom
would call to him and say, "From what city are you?" And he would say,
"Your servant is from one of the tribes of Israel." Then Absalom would
say to him, "See, your claims are good and right, but no man listens to
you on the part of the king." Moreover, Absalom would say, "Oh that
one would appoint me judge in the land, then every man who has any
suit or cause could come to me and I would give him justice."
2 Samuel 15: 2-4

Watch those at the water cooler. Absalom used position and
power to grow influence so that he might manipulate others
for his personal benefit. From the time a child is born, they learn how
to manipulate their parents with a cry. The issue is not whether you
wield the power of influence but whether it will be used for selfish
or selfless reasons. Most kids grow out of emotional manipulation as
they age; however, some in the marketplace grow through manipulating others, which is not God's way.

Absalom positioned himself in a way to steal the people's affections away from his father David so he could steal the throne. There
will always be manipulators in the marketplace. Here are a few ways
in which you can spot an Absalomian spirit:

THE MANIPULATOR: When difficult decisions are made, Absalomians will use the "unhappiness" of the situation to sway emotional support in their direction and away from authority. As they garner support and become a shoulder to cry on, they use their increasing influence to move you toward supporting them in future endeavors. Manipulators are skilled at banking favors today for future use.

THE POWER POINTER: When negativity arises, Absalomians seize the moment and point to it as another example of why change is needed. This elevates their influence and reduces the influence of those in authority. They divert attention and affection away from leaders toward themselves. Politicians practice this with the promise of "change."

THE COMPLAINT COLLECTOR: When uncontrollable circumstances arise, Absalomians camp out at the water cooler or employee lounge, waiting for those with a complaint to show up. Instead of diffusing a situation, they perpetuate it to increase discontent.

REFLECT TO CONNECT

1. Can you sense when someone during conversation is try-ing to sway support toward themselves and away from the authorities in place?
2. What examples can you give of a right and wrong way you have used your influence?
3. What advice would you give to a new coworker who is being invited into the "complaining crowd"?

God hates murmuring and frowns on those that use
the misfortune of others to advance themselves.

THE SUCCESS DRIFT

WEEK 33 | MONDAY

Now when evening came David arose from his bed and walked around on the roof of the king's house, and from the roof he saw a woman bathing; and the woman was very beautiful in appearance.
2 Samuel 11:2

Wrong place—wrong time. In the times of war, a king was to be away from the comforts of the palace and in the field with his soldiers, leading and inspiring them. For David, he had drifted from the place he belonged and had fallen into a complacent lifestyle that led him to sleeping during the day and getting up at night. Being in the wrong place at the wrong time opened the door to David sinning with Bathsheba and then killing her husband to cover it up. Notice the sequence of events that surrounded the king's fall from grace:

1. Comfort: Israel had not taken rest from her enemies, but David had.
2. Conflict: At the intersection of temptation, David failed to count the cost of his actions.
3. Cover-up: Once David realized his sin would find him out, he attempted to cover it up by getting Uriah to sleep with his wife Bathsheba to cover up her pregnancy. Uriah refused, then David had him killed.
4. Confrontation: God confronted David head-on through the prophet Nathan—God didn't mince words.
5. Conviction: David, once confronted, was cut through to the heart with conviction and confessed his sin.
6. Consequence: Although God forgave David's sin, consequences included David's house being at war for the rest of his reign.

Does success make you drift or double down on good work habits? God wants to bring His blessings and prosperity into every area of your life, but not if a season of sustained success will cause you to stumble. If you've gotten off track with your work habits or have drifted from where you know you should be, end the wandering and get realigned doing what you know you should. God prefers a "self-corrector" over one He must correct.

REFLECT TO CONNECT

1. Is there any area of your life that you are getting "pinged" from God that requires a course correction?
2. Success is an inside job—what specifically needs shoring up in your life?
3. Do you have a wandering friend or family member whom God is asking you to "be a Nathan to" so you can speak into their life to pull them back from the consequence of sin?

Everyone is prone to the success drift from time to time—God prefers a "self-corrector" over one He must correct.

BE FIRST TO FACE THE GIANT
WEEK 33 | TUESDAY

Again there was war at Gath, where there was a man of great stature who had twenty-four fingers and toes, six fingers on each hand and six toes on each foot; and he also was descended from the giants. When he taunted Israel, Jonathan the son of Shimea, David's brother, killed him.
1 Chronicles 20:6-7

You may only get a few "giant opportunities" a year to prove yourself. David's nephew was one of a few Israelites who also killed a giant similar to David killing Goliath. However, David was the first to kill a giant. David becomes king, and those who killed giants after him are rarely mentioned. The one who goes first is remembered and honored as a pioneer and a leader. Those who come after the one who first took initiative follow in another's footsteps. But they who go first are LEADERS. Would you like to be known as a giant slayer? If so, be first to step up and speak out, and you will stand out.

Someone is always observing you while you work. Successful people distinguish themselves by going first, starting early, outperforming, and serving others. They are pioneers, not settlers; climbers, not part of the group that gets comfortable and camps out. God uses those who are willing to be aggressive and take action. In the case of David, God orchestrated a public display of courage, but David had to be willing to face Goliath.

Are you ready to pass your test? David's public victory over Goliath elevated him in the eyes of all Israel. What giant is God bringing you to conquer today? Your giant may be a public fight like David's or a private task God is prodding you to complete. God will always provide you opportunities to face your giants privately before bringing you to face them publicly. He will also bring you smaller challenges to ready you for the bigger challenges, so don't miss them.

REFLECT TO CONNECT

1. What is before you now that you are putting off but need to take action on?
2. Are there challenges that, when faced, God may use to brand your reputation with others?

3. Of your colleagues and coworkers, who stands out as a "giant slayer" in your mind?

Seizing smaller challenges is what prepares you for conquering the Goliaths in your life.

———————————◆◆————————————

GET THE "DAVID ANOINTING"

WEEK 33 | WEDNESDAY

And the LORD helped David wherever he went. 2 Samuel 8:6

Problems create promotion. **When God wants to establish** you, He will often use a challenge that no one else can solve but you in order to bring awareness of you to people of position and power. When God established King David in the eyes of his people, He used what kings often face a challenge in war, even an enormous challenge. David went to war, and God was with him wherever he went, establishing David even further in fame, fortune, and victory. God used a similar strategy when it was time to elevate Joseph in the eyes of Pharaoh and the people. Even in Potiphar's house, Potiphar realized that God was with Joseph in whatever he put his hand to, and this elevated Joseph in the eyes of Potiphar, the people, and others in authority.

God allows problems no one can solve but you, but not without His help. Without a problem, a solution is unneeded. Without a challenge, an overcomer's courage goes unnoticed. Without Goliath, David would not have had victory on a national stage. If Joseph had not been in prison, the circumstances that led him to stand before

Pharaoh may not have happened. There are strategies God often uses to establish His purposes in your life. A problem at work that requires a God-sized solution is a clue that God wants to use you in a way that will grow your influence and establish His purposes. These divinely designed strategies can include:

1. **STAND UP:** A problem that comes up that no one can solve, but you volunteer to take it on.
2. **RAISE YOUR HAND:** A relationship no one wants to handle, but you volunteer, are successful, and the high brass takes notice.
3. **STEP FORWARD:** A crisis that causes everyone fear, yet faith rises up in you. You step forward and face the challenge no one else would, and God is with you.

REFLECT TO CONNECT

1. Are there challenges you skirted in your past that later you observed someone else benefited from because they ran toward what you ran away from?
2. What problems or challenges might be hiding under the surface at work or in the marketplace that you have the insight to resolve?
3. What is the "Goliath" in your life or problem your boss faces that God wants you to confront like David did?

To elevate you in the marketplace,
God presents challenges within your environment that require
His involvement and your courage.

THE SIGN OF LOVE

WEEK 33 | THURSDAY

"I will be a father to him and he will be a son to Me; when he commits iniquity, I will correct him with the rod of men and the strokes of the sons of men, but My lovingkindness shall not depart from him, as I took it away from Saul, whom I removed from before you. Your house and your kingdom shall endure before Me forever; your throne shall be established forever." In accordance with all these words and all this vision, so Nathan spoke to David. 2 Samuel 7:14-17

When the desire was birthed in David to build a house for God, God's response was that He would allow Solomon, who would come after him, to be the builder. God goes out of His way in His response to David to prove His love for David's future son when He uses words like "love," "correction," and "establish." And we know that the Lord disciplines those whom He loves, for what child is there whose parent doesn't correct them so their feet are firmly set on a good path?

Pain is the great attention-getter, but God uses it as the master tutor also. It is impossible to be successful in business without the willingness to change, adapt, and shift our behavior on a continual basis. Between the demands of clients, coworkers, and supervisors, you are bound to drop the ball and fall short at times. When the rod of pain or discipline enters your life, God may be gently nudging you to alert you to an adjustment you need to make. When I get corrected, the first question I ask myself is, "Is this input accurate?" Many get defensive or hurt and are unable to receive correction and, therefore, remain unteachable. Consider the following responses as a way of embracing feedback next time you encounter a brush with the rod of correction, whether it be from Heaven or Earth:

1. **Pause:** Reflect, then respond—don't react.
2. **Ask yourself:** Is the input true?
3. **Submit to correction:** What change is needed?
4. **Success:** Thank God for the teachable moment, knowing He will work it together for your good in the future.

REFLECT TO CONNECT

1. When was the last time you experienced a degree of emotional pain as a result of correction?
2. Do you willingly receive constructive criticism, or does the messenger have to contend with defensiveness from you before you are open to input?
3. Do you view correction as an infringement on your "rights" or as feedback as to how you can improve?

God accepts you as you are yet loves you too much to leave you the way you are.

———————◆———————

CELEBRATE TO APPRECIATE

WEEK 33 | FRIDAY

And they brought in the ark of God and placed it inside the tent which David had pitched for it, and they offered burnt offerings and peace offerings before God. When David had finished offering the burnt offering and the peace offerings, he blessed the people in the name of the LORD. He distributed to everyone of Israel, both man and woman, to everyone a loaf of bread and a portion of meat and a raisin cake.
1 Chronicles 16:1-3

When something amazing happens in your life, do you celebrate? After David brought the Ark of God back to Israel, he threw a party and celebrated. Can you imagine everyone in the nation receiving a portion of food from the king? And then they celebrated with a Psalm of thanksgiving which rehearsed and revisited all the great things God had done for Israel. What do you have that you can celebrate in your life? Do you have a song in your heart this week that is energizing you? What are you grateful to God for that you could sing to Him about?

Celebration creates momentum, and momentum creates more wins. Leaders are judged every month by their performance. Performance expectations require that you deliver every month, and some jobs are even in a sink-or-swim environment all the time. Failure to meet quotas, performance metrics, or underdelivering in general can mean less income, fewer bonuses, or even termination. As you sprint through your month, remember to slow down and celebrate when you experience a win. Whether big or small, at home or at work, people like to celebrate. Everyone likes to feel the wind under their wings that comes from a high five in the hallways or a pat on the back, even at home. Celebration opens up bandwidth to create white space everyone needs to consistently perform at high levels. When you celebrate, involve others, pass out credit for the wins, share the rewards, and share gratefulness to God like David did.

REFLECT TO CONNECT

1. When is the last time you stopped down to celebrate something God has done in your ministry, career, or family?
2. Is there something your spouse or children have accomplished this month that you need to celebrate and acknowledge them for?

3. If you were to write God a Psalm of thanksgiving like the one found in 1 Chronicles 14, what would you write?

Celebrating a win recharges and replenishes the soul, and God is a big partier.

A SOLUTION FOR EVERY PROBLEM

WEEK 34 | MONDAY

"It shall be when you hear the sound of marching in the tops of the balsam trees, then you shall go out to battle, for God will have gone out before you to strike the army of the Philistines." David did just as God had commanded him, and they struck down the army of the Philistines from Gibeon even as far as Gezer. Then the fame of David went out into all the lands; and the LORD brought the fear of him on all the nations.
1 Chronicles 14:15-17

G od has a plan for your problem. Once again, David is asking God for advice, and once again, God is specific in answering David's query for a strategy to win. God is as concerned with help-ing His children in the marketplace as much as He is those in the ministry. As a son or daughter of the Highest, you can receive God's outstretched hand. He wants you to come to Him in matters you will face at work, in relationships, and in every area of life. When you are not sure what to do, or you need a divine idea or instruction for what you are facing, follow these steps.

1. **Get quiet and reach out!** Acknowledge to God that you need His help. His line is open and awaiting your call. Whether you pray out loud or internally, have a notepad handy so you can be ready to record what comes to mind. Write your prayer request out, always being specific with requests and questions you ask God.

2. **Lean in and listen closely!** You may hear what feels like a gentle "whisper," God may paint a picture on the inside of you, or He could bring a memory to mind. If God brings someone to mind while you are praying, God may be

directing you to connect with another as a way of answering your prayer. Someone somewhere has likely been through something similar to what you are dealing with in the present. Who are they? Everything God does is through people, so don't be surprised if the answer to your prayer includes pairing you up with someone who can help you. Whether you are leading family, an army like David, a small group, or working alone, God's desire is for you to integrate Him into your daily routines.

3. **Follow!** Whatever you feel God is leading you to do, do it. God's answers and strategies may not make sense to you, but remember, He always sees more than you see. While you may be waiting for one "big" answer, God may only give you one piece of the puzzle at a time. God's strategy is often comprised of small steps. God will often give you an instruction that may come across to you like an idea; follow it.

REFLECT TO CONNECT

1. When you are in trouble, whom do you turn to first?
2. What challenge are you facing now that requires God's insight?
3. Does it matter if you make your query to God vocally or in your heart only?

God delights when His kids reach out to him,
even for the small things.

———————◆———————

ROOTS FOR A REASON

WEEK 34 | TUESDAY

Now Hiram king of Tyre sent messengers to David with cedar trees,
masons and carpenters, to build a house for him. And David realized
that the LORD had established him as king over Israel, and that
his kingdom was highly exalted, for the sake of His people Israel.
1 Chronicles 14:1-2

G od desires to establish everyone in their destiny. The time
had arrived for David to become king of Israel. For years, God
delayed establishing David, knowing that there was a specific date
and time He would all at once bring about the fulfillment of His plan
for David's life. When you are where God wants you to be, you will
find that God will open doors, bring new people and resources into
your life, increase your income and influence, deepen your roots
within an organization and community, and accelerate His blessings
in your life. God established David in many other ways—have you
discerned how God wants to establish you? There are a few other
ways in which God establishes those who pursue Him.

FIVE WAYS GOD ESTABLISHES YOU

1. **PLACE:** He provides a place to live you can call your own.
2. **PURPOSE:** His purposes begin to unfold in your life, and you
   experience uncommon energy, wisdom, and insight in your
   lane of calling.
3. **PRESENCE:** An outpouring of His Presence increases and is
   known by the unexplainable favor you receive.
4. **PLEASURE:** You begin to feel His pleasure as you accomplish
   the work He has given you to do.
5. **PROVISION:** Provision is in the place God has called you to
   serve. Where you find God, there is "more than enough."

Recognizing the providential hand of God is key to your success. God delights to establish you in His ways and in your world. If there is an area you are lacking in or would like God to establish you in, go to God and give Him specifics, then watch with expectation to see what He will do for you. As you wait on Him, be aware that active faith starts with patience and finishes with action. When you ask God for something, He will often give you an instruction. Asking "more" of something requires "more" from you.

REFLECT TO CONNECT

1. Have there been seasons where you sensed God was establishing you?
2. What signaled to you that God was bringing about His purposes in your life?
3. As you interpret the seasons of your life, what do you discern God is doing or about to do through you or for you?

God's blessings are waiting for you in the place of obedience.

———————◆❖◆———————

THE DEPENDABILITY OF DAVID
WEEK 34 | WEDNESDAY

David became greater and greater, for the LORD
God of hosts was with him. 2 Samuel 5:10

Devotion in relationship, coupled with commitment to obedience, unlocks God's divine favor. When David was 15, God chose him to be king and had Samuel anoint him. What was it about David that caused God to not only anoint him but remain with him, fight alongside him, and consider him a devoted friend? Was it David's willingness to defend God's honor against Goliath? Maybe it was David's courageousness in battle or his confidence before the Lord. We know this for sure: God said of David in 1 Samuel 13:14 that he was a "man after His own heart" and would do whatever He asked. David's devotion to his relationship with God and his dedication to obey whatever God told him to do created favor in whatever David put his hands to. Obedience is a serious currency in Heaven, and God richly rewards it. What has God asked you to do that you have not taken action on yet?

Procrastination kills deadlines, dreams, and careers. Have you noticed that when there is something you are delaying doing, the weight of doing it gets bigger and bigger, even compounding, until you get it done? Obedience isn't only doing what you are told by someone in authority; it is doing what you already know you should be doing when you know you should be doing it. God lives in you to work through you, and most often, His interventions in our life are more practical than spiritual in nature. God will often nudge you to remind you of your responsibility, then wait to see if you respond. It is not uncommon that while you feel you are waiting on God to intervene, He is waiting for you to do your part. When leaders fail to fulfill their responsibility, someone's suffering is the result, and people pray to God looking for relief. Getting done what you know must be done is a prelude to receiving greater responsibility.

REFLECT TO CONNECT

1. What does partnership look like with God and you?
2. What have you left undone that needs to be done?

3. If you had to list off what you are waiting on God to do, what does His list look like of what He is waiting for *you* to do?

Delayed obedience is disobedience, even on the things no one has told you to do that you know must be done.

THE NEW SHERIFF IN TOWN

WEEK 34 | THURSDAY

"As the Lord lives, who has redeemed my life from all distress, when one told me, saying, 'Behold, Saul is dead,' and thought he was bringing good news, I seized him and killed him in Ziklag, which was the reward I gave him for his news." 2 Samuel 4:9-10

When a shocking event happens, how do you respond? Do you get fearful, paralyzed, excited, or pause to "consider your ways"? A shift in power within an organization, a new decision-maker on the scene, or the death of someone close creates a shaking at the core of our being. Those who were about to deliver the news that Saul and his sons were dead expected the new authority (David) to react one way, but their misjudgment cost them their lives.

When there is a new sheriff in town, "consider your ways." When there is a shift in authority, it's a signal to re-read the environment, re-learn how the one in authority thinks, and re-visit your assumptions. Here are a few things to consider when a new authority enters your environment.

VISON: What is the new vision? Pieces of the old regime may remain in place; however, change usually always comes with something better to replace what wasn't working.

PRIORITIES: What are the new priorities, and what is no longer considered important? The quicker you can adapt and get on the same page as the one making the new decisions, the better it will go for you.

EXPECTATIONS: What is expected of me? Ask the new decision maker or supervisor you will be working with. Expectations of a new leader for you will be different than what you were accustomed to. Learning how to please those in authority will unlock favor, and the opposite is true.

TODAY'S ACTIONS: What can you do today that will positively impact the new authority and the direction they are moving toward? When new authorities take over, they are sensitive to and notice who is on board and who is sitting on the fence.

REFLECT TO CONNECT

1. How has the ground shaken under your feet with a new boss before?
2. When you go through an emotionally destabilizing event, what is your first response?
3. Some see change as bad, while others see God opening a door; what do you see?

When the ground is shaking under your feet,
leaders shift to adapt to the new environment.

————————◆————————

THE CRAFTSMAN OF DESTINY

WEEK 34 | FRIDAY

David became greater and greater, for the LORD of hosts was with him.
1 Chronicles 11:9

G od is a master mentor who knows how to create His character in you. David was 15 when he was anointed by Samuel to be king, but it was not until the age of 30 that he would enter Jerusalem to rule as king over all Israel. When David's moment had come after to take the throne, he still spent seven and a half years as king of Judah but not over all Israel. And when his time to rule over all Israel came, he had to contend with the Jebusites who were occupying Jerusalem at the time. David had to contend for every square inch of the destiny God had called him to. And in every battle David confronted, God was with him. When God calls and we answer, that is when the epic journey begins. Miley Cyrus wrote the song "The Climb," which chronicles the challenges one faces along the journey toward success. John Wooden once asked, "How do you know you are on the way to success? It's uphill all the way." David had years of struggles—do you think he ever wanted to give up?

The muscle of perseverance is developed the moment you want to quit but keep going anyway. The day-to-day struggles you face as you walk into your destiny are the "material" the master craftsman uses to chisel His character into you. Although unpleasant and difficult at times, the chisel marks left by your master mentor build the spiritual muscles you will need to succeed for the future He is leading you to. David knew his calling 15 years before he would enter it, yet God used this time to prepare him. Many answer the divine call, but not all finish the race. God is looking for "finishers." Keep your eyes fixed on the future promise and persevere until

God brings you into all of His purposes for your life. Growth won't stop unless you cease climbing.

REFLECT TO CONNECT

1. What struggles have you encountered that God is using to fashion you into His masterpiece?
2. What do you need to trust God for today and persevere through?
3. In what ways do you identify with David's 15-year journey from the fields of a shepherd to the steps of the palace?

The muscle of perseverance only develops
when you want to quit but then keep going.

THREE RS OF CREATING CONFIDENCE

WEEK 35 | MONDAY

"There we saw the giants there, the sons of Anak ... and we were
in our own sight as grasshoppers, and so we were in their sight."
Numbers 13:33 (KJV)

G od struggles to get you to see yourself as He sees you. What troubled God when the 12 spies went in wasn't just their lack of faith in God but their lack of faith in themselves. Joshua and Caleb came back with a report that said, in essence, "Let's go; we can take them." The other 10 didn't believe that, even with God's help, they could conquer the giants they faced. Henry Ford once remarked, "If you believe you can, you can. If you believe you can't, you can't." How you see yourself determines your self-image and the ceiling of your effectiveness. Your internal self-talk and your self-image decide your confidence level. Without confidence in yourself, you will struggle to reach and attain all God has for you.

Confidence creates courage. Here are a few ways in which successful saints can create a healthy self-image that perpetuates confidence in themselves and in God.

THREE RS OF CREATING CONFIDENCE

1. **READ** what God says about you in the Scriptures and choose to believe His report over your feelings.
2. **REMIND** yourself of past victories in the Lord, how they were created, and then reproduce them. Nothing creates confidence and a healthy self-image like repeated success.
3. **REPROGRAM** your failures and self-doubts by repurposing past hurts and failures into learning moments. God will help you.

1. What memories or self-doubts chip away at your confidence?
2. When you think of your top 10 qualities, what adjectives come to mind?
3. What is God asking you to do that you've been putting off because you are doubting yourself?

For those who tap into the confidence God has for them, nothing shall be impossible for them.

READ THE ROOM
TO LEAD THE ROOM
WEEK 35 | TUESDAY

Then He told them a parable: "Behold the fig tree and all the trees; as soon as they put forth leaves, you see it and know for yourselves that summer is now near. So you also, when you see these things happening, recognize that the kingdom of God is near." Luke 21:29-31

Jesus reminds us that you can miss important events if your senses are not trained on what to look for. Your ability to read the room (your environment) starts with knowledge and awareness. You must have the know-how (knowledge) of what you are looking for and a high level of awareness (wisdom) so that when signals are sent, you receive them. Chapter 2 in *PERSUADE*, "The Law of Listening," discusses how seasoned communicators and marketplace leaders train their senses so they can pick up verbal and nonverbal communication while speaking to an audience and in one-on-one conversations. Leaders learn to read the room so they can lead those in the room.

Knowledge and awareness are the keys to reading the room. Your eyes, ears, and heart can ascertain visible and invisible communication if you teach them to. There is an invisible energy and communication that is transmitted below the surface of communication many people miss. One of America's greatest business consultants of his time, Peter Drucker, said, "Over 50% of communication is non-verbal." Consider using a notepad to document the clues you pick up on during communication. By studying people and their reactions to yourself and other communicators, your ability to read all that is being communicated will grow dramatically and quickly. If you invite the Holy Spirit to show you what He sees and hears, your ability to discern will fast-track supernaturally. Ask Him to open your spiritual eyes and ears each day and then write down what you "read in the room."

REFLECT TO CONNECT

1. Have you become aware of moments missed in a meeting? Maybe you thought to yourself, "I wish I would have said…"
2. What are the most common communication cues you pick up on during communication?
3. As you reflect on significant conversations you've had in the last week, what moments during the conversation impacted you?

Reading the room precedes leading the room.

———————◆———————

THE GOD DOOR TO WITNESS

WEEK 35 | WEDNESDAY

*I solemnly charge you in the presence of God and of Christ Jesus,
who is to judge the living and the dead, and by His appearing and
His kingdom: preach the word; be ready in season and out of season;
reprove, rebuke, exhort, with great patience and instruction.*
2 Timothy 4:1-2

Witness when the door is open. Doctors are told to "help the patient right in front of them." How do you know if the door to share your story of God's love is open? If there is a need by someone close by, that is your cue that God has opened a door for you to share your story. A few other ways to witness include:

- **Be Alert** for a prompting by the Holy Spirit.
- **Observe** your emotions. If you feel compassion toward them, reach out; this may be God's Spirit emoting through you.
- **Ask** questions to ascertain the need.
- **Listen,** then listen some more. As you listen to them, what is God saying to you?
- **Learn** by asking follow-up questions to areas of the conversation they are emphasizing.
- **Love** them by sharing your story. God may guide you to share a similar situation you were in and how He helped you through it.
- **Hear** what the Holy Spirit would lead you to say. God will often bring a Bible story or Scripture to your memory, which is for them. Let God use it as ointment to a wound.
- **Offer** to pray for them. People rarely refuse an invitation to come into contact with God.

God hears people's prayers at work all day long. Witnessing for God only requires a willing vessel. Walk through the doors God opens for you and watch Him work. The more you step out in faith, the more you will see God show up in your work environment, in relationships, and in chance encounters.

REFLECT TO CONNECT

1. Whom is God prompting you to have a conversation with?
2. Whom are you feeling a burden for?
3. In what ways can you maintain a sensitivity to God's leading as you go through your day?

God will use your witness as often as you let Him.

———————◈———————

THE ART OF SELF-ENCOURAGEMENT

WEEK 35 | THURSDAY

But David strengthened himself in the LORD his God.
1 Samuel 30:6

Where do you go when you are hurting? David had come to a low point in his life. He was still on the run from Saul, and while away from his home base of Ziklag, Amalekites had taken the women and children away, including David's family. The people were so embittered against him that they thought to stone him. Is there something or a series of circumstances you have recently faced that has caused you to feel greatly distressed or depressed?

Learning the "art of encouraging" oneself is one of the most important life skills a person can learn. You, and you alone, are responsible for motivating yourself and keeping yourself energized. Everyone faces emotional ups and downs. Salespeople face rejection when cold calling, managers struggle with rising expectations, employees struggle with injustice, and the list goes on. Regardless of the circumstance, at some point, you will need to learn how to recharge your own emotional tank on the fly. When David was feeling down, he turned to God as his source for renewal.

The word "encourage" comes from two words. "En" means to "add to." And "courage" means "strengthen." So, to do as David did means to turn to God, and He will ADD STRENGTH to you. Next time you are facing a lion, a bear, or just coming off a failure or defeat, follow David's example and strengthen yourself in the Lord. Going to God in worship and word are the fastest ways to invite Him to refresh, renew, and restore your spirit.

There are three ways I strengthen myself in the Lord when I am down, discouraged, or unmotivated:

1. God inhabits the praises of His people (Psalm 22:3). I listen to Christian music and let the words wash over my mind. As I hear with my outer ear, I rehearse the words with my inner spiritual ear by saying them out loud in my mind.

2. "Faith comes from hearing, and hearing by the word of Christ." (Romans 10:17) I will read the Bible slowly as if I am "praying" through the Scriptures and not merely reading. This personalizes the promises of God as I put my name in the verses and watch for the stirring of the Holy Spirit.

3. Remember and rehearse "God memories" of victory. The more I talk to myself about God working through my circumstances in the past, the more power I have in the present.

1. When was the last time you were down and out—did you run to or away from God?
2. Have you developed a way to "strengthen yourself" when you are feeling weak or worn out?
3. Whom can you strengthen today with your words of encouragement and empowerment?

The more I talk to myself about God working through my circumstances in the past, the more power I have in the present.

LET GOD SPEAK THROUGH YOU
WEEK 35 | FRIDAY

"It will lead to an opportunity for your testimony. So make up your minds not to prepare beforehand to defend yourselves; for I will give you utterance and wisdom which none of your opponents will be able to resist or refute." Luke 21:13-15

Jesus promised persecution. At some point, you will suffer for being a follower of Christ and need to give an account of WHY you believe what you believe. Jesus told His disciples not to prepare to defend themselves but to let Him lead them in the moment. Have you had an experience in conversations or from a stage where you felt God flowing through you, and the words just came to you? As words effortlessly came, you knew it was Him. Jesus can provide the *words and wisdom*, not only when speaking of Him but in everyday business situations you will face, for the "mind of Christ" dwells in you. Christ with you is not a reason to avoid preparing for a future conversation; rather, you should be preparing to let Him speak through you as He gives you His thoughts.

You have a story God wants you to tell. To testify is to tell of what you've seen and heard. The disciples walked with Jesus for 3½ years and had a firsthand account of the life of Christ. *While you cannot always prepare your words, you can prepare yourself with prayer.* Praying through precedes breaking through. In what upcoming conversations will you pray for God's words and wisdom to flow through you?

REFLECT TO CONNECT

1. How do you know when God is speaking through you?
2. How have you experienced God speaking through you "in the moment"?
3. Do you believe there are people God wants you to speak to on His behalf this week?

Prayer is the best form of preparation when the stakes are at their highest. Praying through precedes breaking through.

LOOSE LIPS SINK SHIPS

WEEK 36 | MONDAY

Set a guard, O LORD, over my mouth;
Keep watch over the door of my lips. Psalm 141:3

David went through seasons of insecurity and fragility to the point where even what would come out of his mouth concerned him at times. When we are spread too thin or under great pressure, the lid over our heart can sometimes fly open unexpectedly, and we can blurt things out that have not been thought through or considered and, therefore, can do more damage than good. Just as David referred to the "door of his lips," what we say and how we say it can determine whether doors of opportunity open or close, whether people are attracted to us or repelled by us. The words we use create the environment around us—they can create connection or conflict and build relationships or destroy them.

"For of the abundance of the heart his mouth speaketh." **(Luke 6:45 KJV)** If you are feeling like a "city that is broken into and without walls" (Proverbs 25:28) and your lips are running you into trouble, it is a clear sign that you have lost control of your thought life and/or emotions. The first step in taking back your mind is to ask God to keep watch over what is brewing down below and practice the 2-second rule. This is something I like to practice when the lid over my lips is feeling loose. The 2-second rule creates a "pause" in the space between when someone speaks to me and my response. This way, I give careful thought to my words and give God a chance to weigh in and direct them if what is about to come out will damage myself or others. Next time it is your turn to speak, "practice the pause" and give God two seconds to help you gather your thoughts and think through them before you speak. The purpose of the 2-second rule is to bridle your emotional reaction to give you time to respond.

REFLECT TO CONNECT

1. When in recent memory do you recall speaking when you should have remained silent?
2. On a scale of 1-10, how would you rate your level of self-control when you are in a conversation that is disagreeable or confrontational?
3. What are the danger signs to you that your lid has become loose?

> *God will not do for you what He has empowered you to do for yourself. This includes managing your thought life and emotional reactions.*

BECOME A PEOPLE MAGNET
WEEK 36 | TUESDAY

Therefore encourage one another and build up one another, just as you also are doing. 1 Thessalonians 5:11

God works with your nature, not against it. Did you know that the most effective communication skills come right out of the Bible? Biblically influencing and persuading someone for their benefit is an art form that, when done correctly, will pull people toward you. The Apostle Paul was a master at persuasion. Biblical persuasion creates a magnetic "pull"; it doesn't push people to do something against their will.

The Apostle Paul attracted others by how he spoke to them about them. One of the ways to motivate people to action is through encouragement and edification. To encourage another means to add strength to them. To edify means to "uplift" another. Whether you are wanting to strengthen a friend, family member, coworker, kid, spouse, or supervisor, follow this 3-step plan for becoming a "People Magnet."

THREE WAYS TO BECOME A PEOPLE MAGNET

1. **ACKNOWLEDGE:** What strengths, uniqueness, or giftings do you notice in them? Everyone has a "God part" that has been given to them. When you identify the greatness within a person and speak to that greatness, it comes out. The opposite is true also; if you speak to weakness, weakness comes out. Speaking out about a person's uniqueness is how leaders, speakers, sellers, preachers, and all great communicators enlarge others.

2. **ADMIRE:** As you speak to another about what you see in them, speak about it in a tone of admiration. When you see value in someone or something they've accomplished, speaking about it with respect creates an atmosphere of honor. Honor is the ingredient that will create a gravitational pull between you and the one you are honoring.

3. **AFFIRM:** Finally, encourage the one you want to strengthen to "keep up the good work" so as to "let their light shine." By spurring others on to good works, to exercise the gifts God has given to them, and to continue to excel in the greatness you see in them will affirm they are on the right track—and

edify them. When people feel at their best, they perform at their best. Catching someone doing something right and then affirming them for it is one way leaders motivate people.

REFLECT TO CONNECT

1. Whom has God put on your heart to encourage and edify today?
2. What is your opinion on how the Apostle Paul motivates people to action and good works through encouragement and edification?
3. In what ways has God left clues in the Bible to show you how to be more effective in how you communicate with others?

People perform at their best when they feel their best—so encourage them.

THE SECRET TO SUCCESS
WEEK 36 | WEDNESDAY

But his delight is in the law of the LORD, And in His law he meditates day and night. He will be like a tree firmly planted by streams of water, Which yields its fruit in its season And its leaf does not wither; And in whatever he does, he prospers. Psalm 1:2-3

The Bible has a secret to success. The Psalmist above gives a clue to what creates success in these phrases: "His delight is in the law of the LORD," "He meditates day and night," and "Whatever he does, he prospers." This means that *WHATEVER* you put your hand to, it will prosper. How can God make this kind of blanket promise?

Whatever God puts His hand to becomes successful. As you put God first, all things are added unto you (Matthew 6:33). As you delight yourself in the Lord, He puts His desires in your heart. As you meditate on His Word, He makes plain to you what He is doing so you can join Him. Here's the catch: everything He does, He does through you. He doesn't work in your life without you. The secret to success is to think on what God is saying, to desire what He is desiring, and to do what God is doing. The goal isn't to get God interested in what we are doing, but to get involved in what He is doing through us.

Jesus said that He only did what He saw His Father doing (John 5:19). As you spend time with God, He paints His vision for His works upon the canvas of your heart. As you follow His plan, your way is made prosperous in whatever you put your hand to. Meditating on God's word "day and night" doesn't get God to do what we are doing but moves us into the stream of success by doing what He is doing. It is when you do this that you can say, "I only do what I see the Father doing."

REFLECT TO CONNECT

1. As you discern your inward desires, what is God talking to you about?
2. What thought keeps returning to you that God may want to discuss with you?
3. How can you differentiate your desire from God's desire?

Every success starts with a conversation;
what did God say to you last?

SUCCESS AND SIGNIFICANCE

WEEK 36 | THURSDAY

*"Do not store up for yourselves treasures on earth, where moth and rust
destroy, and where thieves break in and steal. But store up for yourselves
treasures in heaven, where neither moth nor rust destroys, and where
thieves do not break in or steal; for where your treasure is,
there your heart will be also.* Matthew 6:19-21

Theologian John Wesley once said, "I judge all things only by
the price they shall gain in eternity." It's so easy to get wrapped
up in the day-to-day grind of life and forget the long-term goal of
what one is working toward. Stress can strip away your joy, and the
demands of life can erase the eternal truth that we are only pioneers
in this life on a journey toward a heavenly home whose maker is
God. Jesus reminds us in Matthew 6:20 to stay focused on eternal
rewards by storing up treasure that will pay in the life to come, not
just in the life we live now.

Achieving success in the earthly realm is important, so don't ever
let anyone tell you differently or try to shame you for your success.
Achieving success is essential to your calling as it creates influence,
wealth, and other necessary resources for you to complete the purposes of God in your life. In fact, the more you make in the earthly
realm, the more you have to serve the heavenly realm. Success can
create money, but it can also pave a path toward significance when it
is stewarded for eternal purposes. Consider how both are important
on your journey. One is not better than the other—each serves an
important role in the different seasons of life.

SUCCESS	SIGNIFICANCE
• Destination focused	• Journey oriented
• Adds value to self	• Adds value to others
• Focused on building a life	• Focused on building a legacy
• Competitive with others	• Completes others
• Creates stepping stones	• Creates cornerstones
• Can leave a hole in the heart	• Can satisfy an ache in the soul

REFLECT TO CONNECT

1. How do you define the difference between success and significance?
2. Have people in the church tried to make you feel guilty for your success?
3. What high levels of success has God called you to achieve?

Success and significance are important;
don't let anyone shame you for wanting both.

FRESH OXYGEN

WEEK 36 | FRIDAY

*Therefore, do not throw away your confidence, which has a great
reward. For you have need of endurance, so that when you have done
the will of God, you may receive what was promised.* Hebrews 10:35-36

A t some point, everyone wants to quit. Weariness has a way
of wearing down our resilience and faith. It's easy to feel and

think right when we feel strong and everything is going well. But what about when things are otherwise? Do you have a strategy for making sure you stay the course and don't grow weary in doing good?

You need a strategy to strengthen yourself and others. Fatigued leaders are susceptible to making bad decisions. Endurance requires more than mental toughness; it requires strategy. There is a reason the flight attendant tells us to put the oxygen mask on ourselves first if the plane is experiencing trouble. If we don't have adequate oxygen, we risk passing out, and this limits our ability to help others. Getting fresh oxygen into your lungs is the first strategy step to staying strong when you are feeling weak. What is your strategy for staying strong throughout your day? Here are a few tactics for renewing and recharging on the run:

1. Read Scripture out loud. Faith is voice activated because "faith comes from hearing" (Romans 10:17). Daniel 10:19 says, "As soon as he spoke to me, I received strength."
2. Find a friend with a hearing ear and ask them to listen.
3. Create a playlist of inspirational music and listen repeatedly.
4. Combine activities you love: exercise, audiobooks, prayer walks, etc...
5. Retreat to a place of beauty and solitude like Jesus did and let God's wonder of creation energize you.
6. Cleanse your mental motor by documenting your self-talk on paper and submitting it to God. This is how you submit every thought and take it captive to the obedience of Christ (2 Corinthians 10:5). Many energy-draining negative self-talk tracks can be eliminated when they are exposed to God's Word.

REFLECT TO CONNECT

1. How do you recharge when life is hectic, and you can't slow down?
2. Have you ever wanted to give up but instead got strengthened to stay in the game?
3. Is there someone you can help to develop their own "refresh and recharge" strategy?

At the moment you want to give up but don't,
endurance is born.

PLAY CHESS WITH GOD

WEEK 37 | MONDAY

Are they not all ministering spirits, sent out to render service for the sake
of those who will inherit salvation? Hebrews 1:14

W ould it surprise you to know that God made the angels "a
little lower" than you and that their purpose is to serve you?
One day you will be astounded at the lengths God has gone to in
order to bring you into your designed purpose.

Just as you are responsible for people in your life, God assigns
angels to look after you. Providence is the hand of God moving
in your life, whether you recognize it or not. Consider that there
is earthly and heavenly assistance working on your behalf, often
behind the scenes, to bring about God's purposes in your life.

Still, when God plants a dream, a vision, or a purpose in your life,
He will often wait for you to act. Acting on what God has planted in
your heart is the evidence that you have heard Him. T.J. Malievsky,
VP for Crista Radio Group in Seattle, once described partnership
with God as a chess game: "He moves, then you move." Partnering
with God in the marketplace is a series of hearing, moving, and
sometimes waiting. Consider the following questions as a way of
recognizing divine assistance that has or can cross your path.

OPEN DOORS: What opportunities are open to you—could God be
opening up a new door for you?

CLOSED DOORS: What doors have been slammed shut, maybe sur-
prisingly? God sees around the corner in our lives and could be
sparing you a future regret.

NEW DESIRE: Has your desire recently changed? If your heart has
changed, it is often evidence God has moved it.

INWARD PULL: Who are you feeling pulled toward? If you are feeling drawn to a person, reach out and start a conversation. The next step in their journey or yours could be revealed in this conversation.

GOD'S HEART: Who are you feeling compassion toward? God's direction to act will flow through you so that you feel as God feels toward a person or situation.

VISION: Do you find yourself mentally roleplaying an act or conversation that is in agreement with the ways and Word of God? If so, just as Jesus could only do what He saw the Father doing, God may be moving you in the same way as you find yourself rehearsing a situation on the screen of your mind.

REFLECT TO CONNECT

1. What was the last divine interaction you experienced?
2. Have you ever experienced a missed opportunity that you knew was from God?
3. How do you know when God has moved or when it is now your turn to move?

Acting on God's purposes activates divine assistance
from all manner of sources to assist you
as you walk into His will.

HUMILITY IN THE MARKETPLACE

WEEK 37 | TUESDAY

*But to the king of Judah who sent you to inquire of the LORD thus
shall you say to him, "Thus says the LORD God of Israel, 'Regarding
the words which you have heard, because your heart was tender and
you humbled yourself before the LORD when you heard what I spoke
against this place and against its inhabitants that they should become a
desolation and a curse, and you have torn your clothes and wept before
Me, I truly have heard you,' declares the LORD."*

2 Kings 22:18-19

The story is told of a man who was once given an award for
being the humblest person in town. Once he accepted the
award, they took it away from him.

Humility gets God's attention. "Humble yourselves in the presence of the LORD, and He will exalt you," James 4:10 promises. Few
things get God's attention more than repentance and humility.
Genuine humility is the intentional lowering of oneself, while false
humility is an act of show. Humility is not only a bending of the knee
but of the heart. Jesus' greatest act of humility was an act of sacrifice
when He took the form of a servant and set aside His heavenly crown
to save mankind from their sins. While most think humility carries
a price, it also carries a reward when God lifts you up. Humility is
a posture of the heart to be practiced. Here are a few expressions of
humility:

- Not promoting yourself, but letting others and God honor you
  in due time.
- Volunteering to do work that is below your station in life.
- Showing kindness to someone who has treated you harshly.
- Taking the high road when wronged and trusting God to make
  it right.

- Choosing to honor those in authority when you don't agree with them.
- Giving up your rights when you have earned the right to demand better.
- Bowing your heart when your head tells you that you don't have to.
- Accepting a lower position when God asks you to serve a purpose above a paycheck.
- The willingness to ask for help, seek repentance, and acknowledge you can't do it alone.
- Admitting when you are wrong to a customer, employee, coworker, supervisor, or family member when you don't have to.

REFLECT TO CONNECT

1. What expression of humility is God whispering in your heart today?
2. Is there an area that God is patiently waiting for you to submit to Him?
3. In what ways are you prideful and struggling to be humble in?

Humility submits to someone or something other than your ego.

———————◆———————

THE HOLY SPIRIT IN THE OFFICE

I will ask the Father, and He will give you another Helper, that He may be with you forever; that is the Spirit of truth, whom the world cannot receive, because it does not see Him or know Him, but you know Him because He abides with you and will be in you. John 14:16-17

Jesus calls you "family," with all the rights of family. Some of these "rights" include God being "with you" in all you do. Here are a few ways God is with you in all that you do:

The Companion: The Holy Spirit is *always* by your side. By remembering Him, acknowledging Him, and talking with Him throughout your day, you will experience unbroken companionship with the One who knows all things. Imagine having God by your side every minute of every day to help you.

The Comforter: The Holy Spirit will always improve how you feel in a given situation. He will not leave you comfortless, but instead, when facing challenges, stress, and what appear to be unsolvable problems, He is there to comfort you with peace and confidence.

The Convicter: When you get off track, the Holy Spirit nudges you to course correct. If you ignore Him and reject His voice of counsel, He won't abandon you. Instead, He will find new ways (circumstances) to reach you rather than leave you on a path where your outcome is to suffer injury. It's not uncommon when decision-making that you will get a "check" in your spirit to rethink your choice if it is wrong. That is God's way of warning you.

The Holy Spirit will be your co-laborer in all that you do to the degree that you include Him in your doing. You will not have a better ally in your day-to-day dealings. Using your work as the backdrop for His working, the more you bring Him into your daily dealings with people and projects, the more He will reveal His ways to you. But He doesn't "butt in"; He waits to be invited in. He is a gentleman awaiting your invitation to join you at work. Won't you ask Him today?

REFLECT TO CONNECT

1. In what ways do you lean on God?
2. Is it okay to ask God for help in all your dealings?
3. Why do some people think God doesn't care about their work life?

The more you include God in your work life,
the more He works on your behalf while you work.

———————————◆———————————

PRAYERS IN UNEXPECTED PACKAGES

WEEK 37 | THURSDAY

Isaac prayed to the LORD on behalf of his wife, because she was barren; and the Lord answered him and Rebekah his wife conceived. But the children struggled together within her; and she said, "If it is so, why then am I this way?" So she went to inquire of the Lord. The LORD said to her, "Two nations are in your womb; And two peoples will be separated from your body; And one people shall be stronger than the other; And the older shall serve the younger."
Genesis 25:21-23

R ebekah is not unlike many of us. She had a desire, talked to those close to her about it (her husband), and no doubt, she prayed along with Isaac that God would answer her prayer. However, when God answered her prayer, His answer did not come to her in the way she expected.

Answers to prayer come in unexpected wrappers. Many of us ask God for something but often miss it if it does not show up in the way we expect. In Rebekah's case, she struggled physically while the answer was being birthed in her. For a successful saint, praying for more business or more success can result in more work; is that what you want? More customers turn into more revenue but also more challenges. With responsibility comes great challenge. Keeping the following in mind will ensure you remain strong through the struggle:

- When God leads you, He also stretches you. That's growth.
- Where there is struggle, perseverance is required. That's stamina.
- When there is no explanation, that is the time to trust. That's faith.

Where God guides you, He will grow you. Keep walking with Him and stay in faith through the seasons of answered prayer, which include seed, time, and harvest. If you're no longer waiting or walking in faith, God is likely waiting on you so He can begin again to work in you.

REFLECT TO CONNECT

1. Is there an answer to prayer you've received that didn't deliver the result you expected?
2. In what way have you relied on God but maybe regretted getting what you asked for?
3. Is there an answered prayer that showed up differently than expected?

If you trust God's answer to prayer more than your request,
then you know He gives you sometimes what you need
over what you want.

———◆———

WINDFALLS OF WEALTH
FROM OBEDIENCE

WEEK 37 | FRIDAY

The LORD appeared to him and said, "Do not go down to Egypt; stay in
the land of which I shall tell you..." Now Isaac sowed in that land and
reaped in the same year a hundredfold. And the Lord blessed him, and
the man became rich, and continued to grow richer until he became
very wealthy; for he had possessions of flocks and herds and a great
household, so that the Philistines envied him. Genesis 26:2, 12-14

Do you know God's instruction to you in this season of your
life? Everyone is assigned to a purpose and a place when God
calls. In Isaac's case, God told him not to depart from where he was
and, as a result, blessed the work of his hands. Isaac's planting that
year reaped a hundredfold return.

Do you follow or find excuses not to obey? It's easy for some
to believe that God is spiritual but not practical. God isn't only in
the business of saving souls but also in the business of blessing.
He knows how to "butter" a saint's bread as they stay in step with
Him. God knows your needs, desires, pursuits, and passions before
you ask Him, for He is in you and always working through you to
provide for you.

REFLECT TO CONNECT

1. To what purpose, place, and group of people has God called you to?
2. What is the evidence that a person is walking in the will of God?
3. Is there a course correction you need to make to ensure you are walking in lockstep with God?

God isn't only in the business of saving souls
but also in the business of blessing.

COMPROMISING CONVERSATIONS

Therefore let him who thinks he stands take heed that he does not fall. No temptation has overtaken you but such as is common to man; and God is faithful, who will not allow you to be tempted beyond what you are able, but with the temptation will provide the way of escape also, so that you will be able to endure it. 1 Corinthians 10:12-13

If you grew up in a church, you have learned about temptation. However, in the marketplace, a saint is *not* surrounded by God-fearing people who have been redeemed. Over time, even the strongest of consciences can be worn down if not kept strengthened and separated from sinful behavior.

Saints spend their day as witnesses in an unredeemed world but also in the midst of souls the Savior hopes to save. It is one thing to identify with those that one hopes to witness to, but entirely another to cross a line of behavior that disqualifies a saint from proclaiming the message of salvation. What are some of the behaviors a saint may encounter in the marketplace they may need to excuse themselves from? Ungodly behavior can include everything from gossip at the water cooler to negative talk to a vulgar and coarse conversation. In what ways can you influence a conversation prior to needing to correct it or exit as a way of escaping ungodly behavior?

1. **Pros and Cons:** Remind those present of consequences if the suggested course of action is followed.
2. **Outcomes Wanted:** Suggesting a productive dialogue that leads those in attendance to a more productive conversation.
3. **Stand up for What is Right:** When all else fails, take a stand against the suggested course of action or direction of the conversation.

4. **Flee Before Faith Fails:** When reason fails, excusing oneself from the company of those who have their course set against what is unacceptable in the sight of the Lord saves pain.

Most saints, at one point, will face a choice to stand up for what is right or remove themselves from a situation that goes against their conscience. If you fail to turn the tide of conversation or the course of behavior, look for the door of exit which God promises He will provide and get out of there. If you can't be successful in steering people away from sin, then successfully remove yourself from the environment that will stain you from sin.

REFLECT TO CONNECT

1. What compromising situations in the marketplace have you faced before?
2. What strategies do you have that turn the tide of momentum away from sinful behavior or conversation?
3. What advice would you give to someone facing a situation of compromise for the first time?

When facing sin, flee. For all other things,
stand and fight.

———————————◆————————————

THE PRACTICE OF
OPEN-MINDEDNESS
WEEK 38 | TUESDAY

"But no one puts a patch of unshrunk cloth on an old garment;
for the patch pulls away from the garment, and a worse tear results.
Nor do people put new wine into old wineskins; otherwise the wineskins
burst, and the wine pours out and the wineskins are ruined; but
they put new wine into fresh wineskins, and both are preserved."
Matthew 9:16-17

Getting people to think in new ways is difficult, even for God. If you try to put a round peg into a square hole, it won't fit. Throughout the Gospels, Jesus was challenged in breaking through old mindsets so people could understand the kingdom He was inviting them into. The difficulty of getting people to change their thinking persists today in the marketplace and in ministry. At one point, even Peter and Paul had an argument to determine if new believers should be forced to follow Old Testament traditions. Everyone tends to bring the past into the present, yet the two may not be compatible. Imagine if you took a new job but kept showing up to your old job, or if you brought old unhealthy habits into new relationships? The old would sabotage the new. It's easy to get stuck in the old mindset, difficult to renew and transform.

If you are not open-minded, you may miss the new mentality God wants to birth in you. At some point, each person gets complacent or stuck in their ways. If you have been born again, your soul was saved, but your mind was not; it requires renewal and transformation. One of the hardest things to do is to change one's mindset, especially if the old mindset is something you held sacred or have found success with. New customers, supervisors, coworkers, and market cycles are all part of life in the marketplace. To guarantee that the bend in the road is not an end in the road for you, here are a few ways in which you can identify a closed vs. open mindset. One God can work in; the other He has to wrestle with.

CLOSED-MINDED PEOPLE	OPEN-MINDED PEOPLE
• Want to be understood	• Want to understand others
• Resist change not their own	• Embrace change that benefits others
• Quick to assume	• Quick to ask questions
• Need to be seen as right	• Want to see what others see
• Stuck on one way of doing things	• Know there is more than one way
• Don't know they are closed-minded	• Work hard to stay open-minded
• Make statements of facts	• Ask questions of curiosity
• Know it all	• Know there is more to learn

REFLECT TO CONNECT

1. Is there anything in your life you are causing God to have to wrestle with you about?
2. What are you wrestling with this year that you were wrestling with last year?
3. Do you think you are flexible or difficult to work with from God's perspective?

What created past success may be what sabotages future success if you don't adapt to a shifting marketplace.

———————◆◆◆———————

THE INHERITANCE

WEEK 38 | WEDNESDAY

*That the communication of thy faith may become effectual by the
acknowledging of every good thing which is in you in Christ Jesus.*
Philemon 1:6 (KJV)

I magine if, at the time of getting a high-paying job, you told
the HR director that you only wanted the salary but were turning
down all the other benefits like stock options, medical, 401k, and
profit-sharing. Many Christians receive salvation when they accept
Christ yet leave everything else behind. Once in God's family, you
receive an inheritance, and you are fully vested on day one.

**Faith is the bridge by which we receive what has been given to
us by grace.** To realize and receive all that has been gifted to us at the
moment of salvation, the Apostle Paul tells us to INVENTORY all of
God's benefits and give thanks for them. Learning how to appropriate "by faith" what has been gifted to you in the Spirit is the exciting
journey God wants to take you on. These benefits are now active reali-
ties that exist within your born-again spirit yet must be *appropriated*
in the natural man. There are gifts, built-in blessings, and promises
from God to you in the Bible which were given to you on the day of
your adoption as a son or daughter of God. How do you appropriate
them? By first having knowledge, then by acknowledging God for
what He has already given. Here are a few things that were reserved
for you from the foundation of the world and given to you in Christ:

YOUR GOSPEL BENEFITS PACKAGE GRANTED
TO YOU AT SALVATION

1. **Chosen Vessel:** As God's child, you are the direct recipient
   of His acceptance and love for you—He made you to live

with Him for eternity, and nothing can separate you from His love.

2. **Endless Wisdom:** You have the mind of Christ—the promise that if you ask Him for wisdom without doubting, He will grant it to you.

3. **Oval Office Privileges:** Direct access has been given to you to enter God's presence and make your requests as you walk boldly into the throne room of grace.

4. **Family:** You have been adopted and are now part of God's family; you have instant fellowship with Him and other believers.

5. **Divine Healing:** By Jesus' stripes you were healed; receive your healing from head to toe.

6. **Fruits of the Spirit:** Right now, your spirit man possesses love, joy, peace, patience, kindness, goodness, faithfulness, gentleness, and self-control, so focus on drawing these out.

7. **Purpose:** God has a plan for your life that is beyond anything you can imagine.

8. **Wealth:** You are promised a multiplied return in this life and the next on anything you give to God's work.

9. **Clean Slate:** All your past, present, and future sins have been forgiven. He washes away your guilt and sin to give you a clean conscience. God is not mad at you; He wants relationship with you.

10. **Identity:** As Jesus was, so are you in this world—Jesus now lives inside of you. The same faith of Jesus is your faith, the same power that raised Christ from the dead now lives in you (Romans 8:11).

11. **Constant Companionship:** God has given you the Holy Spirit, and He has made His abode within you. God will never leave you because His Spirit lives in you. He cannot deny himself.

12. **Victory:** In all things, God has made you an overcomer by giving you a spirit filled with power, love, and self-control. You have the power to defeat sinful desires, stomp out enemy attacks, and overcome any obstacle that would stand in the way of you achieving your God-given destiny. No weapon formed against you can stand.

You can't appropriate what you don't know you have. Continue to inventory everything God has given to you as you read the Bible. As you read, pay close attention to what God highlights in your heart—this is what He is making alive to you. This is signaling the conversation He wants to have with you.

REFLECT TO CONNECT

1. How will your prayer life change now that you know God has already provided everything you need?
2. If you don't "feel" like you've received it, does it mean God has not given it?
3. As you inventory your inheritance given to you by God, how is He leading you to pray?

To activate your inheritance, you must inventory all God has given to you so you can appropriate by faith what grace has gifted.

TIPS FOR YOUR A.S.K.

WEEK 38 | THURSDAY

Jesus said to them, "Suppose you have a friend, and you go to him at midnight and say, 'Friend, lend me three loaves of bread; a friend of mine on a journey has come to me, and I have no food to offer him.' And suppose the one inside answers, 'Don't bother me. The door is already locked, and my children and I are in bed. I can't get up and give you anything.' I tell you, even though he will not get up and give you the bread because of friendship, yet because of your shameless audacity he will surely get up and give you as much as you need." Luke 11:5-8

G od wants you to build your perseverance muscle. There is something about perseverance that attracts the heart of God. In fact, He promises that when you seek Him with all your heart, you shall find Him. (Jeremiah 29:13) Although God loves our pursuit of Him, He also loves to be apprehended by you. He knows what you need before you ask Him because the kingdom of Heaven is within. Jesus provides a simple yet effective way to receive from God. Here is Jesus' simple formula for how to persevere in prayer.

ASK, and it will be given to you. (Tip: Believe you will receive when you pray.)

SEEK, and you will find. (Tip: If the answer isn't obvious, keep seeking, and God will show it to you.)

KNOCK, and it will be opened to you. (Tip: Your answer may manifest in multiple places; remember, prayer comes in unexpected wrappers.)

Jesus promises that everyone who asks, receives; and they who seek, find; and to them who knock, it will be opened. From the moment you begin to ask, seek, and knock, the answer is on the way. God's goodness and love for you is astonishing and almost incomprehensible. He even shows kindness to the unthankful, the evil, and the undeserving. How much more will He answer your prayer when you seek Him according to His will?

REFLECT TO CONNECT

1. What are you seeking God for this week?
2. As you ask, seek, and knock, what insights are you gleaning?
3. What instruction is God giving you as you push on the doors already open to you?

Believe and receive or doubt and go without.

———————————◆◆◆———————————

FAVOR REVEALED

WEEK 38 | FRIDAY

So Joseph found favor in his sight and became his personal servant; and he made him overseer over his house, and all that he owned he put in his charge. It came about that from the time he made him overseer in his house and over all that he owned, the LORD blessed the Egyptian's house on account of Joseph; thus the LORD'S blessing was upon all that he owned, in the house and in the field. Genesis 39:4-5

Favor isn't magic; it's mission-oriented. There are ways in which God orchestrates His work of favor in your life. Here are a few moves God may orchestrate on your behalf when He is creating favor for you. Be sure you do not interrupt or interfere with God in His process, lest you sabotage Him and yourself. You have a role to play in cooperating with His ways of creating favor in your life.

SEVEN CHARACTERISTICS OF FAVOR

1. God causes those in authority to think kindly toward you. This is how God opens doors for you.
2. God prospers the work of your hands, so those in authority over you benefit and, as a result, delegate more responsibility to you, and your influence grows.
3. God creates a public display where your skills are shown to create success, and your influence multiplies.
4. You have an uncommon and unexplainable level of success so that others can see that God is with you.
5. God gives you insight into situations so you can see before others see and perceive more than others perceive. God's INTUITION flows through you.
6. God gives you eloquent words of grace to communicate wisdom and give understanding to those around you and above you.
7. God arranges for you to solve problems no one else can, and word about you spreads. God gives you a reputation for being a problem solver.

Psalm 1:1-3 shows how you can initiate a flow of favor in your life by meditating on God's Word day and night. What is it in His Word that creates favor and prosperity? It's simple. By becoming intimate with His voice, He instructs us day and night as to what we should do and what we should say. As "Christ in you" directs you, you will find favor with those you encounter and success in "whatever you put your hands to," and that's a promise from God.

REFLECT TO CONNECT

1. Who do you know of that has the "Midas touch"?
2. What can you do to cooperate with God's plans to lavish favor upon your life?
3. In what ways could someone make it difficult for God to create favor for them?

God grants favor and success to those who follow
His instructions day and night.

A STUDY OF THOSE IN CHARGE

WEEK 39 | MONDAY

Now therefore, I pray You, if I have found favor in Your sight,
let me know Your ways that I may know You,
so that I may find favor in Your sight.
Exodus 33:13

Moses had been in relationship with God for some time when it dawned on him that the secret to pleasing God would be to learn how He works. Every relationship has nuances to it, and Moses asked God to reveal "His way" to him so that he could adjust himself and adapt to what God likes. In this way, he could avoid the pitfalls of disappointing God and intentionally focus on what creates favor in the relationship. Moses also wanted to express his love through appreciation and obedience.

Adapting yourself to a person and environment is key to success. Imagine yourself single and dating. You are falling in love but not sure what the other person likes. What do you do? You turn your intellectual and emotional receiver on and begin to study the other person to observe what they like and do not like. By learning what pleases them and what irritates them, you adjust your behavior appropriately to garner the response you seek.

Becoming a student of human nature will give you insight into behavior while becoming a student of an individual will reveal a path to earning their favor. Adaptability is the secret to creating successful relationships at will. Following Moses's approach will give you favor with God and man.

REFLECT TO CONNECT

1. Can you describe in detail what the most important people in your life value?
2. What insight do you have of those who have authority over you?
3. How does increasing deposits into the relationship bank account create favor for you?

Adaptability is the secret to creating successful relationships at will.

————————◆————————

ARCHITECTURAL PLANS

WEEK 39 | TUESDAY

"Now Bezalel and Oholiab, and every skillful person in whom the LORD has put skill and understanding to know how to perform all the work in the construction of the sanctuary, shall perform in accordance with all that the LORD has commanded."
Then Moses called Bezalel and Oholiab and every skillful person in whom the LORD had put skill, everyone whose heart stirred him, to come to the work to perform it. They received from Moses all the contributions which the sons of Israel had brought to perform the work in the construction of the sanctuary. And they still continued bringing to him freewill offerings every morning.
Exodus 36:1-3

God is a builder. He has ordained each person to build a life on Earth whereby He is the architect, and we are the builder. Architects create drawings that are a map to articulate every detail necessary for a builder to follow. In the same way, God has your architectural plan written in His book. Do you study His plan for you? Ask Him today what "next" He would like to build into your life. Here are a few ways in which He works when building.

- **God stirs** the heart for what He's gifted you to do. He will put His desire in you, and this desire will act as a magnet to draw you to your purpose, place, career, and more.
- **God puts** a "learn-ed heart" with skill and understanding for the works He calls you to so you are quick to learn in the lane He is drawing you to.
- **God brings** other people alongside you to partner with you, so their strengths bring strength to you and vice versa.
- **God provides** in abundance for every work He has ordained for you. In the case of building the tabernacle, the provision came in daily and over time but was never late.

REFLECT TO CONNECT

1. What is God building in your life during this season?
2. Whom has He brought alongside you to assist in your areas of weakness?
3. Whom is God asking you to help in the building of what God has called them to?

Without the Architect and His blueprint for your life, how can you know what you are to build?

SEASONAL MENTORS

*Moses' father-in-law said to him, "The thing that you are doing is
not good. You will surely wear out, both yourself and these people
who are with you, for the task is too heavy for you; you cannot do it
alone. Now listen to me: I will give you counsel, and God be with you."*
Exodus 18:17-19

Moses's father-in-law (Jethro) was visiting him while hundreds were lined up to see him. Observing how fatiguing this was on Moses, Jethro suggested Moses delegate some of the responsibility of judging the people to others. Moses followed the advice, and it set him free to focus on other priorities for God. Jethro was a seasonal mentor for Moses. In today's technologically advanced world, you can follow someone on YouTube, on a podcast, or in books. In fact, the bookstore is packed with thousands of mentors you can learn from. Nothing can stop you except an unwillingness to grow.

Whom are you following that has a mentoring impact on your life? When God wants to advance you, He will assign you to a mentor. There are two ways to learn: through mentorship and mistakes. Mentorship was designed by God so you can be taught, raised up, and improve. Mentorship allows you to stand on the shoulders of life and avoid the mistakes of people who went before you while learning best practices. You will require mentoring in many areas of life, which is why one mentor is not enough. Here are a few principles of mentorship:

- God will often put you under the authority of someone you may not like. God will use those in authority to test and transform you—if you let Him. Discomfort is the sandpaper God uses to smooth out your rough edges.

- To be able to mine the greatness from your mentor, you must have a student mindset and be able to learn from success, failure, what has been done right, and what has been done wrong.
- Your ticket from your present to your future is often a person. When you learn to thrive under mentorship, those with influence and authority speak well of you, and your reputation as a "learner" will spread.
- Mentorship is often for a season, then your mentor will change. Some can become a mentor to you in one area of life, while others mentor you in another area. It is important that you show appreciation for those who invest in you, and you, in turn, invest in others. Mentorship is God's system for advancement.

REFLECT TO CONNECT

1. Whom has God placed in your life that you should be learning from?
2. Whom has God called you to invest in?
3. What right and wrong ways of doing things can you articulate from observing your mentor?

When God wants to promote you,
He will assign a mentor for you to serve and submit to,
often in the form of a supervisor.

———————————◆———————————

DISCOVER YOUR PURPOSE
IN GOD'S PLAN

Then Joseph said to his brothers, "Please come closer to me." And they
came closer. And he said, "I am your brother Joseph, whom you sold
into Egypt. Now do not be grieved or angry with yourselves, because you
sold me here, for God sent me before you to preserve life ... God sent me
before you to preserve for you a remnant in the earth, and to keep you
alive by a great deliverance. Now, therefore, it was not you who sent me
here, but God; and He has made me a father to Pharaoh and lord of all
his household and ruler over all the land of Egypt." Genesis 45:4-5, 7-8

Is all suffering God's will? When we find meaning in suffering,
that is what makes it bearable. Joseph, in his suffering, not only
found meaning but also discovered God's purposes. In revealing God's
purposes on the day he met his brothers in Egypt, he saw *his* part of
God's plan but not *all* parts of God's plan. God's master plan would
include a season of suffering, sacrifice, and ultimately, a Savior who
would reconcile a world to Himself. God only reveals a piece of His
purpose to you for the season you are in, often hiding what is to come.
Even Jesus has not been told the day He will return to the earth.

Everything that happens is NOT God's will, but that doesn't
mean that He won't weave it into conformity to His overall plan.
Everything that happens is not necessarily ordered or approved by
God. The meaning behind the phrase "everything happens for a reason" suggests that if something happened, it was "meant to be." This
thinking suggests that God wanted it to happen. As God has delegated authority and responsibility to the Son, He has also delegated
authority and responsibility to each person. What might your role
and responsibility be in working with God to fulfill His purposes in
your life? Here are some statements you can recite in the first person:

- I must determine what God's role and my responsibility are and not wait for God to do what He has empowered me to do.
- I must submit to God's purposes even in seasons of suffering, knowing that He will work all things together for good (Romans 8:28) and understanding I see only in part.
- I must "stay in faith" and trust God even when I don't understand why something has happened or why someone has done what they've done, as was in the case of Joseph's brothers. My trust must remain in God, not in other people's behavior toward me.

REFLECT TO CONNECT

1. How does God want to use what I am going through in this season of life?
2. What purposes might be hidden from me that could unfold over time?
3. Whom can I share my journey with so as to get another perspective on what God may be doing that I am missing?

You will see what God wants you to see but not everything He sees.

THE STOPLIGHT INSIDE

WEEK 39 | FRIDAY

And they drew lots for them, and the lot fell to Matthias;
and he was added to the eleven apostles.
Acts 1:26

W hat should I do, God? Just prior to the Holy Spirit arriving on Pentecost, the apostles "cast lots" between two disciples to see who would replace Judas. After the Holy Spirit filled the believers on Pentecost, God was in them and communicated directly to them, yet this did not guarantee that hearing God's leading would not require praying through a matter. Here are a few ways in which God speaks today.

THE BIBLE: More than any other means, His Word and direction can be found in Scripture. As He has breathed on the writers of Scripture, He also breathes on the *reader*. As you read with an open heart, it is as if you are looking through a two-way mirror. It's the only book by which the Author must be present as you read if you are to hear a word for your life that day. Do you have a daily Bible reading plan whereby you have a scheduled appointment with God each day to read and pray?

OPPORTUNE MOMENTS: God will speak in context with what is happening "today" in your life. He will guide you at times with an open door, a closed door, or a "Kairos moment" (an opportune time when you "know in your knower" that He has spoken through circumstance, and it's time to move). If you delay when you should move, you could miss the timing of God. What Kairos moment is before you today?

FREQUENCY: In advertising, it's often necessary to reach a consumer multiple times for the message to get through. If I start to get the same message from multiple sources, I know God is trying to get my attention. If I get three hits on the same message in a short period of time, I know it's time to stop, drop, and pray through the message until I can discern what God is trying to say to me. What message keeps repeating in your life?

THE HEART: God lives in you, and although He will speak to you through people at times, His preferred means of communing with you will always be in your heart, where you first met. In you is where faith lives and where miracles are birthed. God speaks from the inside out, and this is where you'll always find Him. As He knows your every thought, you may sense Him connecting dots on events, stringing together memories, or you may catch yourself meditating on something by reviewing it in your mind over and over again. When you notice this, it's a clue to a conversation He wants to have with you. In what way has God connected the dots for you?

A HOLY UNCTION: Psalm 37:4 says that God will give you the desires of your heart. There will be times you sense His prompting to call someone or do something; take action on what He leads you on. Following invisible instructions carry rewards.

PEACE: We are told to let the peace of Christ rule in our hearts (Colossians 3:15). Peace is like a chief umpire. If you have it and your contemplated course of action does not conflict with the Bible, then it is likely you have a green light to move forward. However, if you are feeling a check in your spirit and have a red or yellow (caution) light going off, know that anxiety is the opposite of peace. God is guiding you to wait or stop and not move forward.

REFLECT TO CONNECT

1. What decision are you contemplating this week in your life?
2. Are you in the habit of taking work, family, and relationship issues to God to seek His counsel?
3. Can you think back to a time when you heard God right or heard Him wrong? What was the outcome, and what did you learn?

God speaks through the context and circumstance of your life by connecting dots you understand so you get the message.

THE POWER OF FOCUS

*Therefore, it is my judgment that we do not trouble those who are
turning to God from among the Gentiles, but that we write to them that
they abstain from things contaminated by idols and from fornication
and from what is strangled and from blood.*
Acts 15:19-20

There was an opportune meeting that arose whereby the apostles would agree which part of the law the Gentiles would be required to follow. Imagine them considering 613 ordinances from the old covenant and then only giving new believers three things they should focus on. Why is this significant? Because the apostles did not want to tie a yoke around the neck of new believers for things that were no longer important. In the context of issues the new believers were facing, they communicated only three priorities of behavior.

Leave God white space to paint His priorities on the screen of your imagination. The easiest way for the enemy to get you off track is to get you focused on doing more than you can handle. "If you chase two rabbits, both will get away," goes an old saying. Unbroken focus and the ability to concentrate over long periods of time are the hallmarks of all great achievers. As you enter each day, consider choosing three priorities and no more for that day's tasking. You will always have more than three things that are important but limit yourself to focusing on three you can accomplish and finish for the day. By focusing on three priorities each day, your efforts will compound over time to achieve great results.

"If you have more than three priorities, you don't have any at all."
Jim Collins, from his best-selling book *Good to Great*

1. What three tasks will require most of your bandwidth today?
2. When can you set aside five minutes each day to plan and prioritize your day?
3. How would focusing on too many priorities impact a person day after day?

Broken focus is the number one enemy of progress.

MESSENGERS WITH A MESSAGE

WEEK 40 | TUESDAY

So then those who were scattered because of the persecution that occurred in connection with Stephen made their way to Phoenicia and Cyprus and Antioch, speaking the word to no one except to Jews alone.
Acts 11:19

God's perspective sees a future you are blind to. One door closes, and another opens. Stephen's death was horrific. Those who witnessed a man being stoned to death must have been afraid and wanted to run. While this may seem like the end of the story, God was only just beginning. In his book *The Circle Maker*, best-selling author Mark Batterson says, "Don't put a period where God leaves a comma."

Those who were scattered were scattered due to persecution, but now, they were armed with a message that was branded on their hearts. God made them messengers as they carried a message of hope, forgiveness, and restoration of relationship with God. And

God made them an eyewitness to a horrible death that would carry such force that its credibility could not be denied. What have you walked through in your life that God may want to use? What horrible event in your life made you a "messenger with a message" as you traveled from one season to the next? Your dirt often becomes another person's soil.

The bend in the road is not the end of the road unless you're traveling without God. The next time your world is shaken, consider how God may want to use it to advance you, someone else, and His purposes all at the same time. Every event, whether good or bad, whether filled with success or failure, can be used by God when we bring it to Him. You may have just been diagnosed with a disease, lost a loved one, or been terminated from employment. Take it to God and see how He wants to turn something bad into something useful. Your dirt, when brought to God, can be repurposed into soil for someone else.

REFLECT TO CONNECT

1. What doors has God closed in your life that led to a better opportunity?
2. What is the message burning inside your heart?
3. What story is locked away inside of you that needs to be told?

God can work a miracle by turning the dirt from your life into someone else's soil—if you let him.

———————————— ◆ ————————————

THE NEW KID ON THE BLOCK

WEEK 40 | WEDNESDAY

*When he came to Jerusalem, he was trying to associate with the
disciples; but they were all afraid of him, not believing that he was a
disciple. But Barnabas took hold of him and brought him to the apostles
and described to them how he had seen the Lord on the road, and that
He had talked to him, and how at Damascus he had spoken out boldly
in the name of Jesus. Acts 9:26-27*

W ho has vouched for you? To be accepted into an inner
circle, someone has to vouch for you so that you can be let
in. Someone speaking favorably on your behalf is *the art of extending influence.* When someone puts their arm around you, they are,
in fact, saying, "If you trust me, you can trust them." It's powerful
when someone is willing to stand up for you. In the case of Paul the
Apostle, early after his conversion, the other apostles were hesitant
to trust him until Barnabas spoke on Paul's behalf. In so doing, he
extended his trust, influence, and stamp of approval over Paul so he
would be let into the group.

They are one of us. When a person is new to an organization, it
can be difficult to make friends, prove oneself, learn a new culture,
and win the approval and favor of people vertical and horizontal to
us. We have all been the new kid on the block before. By speaking
well of a "newbie," you not only elevate them in the eyes of another,
you also empower them when word gets back to them about what
you said. It's counterintuitive, but the more influence you extend to
others, the more yours will increase. Here are a few things to look
for when intentionally talking nicely behind another person's back.

CONTRIBUTION: Catch 'em doing something right and spread a
positive rumor about them.

CHARACTER: Look for something in their overall makeup that you admire, then brag about it.

SUCCESS: Observe them doing something well, then point it out to them and others.

POTENTIAL: Identify an underdeveloped gift and tell others what you see; then, it will one day flourish.

EMPOWERING: When they do or say something that makes another feel good, talk about it openly.

REFLECT TO CONNECT

1. Who has extended their influence as a covering over you in a way that communicated, "They are with me"?
2. Is there someone you can extend your influence to?
3. What positive qualities have you observed in someone you can speak about?

Extending influence to another is like a boomerang;
the faster you release it, the faster it returns to you...
and with increased velocity.

———————————◆———————————

ANOINTED FOR THE ASSIGNMENT
WEEK 40 | THURSDAY

And with great power the apostles were giving testimony to the
resurrection of the Lord Jesus, and abundant grace was upon them all.
Acts 4:33

You are anointed to serve God in a specific area. In the example of the apostles, Peter and John spoke with an unusual confidence and boldness. Stephen spoke with a wisdom the leaders of the day could not resist. The sick who were brought to Peter were healed, and Phillip supernaturally ran up alongside a chariot to witness to a man who would become an ambassador for the Gospel to Ethiopia. What area of service has God chosen to anoint in you?

Where is the power in your life? Is there a lane of service you excel in? What are you doing when you lose track of time (timelessness), experience uncommon success (anointing), are recognized for your work (acknowledgment), are asked for advice (counselor), have a desire to grow in (learning heart), and you feel God's pleasure while doing it? These are all clues to where you will find God's power and anointing at work in your life to bring success to you and His purposes.

God is building a testimony of your story. Your assignment in the marketplace carries the same significance to God as your assignment in ministry. Through the supply of the Spirit, you have access to the same power that gave Peter boldness to speak, Phillip to run, and Stephen to testify. That power can manifest in wisdom as Stephen had, problem-solving power as Joseph had, or courage that Joshua walked with. There is no end to God's creativity, wisdom, or ability to walk you through what you are going through. What do you need to ask God to provide through the supply of the Spirit in your life today for you to be effective in your calling? Lean on Him and let Him lead you.

REFLECT TO CONNECT

1. What is the work of the Holy Spirit in the work environment?
2. In what ways have you seen God show up through your talents and gifts?

3. Do you believe God is as concerned with your witness at work as He is with a message being preached at church from the pulpit?

The supply of the Spirit shows up when you find your lane—it's what allows you to live in the "second wind."

FIVE ATTITUDES FOR SUCCESS OR SABOTAGE

WEEK 40 | FRIDAY

"Why did we ever leave Egypt?"
Numbers 11:20

Longing for the past sabotages the future. Our self-talk creates our attitude. It seems to be a reoccurring cycle. Whenever times would get tough, the children of Israel would revert back to looking on the "good old days" of what they had. When we face difficulty in the present, human nature is to romanticize the past in a way that falsely remembers it as being better than it was. This erroneous picture of the past creates a longing for "former days" while sabotaging the future by complaining about the present. Complaining burdened Moses's (leadership) and angered God. Attitudes are infectious, whether good or bad. The past can tutor or torture you unless you have a God perspective on where you've been and where He is leading you.

Five Perspectives that Shape Attitude

Poor Perspective on Past	Healthy Perspective for the Present
• Longing for what is behind	• Looking toward what is ahead
• Romanticizing the past	• Making the most of the present
• Lessons forgotten	• Lessons learned and leveraged
• Looking at what you don't have	• Thanking God for what you do have
• Complaining about circumstances	• Seeing circumstances biblically

Hope in times of uncertainty is the sure anchor of the soul we hang onto. Navigating difficulty doesn't only build godly character; it reveals cracks in our character. Hope and a healthy perspective delight the heart of the Lord, while murmuring along the road to progress upsets Him. Seeing our situation through God's eyes guarantees we will live forward, not backward, and not long for the "Egypts" of our past.

REFLECT TO CONNECT

1. When was the last time you had to self-correct your attitude?
2. How does God see your situation through His eyes?
3. Whom do you admire that always seems to see the "sunny side of things"?

Like nails on a chalkboard is a bad attitude in God's ears.
The past can tutor or torture you unless you have God's
perspective on where you've been and where
He is leading you.

GRASSHOPPER MENTALITY

WEEK 41 | MONDAY

So they gave out to the sons of Israel a bad report of the land which they had spied out, saying, "The land through which we have gone, in spying it out, is a land that devours its inhabitants; and all the people whom we saw in it are men of great size. There also we saw the Nephilim (the sons of Anak are part of the Nephilim); and we became like grasshoppers in our own sight, and so we were in their sight."
Numbers 13:32-33

F.E.A.R. can stand for "Face Everything and Rise" or "Forget Everything and Run." For every obstacle a leader faces, God has a solution. No matter how tall the barrier or how steep the climb, if God has called you to it, He will see you through it. God has a plan to help you to overcome even the most difficult obstacles. Unfortunately for the children of Israel, 10 spies persuaded the people that the circumstances they were facing were larger than the God they were following. Influence can be a powerful tool to help or hurt people, depending on where the leader leads. In this case, bad leadership led the children of Israel on a 40-year trek around the desert unnecessarily.

At some point, you must choose to believe what God said over what your circumstance is saying to you. A leader's perspective is critical to the group because others follow in their footsteps. If the leader is confident, the people will be, too. If the leader shrinks back, people are prone to take a "wait and see" attitude. At one time or another, everyone must self-correct back to seeing their circumstances through God's eyes and not their own, for it is God who sees beyond what we see.

REFLECT TO CONNECT

1. What obstacles have you faced that caused you to fall from faith and into fear?
2. Can you recall a time when you trusted what your eyes saw more than what God's Word promised?
3. How does one follow a supernatural God while walking through natural circumstances?

Don't let the circumstances you are facing become bigger than the God you are following.

NO "TALK STINK"

WEEK 41 | TUESDAY

Then Miriam and Aaron spoke against Moses because of the Cushite woman whom he had married (for he had married a Cushite woman); and they said, "Has the LORD indeed spoken only through Moses? Has He not spoken through us as well?" And the LORD heard it.
Numbers 12:1-2

The greater your influence, the higher your accountability. It is interesting that it wasn't Moses who heard Miriam and Aaron talking poorly about him; it was God. Why is it important for disgruntled leaders to watch their tongue? Because when people of influence speak, it has a ripple effect. In the case of Miriam and Aaron, God was quick to hold them accountable for even a hint of negativity toward His chosen leader. The greater your influence, the more weight your words are given by followers, so be careful.

Whom do you influence? For every leader, there is a steward-ship one must consider when weighing their words and actions. The standard Jesus spoke of isn't only what is spoken on the outside, but what is allowed to ruminate on the inside. Self-correction is a key sign of maturity for any leader. If you are feeling set aside or offended, bring your case to God before you speak about it to others. Seeking God on the inside first will prevent you from inappropriately speaking negatively about others on the outside.

REFLECT TO CONNECT

1. Have you ever caught yourself saying something you should not have about those in authority?
2. What is your reaction when you hear gossips speaking negatively about other people?
3. How can one positively impact a negative conversation?

If you "talk stink" about others, God isn't the only one who hears it.

STICK UP FOR GOD

WEEK 41 | WEDNESDAY

Then the LORD spoke to Moses, saying, "Phinehas the son of Eleazar, the son of Aaron the priest, has turned away My wrath from the sons of Israel in that he was jealous with My jealousy among them, so that I did not destroy the sons of Israel in My jealousy. Therefore say, 'Behold, I give him My covenant of peace; and it shall be for him and his descendants after him, a covenant of a perpetual priesthood, because

he was jealous for his God and made atonement for the sons of Israel.'"
Numbers 25:10-13

Has anyone ever stuck up for you or defended you publicly? It's easy to forget that God has feelings, and He feels more deeply than we do. He can be hurt, He can be taken advantage of, He feels pain, He can be persuaded, He can be loved, and He desires that we understand His heart.

Will you make God's case when necessary, even if it means risk to you? Phinehas, sensing the heart of God, took immediate action when a dangerous element was brought publicly before the people. How did God respond? In a surprising gesture of appreciation, God showed gratitude toward Phinehas by making a promise to him that would last for generations.

Be ready before the event. You may not encounter the same situation as Phinehas, but at some point, in your work environment or when out with friends, a subject in the news or culture may come into discussion. How will you make God's case for Him? As you prepare to stand up to cultural issues of the day that are in opposition to God's way, God's face will smile on you as He did Phinehas. God smiles on those who stick up for others, too. When you defend the defenseless or helpless, this resonates with the heart of God. When you stick up for what is right, God is on your side.

REFLECT TO CONNECT

1. What situations have you encountered where you have spoken up or held your peace?
2. How do you know when it is time to step up and speak up or stand down and wait on God?
3. Has anyone ever stuck up for you? How did it make you feel?

When you stick up for God,
He stands up for you.

MASTER YOUR MOOD
WITH GOD TALK

WEEK 41 | THURSDAY

Why are you in despair, O my soul? And why are you disturbed
within me? Hope in God, for I shall again praise Him,
The help of my countenance and my God. Psalm 43:5

G od won't do for you that which He has empowered you to do
for yourself. In the Psalmist's prayer for deliverance, he goes
back and forth from petition for help to declaration of God's greatness. He also questions God in his prayers, but how he exits his prayer
provides a clue to how David sets himself up with a winning attitude.

**Watch your thoughts in crisis, for they become feelings that
can influence your future.** David questions his emotions by asking
himself, "Why are you so disturbed within me?" After challenging
his emotions, which he knows are temporary, he leans into God,
who is eternal, by commanding himself to "hope in God for I shall
again praise Him." Your emotions can lead you astray if you don't
learn to master them.

"If you don't talk to yourself, yourself will talk to you."
Joel Osteen

Scientists have proved that the brain is "voice-activated." The
Apostle Paul affirmed this when he said in Romans 10:17, "Faith

comes by hearing." When we say what God says about us, we can feel what God feels toward us. David shows us that one of the best ways to process with God includes leaning on His promises, proclaiming His goodness, and also questioning our own pain out loud. As you question your feelings, then speak out loud the praises and promises of God, you will shift from "feeling your circumstances" to conforming to God's view of them.

REFLECT TO CONNECT

1. When was the last time you had to fight your feelings until they conformed to the Word of God?
2. Other than "hearing," what other strategies do you employ to course-correct your attitude?
3. How often do you prioritize God's mindset over your feelings?

If you want peace, bridle your emotions by wrestling them to the ground with the Word of God.

SERVANT LEADERSHIP THAT BUILDS INFLUENCE
WEEK 41 | FRIDAY

*Then all the tribes of Israel came to David at Hebron and said,
"Behold, we are your bone and your flesh. Previously,
when Saul was king over us, you were the one who led Israel out and in.
And the LORD said to you, 'You will shepherd My people Israel,
and you will be a ruler over Israel.'"*
2 Samuel 5:1-2

God builds relationship equity for you behind the scenes. When it came time for Israel and Judah to unite under King David, the Israelites acknowledged that David's leadership over them had begun many years before they would come under his kingship. Influence isn't built in a day, but over time by adding value to those you hope to lead.

Servant leadership is serving those who follow you. God may use your acts of servant leadership in your current position to build a bridge to your future, even though it may seem as if others are getting the credit in the present. Regardless of where you are in your organization, God wants to build influence right where you are, and He does this by revealing "needs" around you that He has equipped you to meet. When a need arises around you, that is your cue to get into action and add value to someone. As you add value, your relationship equity increases along with your influence. With God's hand guiding your leadership, your influence will grow organically, relationally, and with His hand upon you, supernaturally.

REFLECT TO CONNECT

1. In what ways are you actively serving those around you?
2. Are there service opportunities you could volunteer for?
3. Whom is God leading you to serve in this season?

Influence increases as people benefit from your leadership.

LEADERSHIP DETOURS

WEEK 42 | MONDAY

David was thirty years old when he became king, and he reigned forty
years. At Hebron he reigned over Judah seven years and six months,
and in Jerusalem he reigned thirty-three years over all Israel and Judah.
2 Samuel 5:4-5

G od doesn't call the qualified; He qualifies the called. Some theologians believe that God selected David (a man after His own heart) 8 years before he was born. David was approximately 15 when Samuel anointed him, around 17 when he killed Goliath, still a youth when he remained in the palace with King Saul, around 22 when his wilderness years began, and 30 when he became king over Judah. He would then reign for 40 years. God's plan almost always includes twists and turns we could never predict. What unexpected detours has God guided you on throughout your journey? Were these detours caused by your behavior, others, or God's sovereign hand?

God's preparation process is longer than you'd like but necessary for your longevity. He will often put you under authority or assign a mentor to you that is unfair and harsh (Saul), assign an unexpected ally (Jonathan, who was 30 years older than him), give you a taste of success (fame, victory, or fortune) and then hardship (wilderness years), or could assign a vagabond group of people for you to raise up (David led 400 men for 4 years in the wilderness). The religious leaders during Jesus' time couldn't recognize a King when they saw Him because they misunderstood God's ways and nature. Many leaders God has destined for great assignments miss His hand at work in their lives. Are there fingerprints of God's hand over your leadership based on what you see in David's life story? If so, God may have you "in process" of raising you up like he did David.

REFLECT TO CONNECT

1. What commonalities might your and David's situation share?
2. What is your purpose in this season?
3. Which Bible character do you identify most with and why?

God sees a future you can't, so He prepares character-building opportunities to give you longevity in your leadership.

———————◆———————

GOD'S WAY OF ESTABLISHING YOU

WEEK 42 | TUESDAY

Then Hiram king of Tyre sent messengers to David with cedar trees and carpenters and stonemasons; and they built a house for David. And David realized that the LORD had established him as king over Israel, and that He had exalted his kingdom for the sake of His people Israel.
2 Samuel 5:11-12

Are you established? God isn't only spiritual but practical. Talking about areas of provision often makes people uncomfortable, as if God is threatened by the financial, relational, marital, and other practical aspects of our lives. Getting yourself and your family "established" allows you to focus on the work at hand. What areas in life would you like God to establish you in? Consider making a "needs list" for your work environment, home environment, and future goals, then turn it into a prayer list. Here are a few areas in which God can establish you in practical ways.

Spouse: God can bring you someone who will fit you now and throughout the course of a lifetime.

Favor: God can create desire in the hearts of those around you to serve you and to treat you well.

Influence: God can create an acceleration in magnetism that causes others to follow you.

Relationships: God can bring you into close relationships with people in every area of your life.

Provision: God can provide you with an income that meets your needs and more.

Team: God can draw like-minded people to you who have a similar passion for serving alongside you.

REFLECT TO CONNECT

1. How has God established you where He has called you?
2. Are there ways in which you would like God to establish you?
3. What other "evidences" of God establishing a person are there?

You can't get what you don't expect.
God establishes people
with provision as a piece of His overall purpose.

———————◆◆———————

GET A GOD STRATEGY

WEEK 42 | WEDNESDAY

Now the Philistines came up once again and spread themselves out in
the valley of Rephaim. When David inquired of the Lord, He said,
"You shall not go directly up; circle around behind them and come at
them in front of the balsam trees. It shall be, when you hear the sound of
marching in the tops of the balsam trees, then you shall act promptly,
for then the LORD will have gone out before you to strike the army of
the Philistines." Then David did so, just as the LORD had commanded
him, and struck down the Philistines from Geba as far as Gezer.
2 Samuel 5:22-25

Y ou serve a God of strategy. Scripture records David seeking
God's counsel time and again for specific solutions to wars he
faced. It's easy to assume David always "knew" what to do, but we
see that there are numerous circumstances where he sought God's
advice for both yes/no questions and specific strategy. Whenever
there was a big decision to be made or David was in distress, as when
the Amalekites took the wives and children in Ziklag, he turned to
the Lord. What do you need a "God strategy" for today?

Do you ask God to help you with solutions to the problems you
face? What God did for David, He will do for you. David continued
to have success while he depended on God and sought His advice and
favor. Whatever your need is today, get quiet, get yourself into neutral
emotionally, and pose your question to God. Whether you hear or sense
an immediate answer or not, God knows what to do and will not withhold any good thing from those who seek His counsel. God may provide
you with a full picture or just give you a piece to your puzzle. Whatever
He tells you to do, do that and leave the next step to Him. Your strategy
may include multiple steps, so stay close to the Shepherd and listen for
His steps of strategy as you walk out His solution to the problem.

REFLECT TO CONNECT

1. What strategy has God shared with you to create success in your life?
2. Who do you know that depends fully on God for their leadership decisions?
3. What prayer can you pray today to embrace God as your guide in all your leadership decisions?

> *God lavishes His wisdom on leaders who turn to Him for counsel in the micro-decisions they face.*

SECRETS TO PROTOCOL

WEEK 42 | THURSDAY

But when they came to the threshing floor of Nacon, Uzzah reached out toward the ark of God and took hold of it, for the oxen nearly upset it. And the anger of the LORD burned against Uzzah, and God struck him down there for his irreverence; and he died there by the ark of God.

2 Samuel 6:6-7

G ood intentions aren't enough at the highest levels of leadership; competency and protocol are required. Every leader has a way in which they like to be handled, including God. Every environment has a protocol that, when followed, creates success and, when ignored, creates failure. David, either out of ignorance or forgetfulness, failed to properly handle God and His presence when the Ark was brought up. There is protocol in your work environment, at church, and in the White House. Are you surprised that God has protocols? While there is grace for many situations, there are also consequences. Failure to learn protocol can cause offense, create missed opportunities, and separate you from people and environments you want access to. Are you aware of the protocols in the environments you enter?

With great responsibility comes great accountability. David alone was responsible for the death of Uzzah. The law required the Ark of God to be carried on staves, not on a cart. Anyone touching the Ark would die. Scripture records David's emotions going from anger toward the Lord for killing his friend to fearing God. When you enter a new environment, be aware of:

CULTURE: What are the nuances of the environment?

AUTHORITY: Who has the official say-so?

INFLUENCE: Who has the unofficial say-so?

BEHAVIOR: In what ways do you need to adapt to the environment and people in it?

MISTAKES: What are the big NO-NOs; what do they respect, honor, and hold sacred?

When you are dating someone you care about, it's easy for you to adapt to their needs and become sensitive to the way in which they like to be handled. Doing the same for your employer and those in authority should come naturally. The most successful find ways in which to adapt to the environment and to authorities that control their future. Diplomats adapt, missionaries adapt, visitors adapt, and so can you. Becoming a student to what pleases or irritates those around you will advance yourself and your cause.

1. Have you ever become aware of a misstep in the atmosphere where the room seemed to stop and look?
2. Like going to another country, what else should you be aware of when entering a new environment?
3. What do you believe is God's protocol for entering His presence?

When you value what other people value,
they see you as valuable.

THE HONOR TEST

WEEK 42 | FRIDAY

Mephibosheth, the son of Jonathan the son of Saul,
came to David and fell on his face and prostrated himself.
And David said, "Mephibosheth." And he said, "Here is your servant!"
David said to him, "Do not fear, for I will surely show kindness to you
for the sake of your father Jonathan, and will restore to you all the
land of your grandfather Saul; and you shall eat at my table regularly."
2 Samuel 9:6-7

G od's got a thing for honor. God personally taught David about honor the day he clipped the edge of Saul's robe off in the cave. David not only extended honor to King Saul but also to Saul's grandson Mephibosheth two generations later. David would restore to him all that Saul owned, set up servants to steward everything for him, and insist that Saul's grandson eat daily at his table as one of his own sons. David learned to honor and serve King Saul for seven years—even while Saul was trying to kill him. Honor is a test all leaders must pass before God will increase them. The lack of honor is also the reason Jesus couldn't do miracles in Nazareth. Honor creates an atmosphere for God to work; a lack of honor in the environment inhibits God from working.

Here are a few ways in which leaders can show honor to an individual:

- Tell them what you admire about them, then ask them how they do what they do.
- Praise them publicly, then explain to the team why you value their performance.
- Speak to them about their contribution privately, then tell others how they add value to you, the team, and the organization.
- While in a three-person conversation, turn to one person and tell them what is amazing about the other person by using great and sincere adjectives to highlight their areas of giftedness.

REFLECT TO CONNECT

1. Whom in your life does God desire you to show honor to?
2. Are there people you have failed the "honor test" with?
3. Why do you think "honor" is such a hot button with God?

Honor creates an environment for miracles;
a lack of it can neutralize the power of God.

LESSONS FROM A
STAINED LEGACY

*Now when the wife of Uriah heard that Uriah her husband was dead,
she mourned for her husband. When the time of mourning was over,
David sent and brought her to his house and she became his wife;
then she bore him a son. But the thing that David had done
was evil in the sight of the LORD.* 2 Samuel 11:26-27

Reputation takes a lifetime to build but can be lost in a day.
King David is known as a man after God's own heart, a valiant
warrior, and one of Israel's greatest leaders. Yet, for all his favor and
blessings from God, it was his sin with Bathsheba that stained his
legacy. What leadership lessons can we learn from David's moral
failure?

If you are indulging in anything you wouldn't want printed and
photographed on social media, look behind you—you've stepped
over a line.

WRONG PLACE, WRONG TIME: David wasn't where he was supposed to be when he was supposed to be there. He remained home
when the kings went off to battle. If you are not where you belong,
you open yourself up to enemy attack. Are you working as "unto
the Lord"? Focus on your work, not your appetite.

BAD HABITS: David's success made him comfortable to the point
where he lost his edge and common sense. He was sleeping during the day, staying awake at night, and detaching himself from
real life until he lost his way. Do you have habits that are creating
self-deception? What may be hurting you that is obvious to those
around you?

LEFT HIMSELF OPEN: David's weaknesses are common to many men: beautiful women and power. Never let anything in front of you that doesn't belong in you. While men are seduced by what they see, women are seduced by what they feel. If you are indulging in emotional or physical adultery, stop it.

THE COVER-UP: David could have come clean when Bathsheba became pregnant, but his cover-up would only escalate his crime. His abuse of power led him to killing Uriah, Bathsheba's husband; then God stepped in. The cover-up became worse than the crime.

REFLECT TO CONNECT

1. Have you ever "left yourself open" to moral failure?
2. In what way do you feel David displeased God?
3. What were the steps that led to moral and spiritual failure?

Legacy is like reputation; it is what people remember whether true or not.

THE UNFORGIVEN LEADER

WEEK 43 | TUESDAY

But the king [David] said... "If he curses, and if the LORD has told him, 'Curse David,' then who shall say, 'Why have you done so?'" ... So David and his men went on the way; and Shimei went along on the hillside parallel with him and as he went he cursed and cast stones and threw dust at him. The king and all the people who were with him arrived weary and he refreshed himself there. 2 Samuel 16:10, 13-14

How would you feel if you had a child who interpreted every bad event as if it came from you? Imagine King David traveling on one side of a road with his entourage and mighty men of valor, with Shimei on the other side cursing and throwing stones at him. What person in authority would allow such a thing when they had willing warriors who wanted to stop it from happening? When David was asked why he allowed this, he responded by asserting that it was "God's will." Leaders who won't forgive themselves short-circuit God's ability to lead through them.

Stop blaming God and get over it. Christians are quick to assign motive to bad events suggesting that it is "payback" by God, or they "deserve" bad things happening to them because of something they did in the past. God had forgiven David for his sin with Bathsheba, yet his conscience was so stained that he had not been able to forgive himself. Just because your conscience condemns you doesn't mean God condemns you. David's self-image (internal thought life about himself) was so polluted by his sin that he allowed people to publicly curse him and throw stones at him, assuming it was God's will. God has already forgiven your past, present, and future sins, *whether you feel it or not.* His message is simple: "Let it go. I've forgiven you; forgive yourself." It is not uncommon for people who have failed in business, morally or spiritually, to feel rejected or despondent. If you know someone who has been through this, ask yourself, "what would Jesus do" to help them, then go and do likewise.

REFLECT TO CONNECT

1. Why is it hard for people to forgive and forget?
2. Why do you suppose it is so hard to forgive oneself even though God has forgiven us?

3. Whom do you know that needs to be reminded today that God loves them and has forgiven EVERYTHING?

The stain of sin on a conscience is what will sabotage your self-image; keep your conscience clean by keeping short accounts with God.

THE SCENT OF YOUR CHARACTER
WEEK 43 | WEDNESDAY

But the fruit of the Spirit is love, joy, peace, patience, kindness, goodness, faithfulness, gentleness, self-control; against such things there is no law. Now those who belong to Christ Jesus have crucified the flesh with its passions and desires.
Galatians 5:22-24

L ike fruit hanging on a tree, the fruit of the Spirit should adorn Christian character. I am reminded of smells and "first-time" experiences I had when I was young. The smell of freshly rolled newspapers as I prepared for my morning paper route, the smell of Christmas when I walked into Marshall Field's, and the smell of grass on the field where I used to play baseball. In a similar way, with a different sense, you experience a person's character by how they make you feel when you are around them.

Have you ever admired someone so much that you wanted to be like them? Paul points to the fruit of the Spirit as to what Christ working through us practically looks like. As you go through your day, become aware of "Christ in you"; these fruits are the ornaments of Christ's character manifesting in you. Just as you have a feeling about some people when they walk in the room, the fruit of the Spirit is the feelings others will experience as you model and mimic Christ.

REFLECT TO CONNECT

1. In whom do you often see the fruit of the Spirit manifested?
2 What are the steps one might take to engage the character qualities of Christ?
3. Are some fruits more important than others?

When people can taste and smell the fruit of the Spirit in you, Christ in you is coming through.

THE POWER OF PARTNERSHIP
WEEK 43 | THURSDAY

So King Hiram gave Solomon as much as he desired of the cedar and cypress timber. Solomon then gave Hiram 20,000 kors of wheat as food for his household, and twenty kors of beaten oil; thus Solomon would give Hiram year by year. The LORD gave wisdom to Solomon, just as He promised him; and there was peace between Hiram and Solomon, and the two of them made a covenant.
1 Kings 5:10-12

L eaders create partnerships that are mutually beneficial. Solomon recognized the power of partnership early in his reign. He formed political partnerships, marital partnerships, and economic partnerships. They all served his purposes well, but partnership requires compromise, bartering, and even negotiating. People acting in self-interest are often thought of as sinful or selfish, but that is not always the case. The pursuit of self-interest and having your needs met is human nature. Meeting one another's needs is at the heart of partnership and relationship.

Zig Ziglar once said, "You can have everything you want in life if you will just help enough other people get what they want." What made Solomon so desirous to partner with was that he had something of value the other party wanted, and he was *willing* to trade it in exchange for something he needed. In this way, God's wisdom taught him how to leverage his resources. Next time you have a need, ask yourself, "What do I have that the other person may be needing?" Knowing what you have that the other person may value puts you in a position to form a mutually beneficial partnership.

REFLECT TO CONNECT

1. What qualities embody a successful partnership?
2. What do you have of value that someone may see value in?
3. If you had to make a list of "dos and don'ts" of partnership, what would that list look like?

Partnerships grow strong when value is added from both sides of the table, and it dissolves when value is only one-sided.

SEEKING COUNSEL

WEEK 43 | FRIDAY

But he forsook the counsel of the elders which they had given him, and
consulted with the young men who grew up with him and served him.
1 Kings 12:8

If you hang around five wise people, you will be the sixth. King Rehoboam had enough sense to ask the advice of those with experience around him, but not enough sense to follow it. This one leadership mistake would be the catalyst whereby Israel would split into two kingdoms. God had a hand in orchestrating the way in which it would split; nonetheless, there are leaders today asking advice of inexperienced people and then following it like Rehoboam did.

Watch whose advice you follow. Are you the type of leader who is influenced more by your peers or by a passion to do what is best for the organization? Big leadership decisions come with pressure; recognizing whom to go to for advice can mean the difference between success and failure. Consider the following acrostic next time you need advice.

D: Do your homework. Make a list of people whom you could approach for seeking counsel.

E: Evaluate your list of counselors to ensure those whom you will seek advice from are qualified to give informed and educated advice.

C: Collect a series of questions you can pose to your counselors.

I: Initiate contact with your chosen list of counselors and listen to what they have to say.

D: Decide ahead of time to courageously choose a course of action that is best for the organization, even if it's not what is best for you or popular with others.

E: Engage by making the decision and getting into action.

REFLECT TO CONNECT

1. Have you ever asked the wrong person for advice and then followed it? What was the outcome?
2. Do you always go to the same people for advice, or do you pick and choose your counselors based on the advice you need?
3. How can you evaluate which advice is good vs. bad?

If you don't know, don't ask others who also don't know.

GOOD LEADERSHIP GONE BAD

*Jeroboam said in his heart, "Now the kingdom will return to the house of
David. If this people go up to offer sacrifices in the house of the LORD at
Jerusalem, then the heart of this people will return to their lord, even to
Rehoboam king of Judah; and they will kill me and return to Rehoboam
king of Judah." So the king consulted, and made two golden calves, and
he said to them, "It is too much for you to go up to Jerusalem; behold
your gods, O Israel, that brought you up from the land of Egypt."*
1 Kings 12:26-28

Jeroboam protected his provision and position at the expense
of a nation's relationship with God. It's not the first time this has
happened, and it won't be the last. Many leaders start out strongly,
heading straight, but then veer off the path to put their needs above
the people they serve. God desires to invest in you, and while much
is made about trusting God, can God trust you to stay the course
once influence, power, income, and more are put into your hands?

Self-serving leadership stinks. Servant leaders know that their
position and influence exist to serve others. Self-serving leaders
use their position and influence to serve themselves, often at the
expense of others. God appointed Jeroboam to rule Israel, but when
he sensed his reign slipping away, he turned away from God and led
God's people away from Him. Worship of false gods is not an issue
in today's marketplace; however, leadership that is self-serving is.
What are the signs of a self-serving leader?

- Bad leadership makes decisions for themselves at the expense of
  the organization.
- Bad leadership sacrifices what is right for what is convenient.
- Bad leadership puts self-interest above the interest of others.

- Bad leadership makes decisions with short-term benefits, knowing they end with long-term consequences.

REFLECT TO CONNECT

1. Have you ever worked for a self-serving leader? Explain.
2. Is there a balance between serving self and serving others?
3. What is your definition of servant leadership?

Much is made about people learning to trust God.
But can God trust you?

———————◆———————

FIX WHAT NEEDS FIXING

WEEK 44 | TUESDAY

"He will give up Israel on account of the sins of Jeroboam,
which he committed and with which he made Israel to sin."
1 Kings 14:16

The first quality of great leaders is that they are good followers. In less than one generation of leadership following King David's reign, Israel had forgotten the Lord and began to go after other gods. Under Jeroboam's leadership, they followed his idolatry to abandon God and His ways. It is not God who rejected Israel (us); it was Israel (us) who rejected Him. Yet people find fault with God as children do their parents when they are disciplined. Like in the days of Noah, Israel had become unreachable and unteachable in the prosperity and blessing God had provided. Only through instructive pain points (hardship) would they learn again how and whom to follow. The struggles we face in life are the materials by which God chisels His character into us.

Those who do not correct themselves will eventually be corrected. God, in His goodness and mercy, gives time for repentance, but His patience is not without limits. He has given each of us a conscience whereby we instinctively know the difference between right and wrong (Romans 1:19). If you know there is a change you need to make in your leadership, in your team, or in your personal life, today is the day to course-correct yourself before you are corrected. Pat Robertson, founder of the Christian Broadcast Network, advises that believers should "keep short accounts with God." For a leader, course correction sometimes requires biting the bullet and fixing what needs to be fixed.

REFLECT TO CONNECT

1. When was the last time your conscience smote you?
2. Are you like Adam in the garden, who hides himself when confronted, or are you more like David who confessed when confronted by God?
3. If God freely forgives all your past, present, and future sins, is there someone you need to extend the same grace to?

The struggles you face in life are the working materials
God uses to chisel His character into you.

————————◆————————

A HIGHER CALL

Then David said to Nathan, "I have sinned against the LORD."
And Nathan said to David, "The LORD also has taken away your sin;
you shall not die. However, because by this deed you have given occasion
to the enemies of the LORD to blaspheme, the child also that is born
to you shall surely die." 2 Samuel 12:13-14

L eaders are watched and studied by those who report to
them. After David committed adultery with Bathsheba and
tried to cover it up by killing her husband, the Bible says that God
was "displeased" with what he had done. God forgave David but also
informed him what the consequences of his choice would be. There
is a higher standard required of leaders because their actions, good
or bad, reverberate through an organization. We also see how the
actions and reputation of His children affect God Himself.

When Nathan repeated what God had said with the words, "You
have given occasion to the enemies of the LORD to blaspheme," we
get to peer into how a leader's sin affects the Lord. Whether God
was referring to His accusers in the spiritual realm or the earthy
realm bringing a charge against Him, we see that God is negatively
impacted when we fail to accurately represent Him. David felt the
weight of this when he wrote in Psalm 51:4, "Against You, You only,
I have sinned." David had brought heat and accusations against
God. The realization of how sin causes pain to others and God is
devastating, but God absorbs the brunt and covers us. Thanks be to
God for His enduring mercy to forgive us.

1. What loss does God experience when a person sins?
2. Who is it that stands accusing God?
3. What do you imagine happens in Heaven's courtroom when a person whom God has raised up and anointed falls prey to sin?

Worse than the feeling of failure when we sin is the realization of how God and others have been hurt by it.

THE SCIENCE OF LEADERSHIP LEARNING

WEEK 44 | THURSDAY

Be diligent to present yourself approved to God as a workman who does not need to be ashamed, accurately handling the word of truth.
2 Timothy 2:15

Anyone can teach you, but no one can learn *for* you. You, and you alone, are responsible for becoming an expert in the vocational lane in which you work. Earl Nightingale once said in *The Essence of Success*, "If you study for an hour a day, you will be a national expert within one year." Nowhere in the Bible does it say to "read" the Bible. However, it does say we are to study it, bind it to our hearts, post it everywhere; in short, remember it and do what it says. Following this advice will guarantee you retain what you learn.

The marketplace is moving at the speed of light. Technology and advancements in every field of an organization require people to adapt and learn faster than ever before, and it's not slowing down anytime soon. Alvin Toffler, an American writer, futurist, and businessman, said, "The illiterate of the 21st century will not be those who cannot read and write, but those who cannot learn, unlearn, and relearn." To be successful in the marketplace, you need to have an increasing degree of competence. Your degree of competence will be dependent on your ability to learn and then convert on what you learned over and over again. Here is a quick three-step plan for becoming a learner:

LEARN: Being teachable, humble, and having the right attitude is essential for learning. Without open-mindedness, nothing gets in. Remember, there is always something you don't know.

DISCERN: Some of my greatest lessons came from observing what not to do from poor leaders. Witnessing poor leadership can be one of the greatest teachable moments you can give yourself if you know how to convert on it. There are also some examples you don't want to follow.

RETURN: Repetition is the mother of learning. Rarely do people grasp complex concepts after one input. Frequency is the best way to learn. Returning to key information multiple times, saying it out loud, and then taking action on what you learned will help your retention.

Becoming an expert is easier than ever because expert guidance is available everywhere through technology. You can choose to learn in the lost minutes in the day, like standing in line, in between meetings, and more.

REFLECT TO CONNECT

1. What areas of competency in your work life would you like to shore up?
2. Do you have a time set aside each day to improve yourself?
3. God expects progress, not perfection; what does this mean to you?

Your degree of competence will be dependent on your ability to learn and then convert on what you learned over and over again.

COMMANDED PROVISION

WEEK 44 | FRIDAY

For thus says the LORD God of Israel, 'The bowl of flour shall not be exhausted, nor shall the jar of oil be empty, until the day that the LORD sends rain on the face of the earth.'" So she went and did according to the word of Elijah, and she and he and her household ate for many days. The bowl of flour was not exhausted nor did the jar of oil become empty, according to the word of the Lord which He spoke through Elijah.
1 Kings 17:14-16

Leaders look through the lens of what God has, not what they have. In the days of Elijah the prophet, there was a famine in the land. Elijah was sent on assignment to a widow at Zarephath whom God had already spoken to on Elijah's behalf to provide for his needs. Whom has God spoken to you to provide for? As you provide in obedience, provision is made for you.

Leaders have an abundance mindset. Unless you are in a growth industry that has incredible momentum, you may be surrounded by a scarcity mindset in the workplace. The famines that exist today may not be food, but may instead include encouragement, recognition, a kind word, or critical resources that can fuel or inhibit success. Learn to lean on God by adopting His mindset of abundance. Provision is a two-way street—while you provide what one person needs, God finds someone to provide your needs, according to Ephesians 6:8.

ABUNDANCE MINDSET		SCARCITY MINDSET
Time:	God will help me prioritize.	I don't have enough time.
Hiring:	God will help me find the right people.	There aren't any good people available.
Money:	God will show me how to multiply wealth.	There is not enough money.
Training:	God will help me equip my staff.	Why aren't my people any good?
Capital:	God will show me where to look for investors.	Investors aren't interested in our business.

REFLECT TO CONNECT

1. In what ways do you need to trust God to provide for you?
2. Is there an area of scarcity you need to renew your mind in?
3. What do you have abundance in (kind words/encouragement) that you can provide to people?

As you provide in obedience, provision is made for you.

GOD'S MENTORSHIP MODEL

WEEK 45 | MONDAY

Now the Spirit of the LORD departed from Saul, and an evil spirit from the LORD terrorized him. Saul's servants then said to him, "Behold now, an evil spirit from God is terrorizing you. Let our lord now command your servants who are before you. Let them seek a man who is a skillful player on the harp; and it shall come about when the evil spirit from God is on you, that he shall play the harp with his hand, and you will be well." So Saul said to his servants, "Provide for me now a man who can play well and bring him to me." Then one of the young men said, "Behold, I have seen a son of Jesse the Bethlehemite who is a skillful musician, a mighty man of valor, a warrior, one prudent in speech, and a handsome man; and the LORD is with him." So Saul sent messengers to Jesse and said, "Send me your son David who is with the flock." Jesse took a donkey loaded with bread and a jug of wine and a young goat, and sent them to Saul by David his son. Then David came to Saul and attended him; and Saul loved him greatly, and he became his armor bearer. Saul sent to Jesse, saying, "Let David now stand before me, for he has found favor in my sight." So it came about whenever the evil spirit from God came to Saul, David would take the harp and play it with his hand; and Saul would be refreshed and be well, and the evil spirit would depart from him. 1 Samuel 16:14-23

A problem in the palace is your ticket to transformation. David tended his father's flocks until King Saul needed someone to play the strings in a way that brought him peace. David had a reputation for playing beautiful music, and when the need arose, someone of influence mentioned David's skill (gift) to the king. Once David was able to solve King Saul's "tormenting" problem, Saul loved him greatly, and this "problem-solving lad" became favored by the king. Favor leads to investment and mentorship. Following this season, David killed Goliath, and Saul took notice of him again. Now, David was no longer permitted to tend his father's flock; instead, he remained in the palace.

Some of my greatest lessons came from managers who poorly managed or people who failed. Wise people learn from their mistakes; the wisest learn from other people's mistakes.

You can learn from bad leadership, too. Under Saul's tutelage, David would be trained in the ways of the palace, battle, politics, and many other skills due to his proximity to Saul. This was God's way of readying him for his future. When a problem arises, know that it is God presenting you with an opportunity to increase your influence in a way so He can better position you for your future assignment. Timothy had Paul, Elisha had Elijah, Joshua had Moses, and so on. Here are a few things you can do to attract a good mentor when positioning yourself.

QUALITIES OF A GOOD MENTEE

- Value your mentor's investment in you by doing what they tell you to do, being on time, listening intently, and taking action on what you learn.
- Show gratitude by thanking them often.
- Honor the mentor relationship by returning to show them what you have done with what they gave you.

REFLECT TO CONNECT

1. In what ways have you been mentored before and by whom?
2. Have your greatest mentors been teachers, coworkers, bosses, parents, or someone else of significance in your life?
3. Which mentors has God put you in proximity to? Have you discerned what you are to learn from them?

Wise people learn from their mistakes; the wisest learn from other people's mistakes and successes.

THE RIGHT INFLUENCE

WEEK 45 | TUESDAY

Do not be deceived. "Bad company corrupts good morals."
1 Corinthians 15:33

Behavior rubs off whether you want it to or not. John Maxwell, in his best-selling book *The 21 Irrefutable Laws of Leadership*, said in "The Law of the Picture," "People do what people see." It's not just leaders and mentors who model the behaviors that we pick up; it's our inner circle of friends, coworkers, those vertical to us, and those horizontal to us.

You become like the people you hang around with. You become the average of the five people you spend the most time with. Jim Rohn once said, "If you hang around five people who are rich, you'll be the sixth." The opposite is true, too. It is true for wealth, weight, the things you wish for, and ultimately, for who you will become. If you desire to change your life, surrounding yourself with people who will influence you for the better and not for the worse is essential. Jettisoning the wrong group of friends is not easy for anyone once you know they are not the right fit for you. Even Jesus didn't hang around some of the leaders of the day. How can you identify the right vs. wrong types of people?

The Right People in Your Life Will:	The Wrong People in Your Life Will:
• Believe in you.	• Foster doubt in you.
• Want you to grow past them.	• Want you to stay down with them.
• Want you to grow in your purpose.	• Want you to just get by.
• Run with those ahead of them.	• Stay with those who don't push them.
• Encourage you to go the extra mile.	• Want you to take shortcuts with them.
• Want you to follow a path of success.	• Make excuses to take the easy road.
• Set a good example for you to follow.	• Want you to compromise on principles.
• Challenge you to be more than you are.	• Want to keep you where you are.
• Encourage you to focus on priorities.	• Distract you from reaching your goals.

REFLECT TO CONNECT

1. Is there anyone in your life who doesn't belong?
2. Do you allow them to remain because of their strength or your weakness?
3. Whom is God reminding you to remove from your circle of influence?

Character imprints face-to-face,
so watch whom you hang out with.

———————◆———————

I SPY A MENTOR

WEEK 45 | WEDNESDAY

Paul came also to Derbe and to Lystra. And a disciple was there, named Timothy, the son of a Jewish woman who was a believer, but his father was a Greek, and he was well spoken of by the brethren who were in Lystra and Iconium. Paul wanted this man to go with him. Acts 16:1-3

What qualities attract a good mentor? Timothy stood out to Paul from the start. Timothy was likeable, teachable, young, and impressionable, which meant he was moldable. Mentors who have to do heavy lifting to get mentees on the same page with them eventually move on and find a new student they can invest in. Many hear the call of the Divine Mentor; few heed it.

There are two ways to learn: mentors or mistakes. God may assign you mentors you don't like. A mentor is anyone who is willing to invest in you, either for a season or a moment that adds value to you. Do you know how to spot a mentor when you see them? Consider who within your reach may be a good mentor.

Mentors will be the difference makers in Your life! Mentors...

- May be a teacher, guidance counselor, coach, parent, boss, pastor, or priest who believes in us, invests in us, and cares for us.
- Give us their time and resource us with ideas, tools, and insights.
- Share their experience with us to inspire us and paint pictures of a potential future.
- Believe in us by providing encouragement, confidence, and inspiration.
- Guide us on big decisions and become a friend when life doesn't go our way.
- Help us to see more, travel faster, and go farther than those without a mentor.

REFLECT TO CONNECT

1. Whom might God have placed in your life to mentor you that you have ignored?
2. Do you have mentors (teachers) who rub you the wrong way yet add value to you?
3. Why does God use mentors to advance His children in the marketplace?

The most valuable reward you will receive in life isn't a paycheck; it's a person—a mentor.

F.A.I.T.H. IN ACTION

WEEK 45 | THURSDAY

I sought the LORD, and He answered me, And delivered me from all my fears ... The angel of the LORD encamps around those who fear Him, And rescues them ... Come, you children, listen to me; I will teach you the fear of the LORD. Psalm 34:4, 7, 11

F ear is part of life, even for the courageous. As a child, I had one type of fear; as an adult, I have another. Both reemerge from time to time. After fighting cancer seven times in seven years, I must face and conquer fear whenever it emerges. Fear is an emotion that comes and goes. Have you made a habit of conquering fear? King David killed the 9-foot-tall Goliath and experienced many victories in battle, yet he discusses one particular fear that is within him that is a healthy fear: the fear of the Lord, which means "reverence." God does NOT want you to fear Him but to run to Him when you experience fear (False Evidence Appearing Real) so He can show you your situation through His eyes.

Growth stops when you choose to run from your fears instead of facing them. Leaders can develop a habit of insulating themselves from things that would cause them discomfort, insecurity, or fear. People who are in authority have access to staff and can begin to arrange their lives so they don't receive feedback. They insulate themselves from tough decisions that require courageous leadership or slip into a life of comfort vs. conquest, as David's son Solomon did. David sets an example for leaders by turning to God to wash away his fears. Next time you are experiencing fear, remember who you are, who is on your side, and that you "can do all things through Christ" who strengthens you. When you exercise your F.A.I.T.H. to do what you can, God will do what you can't. With every step you take toward facing your fears, remember that faith stands for…

Forward   Action   Inspired   Through   Him

REFLECT TO CONNECT

1. What are you "avoiding" in your life that may be fear-based?
2. Whom do you know that has created an environment for comfort or a life of conquest?
3. When you are afraid, whom do you run to? This is a clue as to whom you put your trust in.

The evidence of faith over fear is the ground you take
with God in your life as you exercise "F.A.I.T.H":
F-Forward, A-Action, I-Inspired, T-Through, H-Him.

COACHES FIND THE FIT

"See, I have called by name Bezalel, the son of Uri, the son of Hur,
of the tribe of Judah. I have filled him with the Spirit of God in wisdom,
in understanding, in knowledge, and in all kinds of craftsmanship"
… And behold, I Myself have appointed with him Oholiab, the son of
Ahisamach, of the tribe of Dan; and in the hearts of all who are skillful
I have put skill, that they may make all that I have commanded you.
Exodus 31:2-3, 6

G od puts a part of Himself into everyone; which part has He given you? One of the most important leadership skills is to be able to identify the talent God has placed into you, into others and create a plan that develops both.

A bad hire rarely becomes a good employee. When hiring, discerning who fits on the team and in what position is critical for success. When miscast in the wrong position, even talented people struggle when running in a lane that is not a right fit for them. Right placement of talent leads to high performance, and the opposite is also true. Anytime I am dealing with a performance problem, I ask myself three questions:

ABILITY: Does the person have the ability to do the job? If I hire talent, I can train the skill if the raw material is there to develop the individual.

ATTITUDE: Does the person have a willingness to do what I am asking them to do? If there is not a willingness, I cut my losses quickly. I prefer rehabilitation over termination, but you can't help someone who is going to fight you along the way. Even God gets fed up at some point in a wrestling match with the stubborn.

FIT: Does the person belong in the position I have put them in? Genius emerges when it's placed in an environment where it can thrive. If a person is a "fit" with staff, a "fit" in position, and a "fit" with me, I know that low performance can be traced back to ability or attitude. Recruiting talent, finding the right fit, developing the person, and discerning the path to performance is a critical skill of every leader.

REFLECT TO CONNECT

1. If you have ever struggled in a job, has it occurred to you that you might not be in the right position?
2. For the people you know that are struggling in a position, is it due to attitude, ability, or fit?
3. What giftedness has God deposited into the people you are responsible for in your life?

When you find your FIT, it unlocks the greatness of God He's put inside of you.

TESTS OF LEADERSHIP

WEEK 46 | MONDAY

*But one son of Ahimelech the son of Ahitub, named Abiathar,
escaped and fled after David. Abiathar told David that Saul had killed
the priests of the LORD. Then David said to Abiathar, "I knew on that
day, when Doeg the Edomite was there, that he would surely tell Saul.
I have brought about the death of every person in your father's
household. Stay with me; do not be afraid, for he who seeks my life seeks
your life, for you are safe with me."* 1 Samuel 22:20-23

Imagine the weight on David's heart when he heard that he was directly responsible for the death of 85 men from a choice he had made. He didn't directly cause their deaths, but his choice created an "unintended consequence" he could not anticipate. If you were David, would you change your choice only knowing what he knew at the time? The weight of unintended consequence crushed David, but it didn't detract him from the mission ahead.

Good leadership carries a cost and is not always popular. Leaders must make tough decisions from time to time that come with consequences. It is in the crucible of decision-making that a leader is tested. In times of crisis, how will you triage priorities and pains, knowing there will be unavoidable consequences and loss from any decisions you make? Here are a few leadership tests all leaders must pass:

- Will you do what is right or what is popular?
- Will you accept responsibility even when the cost is heavy or public?
- Will you sacrifice "saving face" for doing what is right?
- Will you move forward with what God is calling you to do even when the weight of "unintended consequence" is high?
- Will you serve the team and the greater good when it comes at personal cost to you?

In these leadership tests, God will help you bear the weight but won't carry the ball for you. He expects every leader to step up in their home, their work, and their community when an opportunity to lead presents itself.

REFLECT TO CONNECT

1. In what ways has your leadership been tested?
2. What example can you give of an "unintended consequence"?
3. When have you had to make an unpopular leadership decision?

There is a test every leader must pass to go to the next level of responsibility and rewards.

DON'T BELIEVE EVERYTHING YOU THINK

WEEK 46 | TUESDAY

Would they [sacrifices] not have ceased to be offered, because the worshipers, having once been cleansed, would no longer have had consciousness of sins? But in those sacrifices there is a reminder of sins year by year. For it is impossible for the blood of bulls and goats to take away sins. Hebrews 10:2-4

On the day Adam and Eve ate from the Tree of Knowledge of Good and Evil, they lost their innocence before God. For those who accept Christ, their sins are forgiven, their conscience cleansed, and their relationship is restored to God. When you accept Christ into your heart, He makes a great exchange—your guilt for His love. In many ways, this change is invisible to those around you, yet something supernatural happens. When Jesus forgave your sins, the invisible guilt (consciousness of sin) that haunted you once before is removed. For 4,000 years since the time of Adam, no sacrifice could cleanse the conscience except the one Jesus made. The removal of guilt can't be seen, yet this invisible act of supernatural cleansing is what brings you into the right relationship with God.

Never allow anything in front of you that doesn't belong in you. The human heart is like an imprintable mirror; whatever it beholds will eventually enter in. There may be times following salvation whereby the enemy brings a former memory of sin or guilt to you. When that happens, the enemy is trying to gain a foothold into your consciousness through your memory (former guilt). If you focus on what Jesus did for you, His forgiveness will become greater in you than the guilt you left behind. If you focus on what the enemy is reminding you of, guilt will be reborn and reinstated. What you feed grows within you, and what you starve dies, so feed your faith with what God says about you, not what an old mental tape is playing from your past.

REFLECT TO CONNECT

1. What memories are plaguing your faith that you need to resolve once and for all?
2. What memories of victory does God want you to focus on from your past?
3. Can you think of a time when you became aware that a "thought process" you were experiencing wasn't helpful, and you had to cast it away from you?

Your past is either a mentor or a tormentor.
Make it tutor you—not taunt you.

HUMILITY—THE HALLMARK OF A LEADER'S HEART

WEEK 46 | WEDNESDAY

Surely there was no one like Ahab who sold himself to do evil in the sight of the LORD, because Jezebel his wife incited him ... "Do you see how Ahab has humbled himself before Me? Because he has humbled himself before Me, I will not bring the evil in his days, but I will bring the evil upon his house in his son's days." 1 Kings 21:25, 29

Humility, contrition, and confession are hallmarks of repentance. King Ahab and Queen Jezebel have gone down in history as the worst leaders Israel has known. God uses them as a cautionary tale of what leaders should *not* do when in power. But then God uses Ahab's act of humility after He proclaims judgment to show Elijah what grabs His heart. Ahab then received mercy from God, even though his behavior was wicked.

Humility attracts the heart of God. Some of the greatest growth cycles in my life have followed failures. What makes growth possible after a mistake or failure? Taking responsibility and embracing your role in what led to the failure. While it may be human nature to pass the buck, it's God's nature to handle the heart. God can't work with a stubborn heart, but He will gravitate toward one that is malleable. Leaders who are quick to admit wrong when confronted can move forward vs. leaders who run from humility that must spend their time covering up their mistakes.

1. Are there areas of uncomfortableness God has sent people to confront you in?
2. Why is humility in the heart of a leader so important to God?
3. When leaders lack humility, what are the consequences?

While it may be human nature to pass the buck,
it's God's nature to handle the heart.

———————•❖•———————

NO SURRENDER;
STAND AND FIGHT!

WEEK 46 | THURSDAY

Finally, be strong in the Lord and in the strength of His might.
Put on the full armor of God, so that you will be able to stand
firm against the schemes of the devil. For our struggle is not against
flesh and blood, but against the rulers, against the powers,
against the world forces of this darkness, against the spiritual forces
of wickedness in the heavenly places.
Ephesians 6:10-12

The Apostle Paul was a soldier's soldier. He spoke of an invisible war that was being waged with eternal consequences. For the Christian, we would not intentionally trade what feels good over what is right or temporal benefits for eternal consequences, yet it's easy to do in the micro-decisions we make. Micro-decisions of choosing what feels right over what is right in God's eyes can sneak up on us, even for the seasoned saint. When you consider what God may be asking you to fight for vs. surrender, what comes to mind with regard to your work life, your home life, and your friendships?

Godly Things Worth Fighting for	Things Worthy of Surrendering to God
• Choosing the right people in your life.	• Allowing the wrong people in your life.
• Developing spiritual disciplines.	• Engaging in harmful habits.
• Having the courage to confront bad behavior.	• Being liked by people over being right with God.
• Letting others be heard.	• Dismissing others' opinions.
• Prioritizing quiet time for devotions.	• Using screen time for entertainment.
• Trusting God's Word over your feelings.	• Letting your emotions determine your decisions.
• Pursuing God's purposes for your life.	• Making lifestyle choices that conflict with godliness.

Success in one season of life does not guarantee success in every season. Contending to maintain your surrender to God is an intentional act that must be renewed regularly. At some point, everyone wrestles with God over the "gods" in their life they have put above the one true God. However, we are promised that the short-term pain of letting go will not compare with the long-term freedom and strength we will experience in Christ.

REFLECT TO CONNECT

1. If you had to make a list of things you should be fighting for or surrendering to God, what would that list look like?

2. What could you achieve if the weights holding you down were removed?
3. Why does God not force people to surrender to Him?

We don't need to be told what to surrender to God, only reminded when we are resisting again.

FIRST-TIME MANAGER
WEEK 46 | FRIDAY

[Elisha] also took up the mantle of Elijah that fell from him and returned and stood by the banks of the Jordan. He took the mantle of Elijah that fell from him and struck the waters and said, "Where is the LORD, the God of Elijah?" And when he also had struck the waters, they were divided here and there, and Elisha crossed over.
2 Kings 2:13-14

Everybody follows someone. Modeling is how we learn as infants, kids, teenagers, and adults. Once we see it, we can do it. It's no different for leaders. Whether you have just taken on the mantle of a new position or are a seasoned leader, you are following in the footsteps of another to discover what works and what doesn't work until you find your own leadership style. Once the mantle passed from Elijah to Elisha, the first thing he did was TEST the power that came with the office of head prophet of Israel. As you take on new positions in your career, new people, or increased influence within an organization, consider what will create or cost you equity in your leadership (influence) bank account.

Builds Leadership Equity	Reduces Leadership Equity
• Willing to hear people out.	• Jumping to conclusions without gathering facts.
• Building relationships to get things done.	• Overusing authority early in your role.
• Developing collaboration.	• Making unilateral decisions.
• Taking time to understand.	• Assuming you understand.
• Putting the team above your rights.	• Using the team to serve your position.
• Adapting to the team and environment.	• Exerting what you know over the team and environment.

Good people skills are your best leadership skills. Loren Cunningham, founder of Youth with a Mission, said, "When you use influence to get things done, you gain authority. When you use authority, it costs you influence." When new to a position, proving yourself with the people must precede proving yourself in the organization. If you don't win with your people, you won't win in your new role. The way to guarantee your success is through servant leadership. It's paradoxical, but servant leaders focus on serving those who follow them.

REFLECT TO CONNECT

1. Whom do you know that has had to prove themselves in a new role? What was their experience?
2. Have you ever had to prove yourself in a new role? What was your experience?
3. What advice would you give to someone growing in their career?

Leaders win with the people before they can win in the organization.

PREPARING FOR MY SURRENDER

WEEK 47 | MONDAY

Not that I have already obtained it or have already become perfect,
but I press on so that I may lay hold of that for which also
I was laid hold of by Christ Jesus. Brethren, I do not regard
myself as having laid hold of it yet; but one thing I do: forgetting
what lies behind and reaching forward to what lies ahead,
I press on toward the goal for the prize
of the upward call of God in Christ Jesus.
Philippians 3:12-14

The Apostle Paul had a singular focus on whom he was serving and what his mission was. He didn't want anything to get in the way of his pursuit toward his goal. Paul spoke boldly about the importance of "letting go" of what lay behind, i.e., unnecessary baggage for the journey ahead. Unnecessary baggage is anything that slows us down in pursuit of a higher purpose. This has an application for every area of life. God doesn't force Himself on us, and that includes forcing us to make decisions we already know we must make. We must "willingly" surrender those things He prompts us to, when He prompts us to, lest the delay open doors to pain God is trying to help us avoid down the road.

Along the road toward spiritual maturity, there are things we must give up in order to go up. Growth stops when we are no longer willing to make the tough choices in our lives. Some routines, habits, relationships, or other things from our past we must willingly relinquish. Not surrendering what we know we should can prevent us from moving forward. Is there something in your present God is prompting you to release? Letting go of what lies behind, like the Apostle Paul did, will set you up for something significant God wants to release into your future.

REFLECT TO CONNECT

1. What was the last thing God asked you to surrender?
2. Is there baggage in your life that has detoured your future?
3. Whom do you know who has something they need to surrender or submit to in their life?

When surrendering something God is prompting you to,
you are not only walking away from something
but running toward Someone.

———————◆———————

GOD'S FORCE MULTIPLIER

WEEK 47 | TUESDAY

However, in the Lord, neither is woman independent of man,
nor is man independent of woman. For as the woman originates from
the man, so also the man has his birth through the woman;
and all things originate from God. 1 Corinthians 11:11-12

G od has prepared gifts for you that are hidden within others. God gave a part of Himself to women that He didn't give to men. This can include talents, dispositions, and parts of a personality unique to Him. Whenever my wife and I don't see eye to eye, I ask myself what she may be seeing that I am not seeing or what part of God's greatness is coming through her that I may be missing. There are parts of God's personality uniquely embedded within women that are not inherent or entirely absent within a man and vice versa. For example, women typically are more intuitive, discerning, compassionate, gentle, nurturing, and patient than a man. In

God's grand design, He plants gifts in one that, when combined with another, makes a pair stronger together than when separate. King Solomon said in Ecclesiastes 4:9, "Two are better than one because they have a good return for their labor."

Whether in a relationship with a spouse, a coworker, or an entire team, you can create a force multiplier effect in the home or at the office by leveraging the gifts and personality traits of God that He has planted in those around you. One question to help you get started is to begin talking to God about someone specifically, then ask Him, "What unique part of Yourself did you give to them? Can You show me, please?" Then wait to see what begins to bubble up over the next few days. When you look for the greatness and gifts of God He deposited within others, what you find may surprise you.

REFLECT TO CONNECT

1. God always gives a part of Himself to another that He didn't give to you. What has He planted in those around you?
2. God has planted something in you that someone needs; have you discerned whom you are to serve today?
3. Whom can you strengthen today by communicating why you are stronger with them than without them?

God gives parts of His personality to others
He did not give to you. Discovering and combining God's great
design among people creates a force multiplier effect.

TRUTH IS NOT ENOUGH

WEEK 47 | WEDNESDAY

*All Scripture is inspired by God and profitable for teaching, for reproof,
for correction, for training in righteousness; so that the man of God may
be adequate, equipped for every good work.* 2 Timothy 3:16-17

The first person you must train is yourself. You, and you alone, are responsible for choosing to engage "Christ in you" so that the tutor may tutor you in the ways of God. No one can train your spiritual senses but the Holy Spirit, yet your participation is required.

Have you ever been filled with knowledge on a subject yet still lacked the power to transform or break through? It's been said that the Bible is the only book written that requires the Author to be present when you read it. Without the writer, the reader can partake in a history lesson with good moral teaching but will lack the power that is alive and active, able to transform the person for this life and the life to come. Without an awareness of the Writer's presence (the Holy Spirit), it is possible to read what God wrote but not experience the illumination of what He is saying to you.

Truth and Training + Frequency = Transformation. Where results are lacking, there is a disconnect between my life and the life God wants to bring from Heaven to Earth through me. Am I getting results in my life? If not, I must evaluate what I might be doing that is limiting the power of "Christ in me" to have a transformative impact on my life. God welcomes a desire by us to confront the gaps between what we read and what we experience in Scripture. If there is a disconnect, I must search it out. Here are a few questions I use to challenge the results in my life:

- Am I using His truth to tutor and transform me or picking and choosing what I like to hear?

- Am I using His truth to move His call on my life forward or using Him to advance my priorities?
- Am I acting on what I have learned or accumulating information, being filled with knowledge but not power?
- Is there evidence of "Christ's power" working in me or only His name in my life?
- Is His Word pruning me, or am I pruning the conviction out of His Word?

REFLECT TO CONNECT

1. Do you use God, or do you allow Him to use you?
2. Is there only knowledge, or is there also evidence of power in your life?
3. What truth is God seeding into your spirit today?

You can change without the Tutor of Truth,
but you cannot transform.

THE ROYAL LAW

WEEK 47 | THURSDAY

Even so faith, if it has no works, is dead, being by itself. James 2:17

Whom are you serving when you serve others? Yesterday, I ran through my day in a rush and got a lot done. I ran fast, focused on my tasks for the day, and finished well. Today, I walked through my day without rushing and saw the same people but noticed them differently. I put aside my agenda for the day and served them. While I did not complete my work for the day, I fulfilled the Father's.

"He who waters will himself be watered." (Proverbs 11:25) The Royal Law states that we are to love our neighbors as we ourselves would want to be loved. Imagine the Spirit of Christ hiding within each vessel you see. Christ is in those you run into throughout your day, at the office, in the grocery store line, in some you talk to, and some you ignore. As you see one in need, help them, and serve them as you would the Lord, you are fulfilling the Royal Law and even one higher... the Platinum Law, which says to love God with all your heart, soul, and mind. (Luke 10:27) To the "giver" in you, He promises that the good you do for others, He will do back for you. To serve "Christ in them" is to serve Christ personally. As Jesus said, "as you did it to one of the least of these my brothers, you did it to me. (Matthew 25:40 ESV)

Notice the need and make the ASK. Faith at work can include lending a hearing ear, listening with kind eyes, providing a word of encouragement, giving compassion when judgment is warranted, or simply checking in with someone and asking them if they need anything, as my friend Mark did every day when I was battling cancer.

"You can wish, you can hope, you can pray; but when you pray,
your feet better be moving."
African Proverb

REFLECT TO CONNECT

1. Whom did you run into today where there was a spoken or unspoken need you became aware of?
2. Can you remember a conversation by which you noticed no outward need but sensed an inward hurting in the person you spoke with?

3. To put others first is the Royal Law; how does one do this while "running their race" through their day and still be productive?

While faith is the evidence of a future hope that exists inwardly, the service you do to others is your faith in action outwardly.

TRUST BUT VERIFY
WEEK 47 | FRIDAY

"For thus says the LORD of hosts, the God of Israel, 'Do not let your prophets who are in your midst and your diviners deceive you, and do not listen to the dreams which they dream. For they prophesy falsely to you in My name; I have not sent them,' declares the LORD."
Jeremiah 29:8-9

Influence is a mighty tool that can be used to motivate people toward good or manipulate them for evil. In Old Testament times, the office of prophet carried great influence in the palace. Prophets had the king's ear and could sway decisions economically, militarily, and even spiritually for a nation. The standard of truth was simple for a prophet: if what they said came to pass, they retained their office. If, however, they used their office incorrectly by speaking falsely on behalf of God, they were to be killed.

Do you believe fake news? Fake news in modern culture is an example of "experts" using "selective information" to influence people into believing or doing. How do you know whom you can trust? How do you know when you are being deceived by another or even yourself? Our own desires can sometimes be most to blame for talking us into things we should not be talked into. President Ronald Regan, when considering whether or not to trust the Soviet Union with regard to their missile program, said, "Trust but verify!" Here are a few litmus tests you can give yourself to verify that the information being presented to you is legitimate.

LITMUS TESTS FOR DECISION-MAKING

VERIFIABLE EVIDENCE: Based on the claims being made, are there people you can talk to that do not have a "dog in the hunt" who can verify the facts? Let every fact be confirmed by two or three witnesses.

SELF-DECEIT: If you are in need, especially medically or financially, you are particularly vulnerable. Are you being swayed by relationships that have influence with you for your benefit or for their benefit? The heart can be talked into just about anything if it wants something enough. Are you seeing things as they are or as you want them to be?

CONSEQUENCES: As you count the cost of making your decision, play the tape to the end in a few different outcomes. What will the medical, financial, social, or relational outcome be if you are wrong? What will the cost be if you choose not to move forward with your decision?

TELL THEIR CLAIMS TO OTHER EXPERTS: What would friends OR other respected people not in your immediate circle say about the decision you are considering? For me, I have found that if I am uncomfortable sharing a course of action with others, then it's a good indication something is wrong, or I may be on a road toward self-deception. Remember that in the midst of counselors is wisdom.

REFLECT TO CONNECT

1. In what ways have you been deceived by people you trusted?
2. How can you tell the difference between fact and fiction when being presented with options by experts?
3. Where does one draw the line between presenting something in a positive light vs. going too far and exaggerating?

God hears the inner thoughts of every heart;
He knows when you are talking yourself or someone else
into something you should not.

CEMENTED IN COMMITMENT

WEEK 48 | MONDAY

Shadrach, Meshach and Abed-nego replied to the king,
"O Nebuchadnezzar, we do not need to give you an answer concerning
this matter. If it be so, our God whom we serve is able to deliver us from
the furnace of blazing fire; and He will deliver us out of your hand,
O king. But even if He does not, let it be known to you,
O king, that we are not going to serve your gods or worship the
golden image that you have set up." Daniel 3:16-18

God doesn't give big assignments to unproven people. The three men didn't even consider their options; they had made their decision not to compromise long before their commitment would be tested. They would rather die than break God's commandment. What decisions have you made in your life that you are concrete in your convictions about?

After 30 years in broadcasting, I have been tested with money, sex, power, promotion, and more. How have you been tested? In the marketplace, all Christians are tested in their place of work, in the community, in finances, and in relationships. There comes a time for every believer where their work, will, and character are tested and proved in such a way that after passing the test, God can promote them and point to them as an example of character. Tests in the marketplace can be subtle or obvious. You may be "invited" to partake in something you instinctively know is wrong or, all of a sudden, find yourself in a compromising situation. It may have to do with relationships, finances, horoscopes or tarot cards, a sin of secrecy, convenience, proximity, or opportunity. *Often in a time of testing, God is silent, giving you an opportunity to exercise what you know. God observes to see if you will listen to your conscience or your desires.* As you walk through your test, God will always provide a way of escape and then, on the other side, a path to promotion in character, trust, position, or other thing.

REFLECT TO CONNECT

1. In what ways have you been tested in the last year?
2. In areas you've made mistakes, how has God helped you walk through a failed test and readied you for the next?
3. Why does God test (prove) those He loves?

Often, in a time of testing, God is silent,
giving you an opportunity to exercise what you know.
He always observes to see if you will listen
to your conscience or your desires.

———————◆———————

PAIN—THE ROCKET FUEL
FOR PURPOSE

WEEK 48 | TUESDAY

They said to me, "The remnant there in the province who survived the
captivity are in great distress and reproach, and the wall of Jerusalem
is broken down and its gates are burned with fire." When I heard these
words, I sat down and wept and mourned for days; and I was fasting
and praying before the God of heaven. Nehemiah 1:3-4

What is your first response when pain reels through your soul? "Stop, drop, and roll" is a fire-safety technique to practice in order to minimize injury if your clothes catch on fire. Some people run and hide to avoid pain, but then it chases them. Mature saints train their senses to see pain as a conversation starter with God. Nehemiah's first response when pain reeled through his soul was to stop, drop, and roll into God's presence.

It may be counterintuitive, but run toward your pain and let God repurpose it. Pain is often a point of contact God will use to get your attention, birth a new vision in you, or send a message of correction. How you respond when pain hits will determine what happens next in your relationship with God. The first and highest view of your situation is to ask God for His perspective on your pain. Until you see your pain through God's eyes, you won't know how He wants to leverage it for your future and His purposes. Nehemiah's pain drove him to his knees to seek God. Why is prayer so important when experiencing pain? Because a conversation with God about pain turns pain into fuel that produces a force multiplier in your faith. In what ways might God leverage pain in your life?

- Pain creates vision.
- Pain unlocks passion.
- Pain searches for answers.
- Pain seeks resolution and results.
- Pain creates momentum that drives behavior.
- Pain creates a common purpose among people.
- Pain recalibrates focus to get you moving in the right direction.
- Pain can be a launching pad for the larger story God has for your life.
- Pain clears the clogged channels of communication so you can hear God clearly.

REFLECT TO CONNECT

1. What are the pain points you are facing?
2. What pain points in your past has God leveraged to help create a better future for you?
3. How can you use your "pain points" to help another person break through in their circumstances?

If you let Him, God will repurpose the pain in your life into a fuel that produces a force multiplier for you.

THE PRAYER OF PERSUASION
WEEK 48 | WEDNESDAY

"O Lord, I beseech You, may Your ear be attentive to the prayer of Your servant and the prayer of Your servants who delight to revere Your name, and make Your servant successful today and grant him compassion before this man." Now I was the cupbearer to the king.
Nehemiah 1:11

Have you ever quoted God to God while praying? It works! Nehemiah had just received a report of a remnant of his people who were suffering in Jerusalem. With sadness of heart, he wept, prayed, and fasted. Most of his prayer was a combination of confession and reminding God of what He said would happen if His children abandoned Him, but then also how He would rescue them and bring them back together. There are a few clues Nehemiah gives us on how he interceded and then asked God to help him persuade the king.

1. Nehemiah's cause was noble; he was on the right side of right and pleading with God to do what He was eager to do, which was to restore His people. You will have many opportunities to ask God to help you do the right thing in your career. God is eager to help you bring His ways into your work. When asking God in prayer, be sure to ask Him according to His "heart," submitting your desires to His so He can fashion them for eternal success, not just temporary gain. When you put yourself in Nehemiah's shoes, consider His situation and the big ask He was about to make to the king.

2. Nehemiah asks God's help in making his ask to the king. Nehemiah is about to make a big ask of a non-Jewish king but first asks God to grant him favor that the king would have compassion on him. It's difficult to get things done without the support of those in authority. You need influence *and* favor. As a young professional, I made it a habit to ask God for favor with "God and man" each day. You will need both for your assignment.

3. Nehemiah had access to the king as the cupbearer. Wherever you are in an organization, you have to ask yourself, "Whom do I have access to?" Regardless of where you start, no door is so shut that God cannot open for you. It is often God who is waiting for you—a willing heart is harder to come by than an open door. When an injustice hits your heart hard, that may be God's heart imprinting on yours. Follow the thread of compassion and go to your knees. It's possible that God wants to empower you in your position to accomplish a great work.

1. Are there injustices you see that God could use you to help correct?
2. Nehemiah was a "builder" of people and walls; what has God called you to build in your career?
3. What work project is resonating in your heart that God may want to become a builder with you in?

Praying the promises of God creates favor
for you and your cause.

PRAY FOR SUCCESS

WEEK 48 | THURSDAY

"O Lord, I beseech You, may Your ear be attentive
to the prayer of Your servant and the prayer of
Your servants who delight to revere Your name, and make
Your servant successful today and grant him compassion before
this man." Now I was the cupbearer to the king.
Nehemiah 1:11

Nehemiah prayed for success, and so can you. Praying with an open heart opens a two-way channel of communication between you and Heaven. Praying God's Word (the Bible—what God said) as Nehemiah did says to God, "I heard what You said before, and I want to hear You now." Mark Batterson, in his best-selling book *The Circle Maker*, said, "The Bible wasn't meant to be read through but prayed through." Praying God's will guarantees

God's involvement in your success as you follow His lead and do your part. What does it mean to pray with an open heart? When you pray as Nehemiah did, you pray with sincerity, transparency, reverence, and a specific request—then you LISTEN. The "open heart" approach when praying for success carries a conviction of purpose to get something done, and this attracts God's favor.

God breathes success on those who involve Him in the micro-decisions of their day. God is delighted when you come to Him for help, just like any father would be when their son or daughter reaches out. Asking God to make your way prosperous doesn't move God, but it moves you to work with His Spirit to accomplish something with Him you could not accomplish without Him. When I was 20 years old, selling advertising to clients twice my age, I would often prepare for meetings by writing my statements and questions on a pad of paper I kept in my car before I walked into the meeting. As I wrote, I would pray, "Lord, please give me the right words to say and the right questions to ask and grant me favor with this customer." So much of success is nuanced in a moment of timing. Bringing God into the micro-moments of your day-to-day work activities allows Him to breathe inspiration over your decisions, your deliberations, and the outcomes of what you set your hand to. When should you pray the prayer for success? Any time you are meeting with someone you desire favor with or someone who has authority to make your life better or worse. This can include supervisors, customers, coworkers, coaches, pastors, parents, and more.

REFLECT TO CONNECT

1. What meeting might you need God's help or hand with? What outcome are you hoping for?

2. Can you give an example of a meeting you had where you said the wrong thing that sent the meeting in a wrong direction?
3. Have you ever tried writing out your prayer requests to see how God might answer you on paper?

Bringing God into the micro-moments of your day-to-day work activities allows Him to breathe inspiration over your decisions and deliberations and influence the outcomes of what you set your hand to.

NEHEMIAH'S SECRET STRATEGY

WEEK 48 | FRIDAY

So I came to Jerusalem and was there three days. And I arose in the night, I and a few men with me. I did not tell anyone what my God was putting into my mind to do for Jerusalem and there was no animal with me except the animal on which I was riding. So I went out at night by the Valley Gate in the direction of the Dragon's Well and on to the Refuse Gate, inspecting the walls of Jerusalem which were broken down and its gates which were consumed by fire. Nehemiah 2:11-13

Do you believe God has a specific strategy for everything He does or that He is haphazard in His work? If you said yes to the first option, then you must go back to God and get the strategy and details for the vision He is leading you to walk out. When God plants a vision in you for your life or career or puts a work to be done on your heart, He also has insight about the person or the circumstances you will face. For the work Nehemiah was about to embark on, consider the process God led him through before the work began.

1. Nehemiah prayed in the micro-moments at work before, during, and likely after conversations. Nehemiah prayed to God before his moment to make the big ask of the king. He "paused" by practicing the 3-second rule, allowing God to weigh in and direct His answer. Whom do you need to practice the "3-second pause" with in conversation?

2. Nehemiah architected his plans with God privately before sharing them publicly with the king or his team. Nehemiah, when answering the king, had detailed plans with an outline of a timeline so as to infuse confidence and win favor with the king. When meeting with the kings of this world, kings won't extend their authority and influence to you unless you can demonstrate competence. Delegating responsibility or extending influence to "unproven" people or those who are not good planners is too much risk for them.

3. Nehemiah walked the ground secretly at night, away from the big crowds, so he could survey the work undisturbed. Leaders always survey the terrain before putting their hand to the plow so they can see what God sees, hear what God wants them to hear, and feel what God feels for the work He has called them to. The more time you invest planning in private with God, the more you will produce when it's time to take action. Every vision faces resistance; walking the ground ahead of time will allow God to whisper insights into your spirit. Naysayers always surround the work and purposes of God, so keep quiet what you need to keep quiet.

4. Nehemiah spoke God's words. Nehemiah shared with his inner circle about the process God had brought him through with the king and how God had granted him favor to persuade the king. When enlisting support, saying what God said to you is what persuades people to follow. When what you

say out loud is the same as what God whispered in the Spirit, people will hear God speaking through you.

5. Nehemiah knew what to share with people and what NOT to share with people. Some things that God shares are between you and God only; discern the difference.

Doing as Nehemiah did will give you insights into how God likes to work with wall builders. What wall is God calling you to build in your life during this season?

REFLECT TO CONNECT

1. What can you learn from Nehemiah for an important meeting you have coming up?
2. What "ground" does God want you to walk as Nehemiah did so He can survey the land with you?
3. Have you ever practiced the 3-second rule, allowing the pause to mute your emotions so God can speak to you in a micro-moment?

The more time you invest planning in private with God, the more you will produce when it's time to take action.

LEADERSHIP LEVERS OF MOTIVATION

WEEK 49 | MONDAY

Then I said to them, "You see the bad situation we are in, that Jerusalem is desolate and its gates burned by fire. Come, let us rebuild the wall of Jerusalem so that we will no longer be a reproach." I told them how the hand of my God had been favorable to me and also about the king's words which he had spoken to me. Then they said, "Let us arise and build." So they put their hands to the good work. Nehemiah 2:17-18

Persuasive elements embedded within your vision are what will make people buy in. Passion, pain, purpose, pleasure, or pursuit of solving a problem are the energy forces leaders tap into to rouse a sleepy workforce. These are the inherent motivators within people that spark the wellspring of motivation lying dormant within and unleash a drive to work without ceasing. Why do they work without ceasing? Because they are not just working for a paycheck but for a purpose that takes them to a future that transcends their present. Nehemiah knew how to tap into this wellspring of emotion and energy buried within the people. He knew what was sacred in them and pushed on the right leadership levers. How did he do that? He baited his hook with what he knew the fish would bite. Here are a few ways in which you as a leader can bait the hook of buy-in using the people's "why" to draw them into a cause worth fighting for.

CAST VISION WITH SELF-INTEREST ATTACHED: Paint a picture of a future that is better than the present for the organization and the people. If a person can't "see" how your vision benefits them and not just the organization, you will not convince them to buy in wholeheartedly. The strongest visions help people to see what they can achieve, who they can become, and what they can attain, whether it be financial, emotional, or social.

CAST PURPOSE WITH STICKINESS: People want to be part of something bigger than themselves. Leaders look for angles that will help them position their vision as "first times," "never been done befores," "impossible odds," "victorious outcomes," and "history-making." When you help people achieve and become *with you* what they could not *without you*, they will follow you into the uncertainty of an adventuresome future.

CAST ACCOUNTABILITY WITH CONSEQUENCES: Share with people what their role and responsibility will be, then expect it. Without risk and reward, there is no significance in the success or consequence in the loss if the vision doesn't come to pass.

CAST WITH PASSION: Emotion creates motion. When people feel your heart, you unlock the door of emotion and passion within them. The picture of passion in your heart imprints on their heart and partnership is formed. People must buy into the messenger before they buy into the message, so always show your heart before you sell your vision. As the messenger becomes the message, the mission transfers.

REFLECT TO CONNECT

1. What bait do you use to get people excited about what you are excited about?
2. What is the vision hidden in your heart you want your family, friends, or coworkers to buy into?
3. What is the passion or pain point right now in your life that God is using to start a conversation with you?

People must buy into the messenger before they will buy
into the message, so always show your heart before
you sell your vision. As the messenger becomes the message,
the mission transfers.

———————————◆◆————————————

ENEMIES AT THE GATE

WEEK 49 | TUESDAY

So I answered them and said to them, "The God of heaven will give us
success; therefore we His servants will arise and build, but you have no
portion, right or memorial in Jerusalem." Nehemiah 2:20

S tand your ground. Confrontation makes people uncomfortable. Successful leaders know how to get comfortable with the
uncomfortable. That is what separates them from the pack. Knowing
how to navigate conflict, attacks, and serious threats to your leadership
is critical if you are to succeed. Every worthwhile vision will attract
enemies. Enemies are the people and forces, both visible and invisible,
that will stand against you as you build your dream. Leaders must
anticipate conflict, then be willing to contend with resistance. Here are
a few strategies to neutralize an enemy or tactic being used against you:

- Call it out.
- Face it and fight it.
- Accept it and work through it.
- Make peace by negotiating with it.
- Marshal your resources against it and overwhelm it.

Nehemiah, going into his building project, was full of prayer, purpose, and plans. He anticipated resistance and equipped his people

to work on the wall while being "enemy conscious." Nehemiah didn't soft-shoe his enemies, placate them, or negotiate with them. Nehemiah said "no" to them and stood his ground, and then his team followed his lead. It wasn't easy, but courageous leadership never is.

REFLECT TO CONNECT

1. What stands have you made that required you to fight through enemy attacks?
2. What enemies are you facing as you contend for the ground God wants you to take?
3. Are there people God wants you to defend that are within your circle of responsibility?

Enemies to the purposes of God won't stand down
until you stand up to them.

ENEMY TACTICS AND TRICKS

WEEK 49 | WEDNESDAY

When I saw their fear, I rose and spoke to the nobles, the officials and
the rest of the people: "Do not be afraid of them; remember the Lord
who is great and awesome, and fight for your brothers, your sons,
your daughters, your wives and your houses." Nehemiah 4:14

The team Nehemiah had raised up had a mind to work (Nehemiah 4:6). With this unity of purpose, nothing could stop them. The greatest enemy you will face is always yourself. The enemy will interfere with you but doesn't have power over you to force you to do anything without your permission. Once you purpose to accomplish something, nothing shall be impossible for you as you work alongside God. But like Nehemiah, who had to lead himself and his team, here are a few strategies the enemy will use to trip you up:

FIVE TACTICS FROM THE ENEMY'S BAG OF TRICKS

1. **CONFUSION:** Uncertainty or misdirection will halt any work in its place. Leaders bring clarity and organization to diminish confusion.

2. **CONFLICT:** Seeds of conflict redirect the energy away from productive work to unnecessary and destructive emotional warfare. Leaders quickly resolve and eliminate conflict that interferes with progress.

3. **FEAR:** Focusing on circumstances around you vs. the God working in you will weaken even the strongest of saints when facing daunting challenges. Leaders keep people's eyes focused on the future prize, not the price being paid in the present.

4. **UNBELIEF:** The mixing of doubt with your belief will create a counterbalancing effect to neutralize the power that fuels your faith. Leaders teach people to be single-minded about the cause lest they get overwhelmed with the circumstances surrounding the project.

5. **DISTRACTION:** If the enemy can't stop you, he will entice you with something that looks appealing to break your focus. But stay strong by following what King David did when he said, "My heart is FIXED" (Psalm 57:7 KJV, emphasis added). Leaders keep people's eyes forward.

The enemy can't force you to surrender, but he can wear you down until you want to give up. The enemy can't take control of your will or volition, but he *is* allowed to woo you with promises and lies of an easier path. The enemy can't make choices for you, but he can present alternatives to you like he did with Eve in the garden and entice you to follow another voice.

"We have nothing to fear but fear itself."
FDR, 1933 Inaugural Address

REFLECT TO CONNECT

1. What strategies do you use to help you maintain your focus when distractions abound?
2. What tactics have you seen the enemy use against you in the work environment?
3. How can you fortify yourself against your most vulnerable area of attack?

Leaders keep people's eyes focused on the future prize,
not the price being paid in the present.

———————◆◆◆———————

THE CHRONICLES OF THE WALL BUILDER

WEEK 49 | THURSDAY

When our enemies heard that it was known to us, and that God had frustrated their plan, then all of us returned to the wall, each one

to his work. From that day on, half of my servants carried on the
work while half of them held the spears, the shields, the bows and the
breastplates; and the captains were behind the whole house of Judah.
Nehemiah 4:15-16

You were made to be an "overcomer," so fight for the right things. Do you think that because God is on your side that life and work will always be smooth sailing? Or that opposition is only faced by those who don't know God? Nehemiah had a God-ordained mission to rebuild the wall in Jerusalem, yet he would have to face enemies who would discourage his builders, threaten the lives of those helping, and more. If you've ever set out to build something significant in your life, you know what it's like to be a "Nehemiah." Nehemiah's team had to multitask under terrible circumstances, yet they prevailed. What are you building, and what are you facing?

If the work you are doing didn't require God's help, it wouldn't be big enough for you. Nehemiah wasn't the only laborer called to the greatness of servanthood who would suffer hardship along the way. Joshua led Israel into the Promised Land with the power of God at his side, yet had to fight for every square inch of "Heaven on earth" that was promised to him and Israel. Even Jesus said that Christians would face persecution. If the road you are walking in your vocational calling didn't require the miraculous, it wouldn't be a miracle. Every struggle you are facing is leading to not only a breakthrough but a testimony. Consider making a list of all the struggles you face, whether they be outward circumstances or inward emotional struggles, and lay them before God. This is your future "victory list" God desires to help you walk through so you can break through. Your breakthroughs will make up "book one" someday in the Chronicles of Wall-Building for your life.

REFLECT TO CONNECT

1. How can you help a "Nehemiah" build their wall? How can you become a Nehemiah?
2. What are you building in your life that requires God's help for it to succeed?
3. Who is a "wall builder" you could go to for advice?

God Himself faces opposition and battles, yet
He still builds daily with those willing to work alongside Him.
What wall does He want to build with you?

RESPECT IN THE RANKS

WEEK 49 | FRIDAY

Moreover, from the day that I was appointed to be their governor in the
land of Judah, from the twentieth year to the thirty-second year of King
Artaxerxes, for twelve years, neither I nor my kinsmen have eaten the
governor's food allowance. But the former governors who were before me
laid burdens on the people and took from them bread and wine besides
forty shekels of silver; even their servants domineered the people.
But I did not do so because of the fear of God. Nehemiah 5:14-15

J ust because you can, doesn't mean you should. As a leader, your behavior is always being observed and evaluated in the ranks. For there to be respect, authenticity and credibility must exist, as they are the currency that increases or reduces your influence. If people are to buy into you as a leader and perform beyond minimum expectations, they must feel you identify with them. Leadership positions often come with perks, rewards, even special treatment not available to employees in the lower ranks. Nehemiah knew his people were struggling, so he passed on the perks that were normally available to a leader in his position. In so doing, his people went above and beyond, finishing the wall-building project in record time.

"If your actions seem to undermine your words,
you'll create problems no amount of jawboning can fix."
John W. Gardner

REFLECT TO CONNECT

1. When you ask others to tighten their belt, do you do the same?
2. When you ask others to sacrifice, is your sacrifice visible?
3. What examples of leaders asking for one thing then doing another can you give?

For there to be respect, authenticity and credibility must exist,
as they are the currency that increases or reduces your influence.

RELINQUISHING RIGHTS IN THE OFFICE OF LEADERSHIP

WEEK 50 | MONDAY

I did not demand the governor's food allowance, because the servitude was heavy on this people. Remember me, O my God, for good, according to all that I have done for this people. Nehemiah 5:18-19

Leaders lighten the load for their people with strategic sacrifices. Nehemiah distinguished himself in the eyes of the people and God by giving up what he had a right to have. Privileges of leadership exist, yet when a leader passes on them or returns them back to the people, it does not go unnoticed by God.

Your position exists to serve the people, not the other way around. There is a street credit that exists for a leader who sacrifices for their people. Nehemiah knew that if he exercised his right for the governor's portion, it would come at the expense of the people. Great leadership doesn't think twice about laying down personal rights so the organization can benefit. Sometimes a leader may sacrifice time, income, expense accounts, vacation plans, and more that they may be entitled to so the team can benefit or be relieved from a burden. Leaders can't just be aware of what something is; they must be aware of how something looks. Remaining "above reproach" in leveraging the benefits that accompany the office of leadership is as important as avoiding the hint of impropriety in issues of character.

REFLECT TO CONNECT

1. Are there "rights of leadership" you feel led to lay down?
2. What do people say about leaders who abuse perks?

3. Why is it both good and bad to enjoy the privileges of leadership?

Remaining "above reproach" in leveraging the benefits that accompany leadership is as important as avoiding the hint of impropriety in issues of character.

THE FINISHER

WEEK 50 | TUESDAY

So I sent messengers to them, saying, "I am doing a great work and I cannot come down. Why should the work stop while I leave it and come down to you?" They sent messages to me four times in this manner, and I answered them in the same way. Nehemiah 6:3-4

Distraction is the enemy's plan for you because it breaks your focus. Nehemiah had a number of distractions (good reasons) to stop building the wall. Some included fear, complaints by the people, and real physical threats he and his team faced while they built. Nonetheless, he let nothing stop the building. Metaphorically, there are many things that will "break your focus" and attempt to divert your attention away from starting projects and then finishing the projects you start. For myself, I tend to take on too much, which fractures my attention in a way that leaves important projects left undone. Has it also been your experience that taking on too many projects siphons a little bit of energy for each, leaving them all unfinished?

In the world of procrastination, tomorrow is the busiest day of the week. In *PERSUADE*, I discuss the dangers of multitasking and why it retards the concentration muscle, making it difficult for people to stay on task. Leaders must keep themselves and their team focused if they are to consistently move projects and people into the end zone of victory. Here is a strategy to stay focused when managing projects:

- **Time Block!** Shut yourself into a room with your project and refuse to come out until your project is complete. For some, this is a physical room; for others, it may be a mental room I call the "Focus Box" that allows nothing in but "the one thing." The Apostle Paul once said, "One thing I do" (Philippians 3:13).
- **Refuse Mental Interruptions!** The thoughts of the mind must be directed in a specific direction. The mind hates to be focused on only one subject at a time. It must be brought into subjection to its master—YOU.
- **Set Technology Aside!** Focusing is a mental exercise in REFUSING to do anything but the "one thing" you have decided to do. Refuse to respond to email, social media posts, and alerts. The dopamine hit your brain receives by constantly looking and reacting to your smartphone is what breaks your concentration and weakens your attention span, making it dependent on quick-fix, feel-good distraction bursts that hinder your mental focus.

REFLECT TO CONNECT

1. What unfinished project has been haunting you?
2. What successful strategies do you have for staying focused?
3. Of the people you know who are successful, how do they manage their tendency to procrastinate?

*Focus is the byproduct of building your concentration muscle;
it grows with use.*

A LEADER'S MUSCLE
OF DISCERNMENT

WEEK 50 | WEDNESDAY

*Then I perceived that surely God had not sent him, but he uttered his
prophecy against me because Tobiah and Sanballat had hired him.
He was hired for this reason, that I might become frightened and act
accordingly and sin, so that they might have an evil report in order
that they could reproach me.* Nehemiah 6:12-13

The power of discernment shows you what is unseen, helps
you to hear what is unsaid, and senses what is hidden. A leader's
success or failure is dependent on knowing whom to trust, whom to
question and what data to follow. Nehemiah, through the use of his
trained senses and relationship with God, developed strong powers
of discernment.

The muscle of discernment can be built. One of the most powerful yet intangible gifts a leader must develop is discernment. When
making decisions, I will often ask God, "Please show me what is
unseen." Knowledge, experience, and nudges from the Divine all
play a role in a leader's ability to listen, learn, and lead by leveraging their intuitive senses. Powers of discernment can come from
sources that include:

- A word of knowledge about a situation. Sometimes God will
  whisper an insight about a situation or person, pose a question
  in your mind, or give you a gut feeling causing your "Spidey
  senses" to tingle.
- Your strengths and former experience. In "The Law of the Sixth
  Sense" from *PERSUADE,* I discuss a number of ways in which a

person can develop their intuitive sense. A snap-judgment call can be the result of experience, a memory becoming present for no reason but to plant a feeling or picture in your subconscious (your spirit), or a burden you feel to act in a certain way, call someone, or hit "pause" on a decision you are contemplating.

- Messengers that come into your life. The list of ways in which God can give you a warning or push you in one direction or the other is endless. Being committed to God's way (best over better) and putting people over personal gain are character-building behaviors to ensure you are receiving the right signals to help your powers of discernment.

REFLECT TO CONNECT

1. Whom do you rely on for sound counsel?
2. Can you remember a time when you trusted the right or wrong person? What was the outcome?
3. How can you tell when someone is giving you sound advice or leading you astray?

Your muscle of discernment can be developed to see what is unseen, to hear what is unspoken, and to sense what God senses.

HIDDEN AGENDAS

WEEK 50 | THURSDAY

Remember, O my God, Tobiah and Sanballat according to these works of theirs, and also Noadiah the prophetess and the rest of the prophets who were trying to frighten me. Nehemiah 6:14

Two great motivators are fear and desire; wise leaders sniff them both out. It is human nature to follow pleasure and avoid pain; tapping into both creates a motivating force. In Nehemiah's case, and in many instances in the Old Testament, false prophets said they were speaking on behalf of God when they were not as a way to move their personal agendas forward. In today's society, news organizations parse stories and use politics to move their agendas forward. We call this "fake news." Using facts, figures, storytelling, and other powerful forms of influential communication skills to move your personal agenda forward at the expense of others is dishonest, disingenuous, and manipulative. How can you avoid being moved off your agenda and onto another's? Do what Nehemiah did.

GET A CLEAR WORD! Nehemiah had a word from God and knew that anything that attempted to move him off "what God said" was misdirection. Nehemiah was successful because his agenda came from God. In contrast, Eve in the garden and Balaam the prophet both let themselves be talked into something they wanted over what God directed, and both succumbed to another's agenda.

GET INFORMED! Nehemiah had a sense ahead of time of who his enemies were. He questioned their motives from the start. Question the motives of anyone who tries to move your leadership off mission.

GET READY! Nehemiah anticipated resistance before the project of rebuilding the wall started, so when it showed up, his antenna picked up on it, and he was prepared to answer those who would stand against him.

GET PRAYED UP! Nehemiah relied on God and prayed frequently before and during the wall-building project for himself, his team, and the work which God gave him to do. Anytime you bring prayer into your project and pray over your people, you engage the supernatural powers of Heaven to come to your aid.

REFLECT TO CONNECT

1. What resistance do you face in following God's best for your life?
2. What work has God given you to do in building your life and His kingdom?
3. Have you had the experience of people using information incorrectly to manipulate you?

God resists leaders who use their giftings to manipulate others for their personal agendas.

———————◆◆◆———————

THE POWER TO REFRAME
WEEK 50 | FRIDAY

So they set up the altar on its foundation, for they were terrified because of the peoples of the lands; and they offered burnt offerings on it to the LORD, burnt offerings morning and evening. Ezra 3:3

Leaders develop the skill of coaching others to walk through fear and into freedom. Imagine participating in a building project whereby as you build, enemies threaten you. The people of God, when reconstructing the altar, temple, and walls in Jerusalem, faced real opposition, including physical threats, plus undermining influences that aimed to stop their progress. Yet, they pressed on.

Courage is the intentional decision to walk through fear to get to freedom. In your lifetime, you will face many types of fears, including financial, medical, emotional, family, career, and more.

Fear can be real or imagined, but focusing on fear or worry is a sin. Focusing on fear is what gives it energy, which is what causes it to grow. Faith grows the same way. By focusing and meditating on it, you feed it emotionally. Leaders must learn to manage their own fear, then lead others to do the same. The moment you teach people how to reframe how they view their situation, strength begins to emerge. Following are a few ways to help yourself and others change the optics of a circumstance. These include using our mindsets and imagination in the way God intended us to.

- Instead of looking at loss or consequences, remind yourself of the rewards you are walking into.
- If your circumstance creates fear, focus on how God might view it.
- Fix your attention on your long-term goals, and the pain of the present will become smaller in the bigness of the future God has for you.
- See yourself running to someone instead away from something and watch fear dissolve in your rearview mirror.
- Set your eyes on serving a purpose greater than yourself, and fear becomes small in the presence of God.
- Say what God says about your circumstance out loud, for faith comes by hearing the word of God spoken over your life.

Just as faith is a decision, so is fear. One creates freedom; the other takes you hostage. Faith is not a "blind trusting"; it is an active confidence in something or Someone, who is Jesus Christ.

REFLECT TO CONNECT

1. What would you be capable of if you knew you could not fail?
2. If you had to write down your faith vs. fears, what comes to mind?

3. What is God's perspective about that one thing that you feel apprehension about?

> *Faith is not a "blind trusting"; it is an active and purposeful confidence in something or Someone.*

BAD APPLES IN THE BUNCH

WEEK 51 | MONDAY

Then the people of the land discouraged the people of Judah, and frightened them from building, and hired counselors against them to frustrate their counsel all the days of Cyrus king of Persia, even until the reign of Darius king of Persia. Ezra 4:4-5

Mark the momentum breakers. Whether building a building, leading a team, or working toward a vision, resistance goes with the territory. Sometimes the resistance shows up in people, finances, or forces around you. When leaders make organizational changes, there are almost always "resisters" they must contend with. The Apostle Paul said leaders are to "mark" those who cause division or strife.

Learning to lead through resistance is critical if you are to be successful. What does "people resistance" look like, and how should you handle it? When making change, I allow time for acceptance but am aware of those who are set on fighting progress. These are the negative, poison-spreading people talking and spreading discontent at the water cooler. Naysayers never miss an opportunity to weaken people with their words. Make sure you "mark" the "bad apples" and address the behavior before they spoil your good apples.

FENCE SITTERS: When change occurs, there are always those who need time to download the change. Fence sitters can be converted to embrace change with a positive attitude but be aware of those who are "unconvertable."

UNDERMINERS: These are enemies to your leadership and your culture. They may tell you what you want to hear while with you, then work against you the moment they are mixing among the people.

Like a cancer, their bad attitude spreads, and if they are not identified and eliminated from the environment, they can poison the team like a bad apple spoils a bunch.

GAMERS: Gamers are watching to see when you are watching so they can "get away" with what they do behind your back when you're not looking. They look to leverage a situation only for their benefit but won't fight for the benefit of others when they are asked to step up. Gamers are not intentionally destructive to an environment but can set a bad example for the team. Left unchecked, people will assume their behavior is approved by leadership if it goes uncorrected.

Dealing with momentum breakers may take time. Identify them, then formulate a plan to work them out of your business and away from the team who has your high contributors.

REFLECT TO CONNECT

1. What and who are the momentum breakers in your organization?
2. Who are the momentum creators that bring positive energy to your life?
3. Who in your experience has been a backstabber, underminer, or gamer?

Naysayers never miss an opportunity to weaken people with their words at the water cooler.

A REPUTATION FOR COMPETENCE

WEEK 51 | TUESDAY

*This Ezra went up from Babylon, and he was a scribe skilled in the law
of Moses, which the LORD God of Israel had given; and the king granted
him all he requested because the hand of the LORD his God was upon
him... For Ezra had set his heart to study the law of the LORD and to
practice it, and to teach His statutes and ordinances in Israel.*
Ezra 7:6, 10

The God of Heaven and the kings of Earth have one thing in
common: they both need people they can trust. The Bible is
filled with stories, analogies, and principles that point people to
trusting God. Have you considered that God needs to be able to
trust you?

The big assignments go to people of competence. Ezra had proven
himself to God and to the king over a long period of time through his
diligence, consistency, and performance as reliable and competent.
Leaders must have people next to them whom they can pass the ball
to when the stakes are high or when there is a big job that needs doing.
How did Ezra attain such a high reputation for competence?

- Ezra was considered a scholar, but to attain that, he became a
  good student. Day after day, he devoted himself to learning in
  his chosen lane of assignment. What lane of expertise are you
  studying in?
- Ezra was known as a person of skill. Ezra became skilled through
  study and repetition. Without repetition, mastery is not possible.
  God will give you opportunities to practice in private before you
  are put before an audience of authority and influence where you
  are tested and observed publicly.

- Ezra was influential. He developed relationships with the king, with God, and with the people so his influence and reputation grew. When the big job came open to reestablish the Law in Jerusalem, both the God of Heaven and the king of Babylon picked him to carry out the task because he had proven himself in character and competence.

REFLECT TO CONNECT

1. What skill(s) have you decided to become a master of?
2. Whom are you surrounding yourself with to mentor you?
3. Do you have a sense of how God might want to use your talent now or in the future?

Competence is developed one day, one decision, and one repetition at a time.

THE FLOW OF FAVOR
WEEK 51 | WEDNESDAY

"You, Ezra, according to the wisdom of your God which is in your hand, appoint magistrates and judges that they may judge all the people who are in the province beyond the River, even all those who know the laws of your God; and you may teach anyone who is ignorant of them."
Ezra 7:25

Favor is the invisible current of grace that attracts people to you who are predisposed to assist you. How God moved the heart of King Artaxerxes to empower Ezra to do what He had called him to do is a picture of the ways in which God will use favor to empower you. Favor is assigned to you for your assignment; whom has God called to assist you?

Favor shows up in the way in which you are needing God to move. Someone who possesses a position of authority, influence, wealth, relationships, government, or protection will allow what they have to flow to you so God can leverage it through you to serve His purposes. In Ezra's case, the very words spoken by King Artaxerxes to Ezra mimicked the very calling and gift set Ezra had. What "mountain" do you need the invisible hand of favor to move for you today?

Favor is in your control. There are ways you can attract favor, including performing your job with excellence and integrity, that will help you to stand out from the crowd. God helped Joseph, Daniel, Ezra, and more stand heads and shoulders above the crowd because of their consistency and commitment in their fields. God's "hand of favor" rests on those who have developed excellence and are of a trustworthy spirit to lead people in the marketplace or ministry.

REFLECT TO CONNECT

1. In what ways have currents of favor flowed to you?
2. Whom in your life has God granted you favor with, and for what reason?
3. To what degree are leaders tempted to use the currents of favor to serve themselves and not others?

Favor is the invisible current of grace that attracts people to you who are predisposed to assist you.

PROTECTION IN OBEDIENCE

WEEK 51 | THURSDAY

"So now do not give your daughters to their sons nor take their daughters to your sons, and never seek their peace or their prosperity, that you may be strong and eat the good things of the land and leave it as an inheritance to your sons forever." Ezra 9:12

The grass isn't greener on the other side; there is just more to mow. When Ezra said to "never seek their peace or their prosperity," he recognized that there were enticements that would be appealing to his people. If the people were wooed by these trappings, they would be a pathway to destruction. It's easy to look over the fence, see only the benefits of another way of life, and desire it without counting or knowing the cost of what else a life on the other side of a decision looks like. It's in this same way the enemy uses temptation without showing consequences.

In recruitment, enticements in the work world include a higher salary, more vacation time, a better position or title, the ability to work from home, or affirmation that may be lacking where you currently work. I was once offered a $100k bump in annual pay that would have solved my money problems and more. After praying about it, God said, "Slowly back out of that door." After obeying, I felt depressed for about a month. But God always sees something you don't. That is why trusting Him requires faith and obedience. In the not-so-distant future, the person who took the job lost it, and the company went through difficult times. God always sees a future you don't see.

REFLECT TO CONNECT

1. Has there ever been a "money test" or other type of test you passed or failed?
2. In what ways have you been wooed or enticed with new and exciting opportunities?
3. How can you tell the difference between what opportunities are good vs. bad when the present looks tempting and the future uncertain?

When God asks you to give up something can see,
it's because He has something better for you that you can't see.

WORDS THAT STRENGTHEN

WEEK 51 | FRIDAY

"Arise! For this matter is your responsibility,
but we will be with you; be courageous and act."
Ezra 10:4

S ay it so they feel it. When I was young, I used to see my parents as all-knowing, unwavering, strong people all the time. But as I grew from adolescence to adulthood, I began to understand that they were regular people who experienced all the emotions I did. They could feel, be happy, or hurt. Plus, they knew when I was supporting them or resisting them. Those in authority in your life are the same way; they need your help. They need to feel your support.

Speak your support so they can feel your support. Shecaniah, one of the people in support of Ezra, spoke up and, with his words, strengthened Ezra for a very difficult decision he would have to make. Pastors, parents, teachers, and leaders from every vocation can be supported and strengthened by your words. I always make it a point to strengthen those above me, not just those horizontal to me. People assume those higher up are fine on their own, but they, too, need encouragement. Here are a few ways in which you can support those you answer to.

- Words of Affirmation: I believe in you and what you are doing.
- Words of Commitment: I am with you to support you.
- Words of Suggestion: Here is an idea that may help. What else can I do?
- Words of Empathy: I know what you're going through. How can I help?
- Words of Action: You can count on me to be there for you.

REFLECT TO CONNECT

1. Is there someone you long to hear words of support from?
2. How much emotional intelligence is required to feel what others feel?
3. Whom in authority over you can you verbalize words of support to today?

See someone struggling, say something encouraging, and you have lived the Golden Rule.

CHIEF FUNDRAISER
FOR THE GOSPEL

WEEK 52 | MONDAY

Now this I say, he who sows sparingly will also reap sparingly, and he
who sows bountifully will also reap bountifully. Each one must
do just as he has purposed in his heart, not grudgingly or under
compulsion, for God loves a cheerful giver.
2 Corinthians 9:6-7

S uccessfully asking people to part with their time, money, or
talents is an art form you must learn. How do you make your
"ask" when you are recruiting people to your cause? Paul was mas-
terful at connecting human desire to Heaven's purposes. The Apostle
Paul utilized his gifts of communication in raising finances to move
the Gospel forward. How did he do that? Consider how Paul added
meaning multiple times during his "ask" by hitting on hot buttons
his audience might resonate with.

1. **PAUL PREPARES THE GROUND WITH GRACIOUS
   COMPLIMENTS:** Paul opens his "ask" by speaking about
   their reputation of generosity, suggesting it's not even necessary to bring "giving" up, then tells them how their promise
   to support the Macedonians has created a zeal.
2. **PAUL OBLIGATES THE GIVER:** Paul interjects a twinge
   of consequence to the Corinthians that if they don't follow
   through and give as Paul said they would, it could look bad
   for them *and* him.
3. **PAUL DEALS WITH THE ELEPHANT IN THE ROOM:**
   The tendency when giving can be to shrink back from what
   one has purposed in their heart to do. Paul deals with this
   head-on by interjecting the word "covetousness" into the

conversation, which means to "desire something that belongs to someone else." Why does Paul do this? He wants to address the inner wrestling his audience will have as a way of helping them get past it before it comes up.

4. **PAUL POINTS OUT A PROMISE:** Paul finishes his "ask" by reminding the Corinthians of the ROI (benefits) they can count on by their generosity which includes:

- A giver's gift produces thanksgiving to God by others.
- God's supply of grace provides for the needs of the giver.
- The more they give, the more they receive back from God.
- Giving to God creates pleasure for Him as God loves a cheerful giver.
- God gives seed to sowers, then multiplies it so that person's "account of righteousness" will increase.

REFLECT TO CONNECT

1. Do you agree with how Paul persuaded people to give?
2. Is a person's problem with giving in parting with the money or in how the "ask" is done?
3. Should people be challenged to increase their giving to God? If so, why? If not, why?

The Apostle Paul always provided reasons for giving and ROI that would resonate with people. That's how he raised finances to move the Gospel forward.

———————————◆———————————

THE COST OF DISRESPECT

WEEK 52 | TUESDAY

But Queen Vashti refused to come at the king's command delivered
by the eunuchs. Then the king became very angry
and his wrath burned within him. Esther 1:12

Vashti vanquished—disrespect displaces influence and position. When a person of authority makes a decision that is not followed, it leaves them questioning their subordinate's commitment to them and the organization. In today's team-oriented and concentric workflow environment, there is not always a direct line of authority, which can make some in a dotted-line reporting relationship think that obedience is optional. Keep in mind that whether in a direct or dotted line, authorities who feel snubbed by subordinates will search out solutions to find the support they need or find another subordinate who is supportive of what they need done. Disrespect comes with a price.

If you must resist or reject, handle it carefully. In every person's work experience, there will come a time they will be asked to do something they will not want to do. The task given by an authority-on-high may seem beneath you, not a "fit," not your job, inappropriate, or not suited to you. However, how you reject or handle the request from an authority can determine whether or not you continue to advance in your career, stall your career, or lose invisible currents of influence and favor. How should you handle yourself in this situation?

1. **Submit to a Higher Purpose:** If you are feeling "rubbed the wrong way" in the request, count the cost of taking the high road to fulfill the request vs. risking your greater goals, your position, and how your relationships might suffer if you refuse a supervisor's request. Could this be a test from God?

2. **Speak Truth to Power:** If the request being made of you is immoral or illegal, you have an obligation to speak truth to power; however, be careful in your approach. Your "viewpoint" of the situation may differ from that of a supervisor's, and suggesting they lack integrity while you stand on the "high ground" can come across as insulting. For such a situation as this, seek God in prayer for strategy or implementing a strategic silence for your situation.

3. **Swallow Your Pride:** Everyone feels "snubbed" or disrespected by an authority at one time or another. Although we guess at its meaning, it is often not an intentional act, and interpreting it as such can create an injury that leads to anger. It is in times like this that you must remember you are in subjection to authority and that everyone reports to someone, so suck it up and do your job.

REFLECT TO CONNECT

1. When was the last time you were rubbed the wrong way by a supervisor? What was your inward response?

2. What counsel have you had to give to a friend who was asked to do something by a supervisor they felt uncomfortable with?

3. Who in your work experience was a favorite and least favorite supervisor of yours and why?

Disrespect displaces your influence and favor,
but honor and submission with excellence elevates you
in the eyes of authority.

SIGNS OF A MANIPULATIVE LEADER

WEEK 52 | WEDNESDAY

Then Haman said to King Ahasuerus, "There is a certain people scattered and dispersed among the peoples in all the provinces of your kingdom; their laws are different from those of all other people and they do not observe the king's laws, so it is not in the king's interest to let them remain. Then the king took his signet ring from his hand and gave it to Haman, the son of Hammedatha the Agagite, the enemy of the Jews. The king said to Haman, "The silver is yours, and the people also, to do with them as you please." Esther 3:8, 10-11

Bad leadership is more common than it should be. Haman is an example of a leader who rose to a position of influence and authority, then used it to hurt others. Leaders who use their position to serve themselves and not others fall into malicious motives when feeling threatened like Haman did. Fortunately, God looks out for His people in the marketplace, exposes plots against His people, and proves once again that nothing is hidden from His sight. What are the signs of a manipulative leader?

- Haman's motivation was birthed from resentment because Mordecai would not bow to him, so Haman sought to kill him. People with plots to hurt others are not uncommon in organizations. Have you known people whose mindsets are to think in terms of revenge, resentment, and making plans of retribution toward those they view as enemies?
- Haman only told the king one side of the story as a way to manipulate the king so he would be granted authority to carry out his personal vendetta. Have you ever observed people close to a supervisor who withhold information as a way to sway a decision in their direction?

- Haman used his influence and position with King Ahasuerus to serve his pride and lust for power. There will always be people close to power whose goal is to gather all they can for themselves—and often at the expense of others.

REFLECT TO CONNECT

1. Do you know of leaders you would characterize as bad leaders? Why?
2. Have you ever known someone who was always talking about an "enemy" as if they need to be watching their back or plotting against another?
3. If you saw one leader manipulating someone, under what circumstances would you have the courage to expose the plot?

The providential hand of God has foresight to know everything before it happens, so you will have a heads up when He wants you to be in the know.

PROTECTION UNSEEN

WEEK 52 | THURSDAY

During that night the king could not sleep so he gave an order to bring the book of records, the chronicles, and they were read before the king. It was found written what Mordecai had reported concerning Bigthana and Teresh, two of the king's eunuchs who were doorkeepers, that they had sought to lay hands on King Ahasuerus. The king said, "What honor or dignity has been bestowed on Mordecai for this?"
Esther 6:1-3

G od rarely shows us His "360-degree perspective" on all the ways in which He is working behind the scenes on our behalf. The story of Esther shows that God is at work night and day whether you are awake or asleep, and He is working in many ways whether or not you know how He is working your circumstances together for good. Consider the many strings God was pulling behind the scenes in just one aspect of the Esther story when Haman conspired to kill Mordecai.

- God caused the king to have a restless night, which led to him waking up and desiring to see records of the past. Then ironically, the king stumbled upon an incident where a person named Mordecai saved his life, and gratefulness welled up in his heart to reward him.
- Mordecai did not know that Haman was plotting to have him hanged and that God was already at work behind the scenes to thwart the plot and save his life.
- Haman did not know that God was working in the king's heart to honor the very person he wanted to hang, or else he never would have suggested such lavish honor on a person he was planning to hang.
- Esther was unaware that while God was working through her to save her people, He was also working behind the scenes to save her uncle Mordecai.
- Haman's wife did not know that her suggestion for her husband to build the gallows to hang Mordecai on would result in her husband being hung on it instead.

Only God knows everything going on behind the scenes. While you see a piece of the picture, God sees the whole thing. It's quite possible that one day He will show you movie scenes from your life wherein He lets you see all the ways in which He was involved in it.

REFLECT TO CONNECT

1. Are you aware of the invisible hand of God that has worked on your behalf in the past?
2. Have you ever considered asking God to show you what He sees in your circumstance?
3. When you can't see God's hand at work, do you believe it is still there, or do you lose faith, thinking you are alone?

The invisible providential hand of God is always at work in your life.

———————◆◆◆———————

THE LARGER STORY OF MORDECAI

WEEK 52 | FRIDAY

For Mordecai the Jew was second only to King Ahasuerus, and great among the Jews and in favor with his many kinsmen, one who sought the good of his people and one who spoke for the welfare of his whole nation. Esther 10:3

The BIG PICTURE you don't see comes after you. Mordecai, like Daniel and Joseph, shows how God can take someone in the worst possible circumstance (captivity) and elevate them to a place of prominence, power, and influence while serving the kings of Earth and the King of Heaven simultaneously. Mordecai, in the story of Esther, was not the hero or savior of the Jewish people like Esther was; his only influence was behind the scenes as a minor player until a major plot was revealed at the end. God's end game didn't conclude with Esther but began with setting up Mordecai. He was a person tested and approved every step of the way to work justice, do what was right regardless of risk, and look out for God's interests and those of His people. Character is said to be who you are when no one but God is watching. Consider how Mordecai proved his integrity and wisdom in a way that caused God to use him so mightily.

THE ACTS OF MORDECAI

- **ACTED SACRIFICIALLY:** Mordecai took Esther in while she was a child and raised her as his own but released her when her time came to leave.
- **PROTECTED PEOPLE:** Mordecai reported on a plot to kill the king because it was the right thing to do.
- **PROVED HIS INTEGRITY:** Mordecai refused to violate the law of God by bowing to Haman but instead risked his life so he could maintain his conscience and his good standing with God.
- **DEMONSTRATED WISDOM:** Mordecai discerned God's hand early on as Esther was elevated to the palace.
- **SAW THE BIG PICTURE:** Mordecai boldly stepped forward, challenging his niece to risk her life by remembering God's "why" for positioning her for "such a time as this." (Esther 4:14)
- **ALLOWED GOD TO WORK THROUGH HIM:** Mordecai quarterbacked the strategy in how the Jewish people would unite, protect themselves, eliminate their enemies, and thrive in a foreign land under foreign rulers.

The acts of Mordecai show how he achieved greatness and honor and fulfilled his purpose in serving God and the people God loved.

REFLECT TO CONNECT

1. In what ways have you or would you like to prove yourself as Mordecai did?
2. Are there limits to your commitment to integrity, or would you risk everything as Mordecai did?
3. Are there currently opportunities in your work environment for you to step up and take initiative in?

God is writing a great narrative in your story which requires you to choose "the right regardless of sacrifice"; what is it?